Electoral
Authoritarianism

Electoral Authoritarianism

The Dynamics of Unfree Competition

edited by
Andreas Schedler

LYNNE
RIENNER
PUBLISHERS

BOULDER
LONDON

Published in the United States of America in 2006 by
Lynne Rienner Publishers, Inc.
1800 30th Street, Boulder, Colorado 80301
www.rienner.com

and in the United Kingdom by
Lynne Rienner Publishers, Inc.
3 Henrietta Street, Covent Garden, London WC2E 8LU

Library of Congress Cataloging-in-Publication Data
Electoral authoritarianism / edited by Andreas Schedler,
    p.   cm.
    Includes bibliographical references and index.
    ISBN-13: 978-1-58826-415-2 (hardcover: alk. paper)
    ISBN-10: 1-58826-415-7 (hardcover: alk. paper)
    ISBN-13: 978-1-58826-440-4 (pbk.: alk. paper)
    ISBN-10: 1-58826-440-8 (pbk.: alk. paper)
    1. Elections. 2. Authoritarianism. I. Schedler, Andreas, 1964–   II. Title.
JF1001.E386 2006
321.9—dc22   2006002384

British Cataloguing in Publication Data
A Cataloguing in Publication record for this book
is available from the British Library.

Printed and bound in the United States of America

The paper used in this publication meets the requirements
of the American National Standard for Permanence of
Paper for Printed Library Materials Z39.48-1992.

5 4 3 2 1

Contents

Tables and Figures

Tables

vii

Figures

Acknowledgments

If authors, when turning in their final book manuscripts after several rounds of detailed commentary and revision, thank the editor and express their appreciation for his "rigorous editing skills," you know they are telling you: You shall be forgiven. They are telling you, there is life after the edited volume, and we will be friends again. So, now it is my turn to thank the authors—for their admirable patience, their gracious acceptance of my high-flying demands, their professionalism, their friendship.

This book was conceived at a conference on "The Dynamics of Electoral Authoritarianism" at CIDE in Mexico City. The meeting, an outstanding exercise in critical deliberation described by one participant as "perhaps the most stimulating conference in my life," was cosponsored by the Mexican National Council for Science and Technology through research grant 36970-D and the National Endowment for Democracy's International Forum for Democratic Studies (IFDS) in Washington, DC. My gratitude goes to both institutions. In particular, I wish to thank the directors of IFDS, Larry Diamond and Marc F. Plattner, as well as its program director, Thomas W. Skladony, for their invaluable trust and support.

—Andreas Schedler

1

The Logic of
Electoral Authoritarianism

Andreas Schedler

A specter is haunting the developing world—the specter of electoral authoritarianism. The good thing is that scaring off specters is an easy assignment,
in particular for those who fail to believe in scary metaphysical creatures.
The bad thing is that the specter is a metaphor, while electoral authoritarianism is a reality.[1] A large number of political regimes in the contemporary
world, ranging from Azerbaijan to Zimbabwe, from Russia to Singapore,
from Belarus to Cameroon, from Egypt to Malaysia, have established the
institutional façades of democracy, including regular multiparty elections
for the chief executive, in order to conceal (and reproduce) harsh realities
of authoritarian governance. Although in historical perspective the authoritarian use of elections is nothing new, contemporary electoral authoritarian
regimes take the time-honored practice of electoral manipulation to new
heights.

This book contains original comparative research into the conflictive
interaction between rulers and opposition parties in the central arena of struggle under electoral authoritarianism—the electoral battlefield. This introduc-
tory chapter addresses three analytical core issues with which the emergent
comparative study of electoral authoritarian regimes is grappling: the concept
of electoral authoritarianism, its observation and measurement, and its endogenous dynamic. The first section, on conceptual issues, explains how students of comparative democratization have responded to the proliferation of
political regimes that couple formal democratic institutions (multiparty elections) with authoritarian practices. In addition, it offers and justifies a formal
definition of electoral authoritarian regimes that looks at both constitutional
properties and democratic qualities of electoral processes. The second section, on issues of measurement, discusses a fundamental methodological
problem: in electoral authoritarian regimes, official election results are the
combined outcome of two unknown and unobservable variables—popular

preferences and authoritarian manipulation. We can resolve this observational problem either by using the competitiveness of opposition parties as a proxy for authoritarian manipulation, or we may seek to gather extensive knowledge about the case at hand in order to reach a comprehensive judgment about the overall democratic quality of a given electoral process. The third section, on the endogenous dynamic of electoral authoritarianism, analyzes authoritarian elections as "creative" institutions that constitute a certain set of actors (citizens, opposition actors, and ruling parties), endow them with certain sets of strategies, and push them into a conflictive "nested game" in which the competition for votes *within* given rules takes place alongside the competitive struggle *over* the rules of the game.

The Concept of Electoral Authoritarianism

The early 1990s were a time of democratic optimism. South America had completed its journey to electoral democracy, the Soviet empire had disintegrated in relative peace, and sub-Saharan Africa was passing through an unprecedented series of multiparty elections. We were reading about the end of history, the triumph of democracy, and the liberal world order. Both academic and political observers, however, are trained to be skeptics. Few, if any, ever embraced teleological illusions about the expansion of democracy. If the world was ever to become overwhelmingly liberal, democratic, and peaceful, it would not happen at once, but in bits and pieces, ups and downs, and over the long run. From its very inception, the idea of global "waves" of democratization was accompanied by warnings against "reverse waves" of authoritarian regression. Waves come and go.[2]

Since the Portuguese Revolution of the Carnations in 1974, the political drama that marks the official starting point of the "third wave" of global democratization, the number of democratic regimes worldwide has roughly doubled. Although different counts yield different pictures, the overall trend is quite clear. For instance, the annual Freedom House report on political rights and civil liberties in the world identified forty-two "free" countries in the year 1974. Three decades later, in 2004, it judged eighty-nine countries to be free (out of a total of 118 countries it classified as "electoral democracies").[3] Without a doubt, these numbers are impressive. The breadth and resilience of the third wave of democratic expansion is without precedent in the history of the international system. However, today the flurry of optimism that accompanied the end of the Cold War has subsided. The resurgence of ethnic violence in former communist countries and sub-Saharan Africa explains part of the new skepticism, as does the terror unleashed inside advanced democracies by the transnational crime syndicate Al-Qaida. Persisting realities of authoritarian rule explain the other part.

On the one hand, a significant number of old autocracies survive in different parts of the world, untouched by the stirs of regime crisis. This is true, for example, for the single-party regimes of Cuba, China, Laos, North Korea, Vietnam, Eritrea, Libya, and Syria; for the military regimes of Pakistan, Burma (Myanmar), and Sudan; and for the traditional monarchies of the Arab world (despite some facile talk about the "Arab spring" after the January 2005 legislative elections in Iraq). On the other hand, numerous transition processes, even if they led to an initial opening crowned by free and fair elections (as in parts of sub-Saharan Africa and the former Soviet Union), ended up in new forms of authoritarianism behind electoral façades. They ended up establishing what today represents the modal type of political regime in the developing world: electoral authoritarianism.

Electoral authoritarian regimes play the game of multiparty elections by holding regular elections for the chief executive and a national legislative assembly. Yet they violate the liberal-democratic principles of freedom and fairness so profoundly and systematically as to render elections instruments of authoritarian rule rather than "instruments of democracy" (Powell 2000). Under electoral authoritarian rule, elections are broadly inclusive (they are held under universal suffrage) as well as minimally pluralistic (opposition parties are allowed to run), minimally competitive (opposition parties, while denied victory, are allowed to win votes and seats), and minimally open (opposition parties are not subject to massive repression, although they may experience repressive treatment in selective and intermittent ways). Overall, however, electoral contests are subject to state manipulation so severe, widespread, and systematic that they do not qualify as democratic. Authoritarian manipulation may come under many guises, all serving the purpose of containing the troubling uncertainty of electoral outcomes. Rulers may devise discriminatory electoral rules, exclude opposition parties and candidates from entering the electoral arena, infringe upon their political rights and civil liberties, restrict their access to mass media and campaign finance, impose formal or informal suffrage restrictions on their supporters, coerce or corrupt them into deserting the opposition camp, or simply redistribute votes and seats through electoral fraud.[4]

An incomplete list of contemporary examples of electoral authoritarian regimes (as of early 2006) includes, in the former Soviet Union, Armenia, Azerbaijan, Kazakhstan, Kyrgyzstan, Russia, and Tajikistan; in North Africa and the Middle East, Algeria, Egypt, Tunisia, and Yemen; in sub-Saharan Africa, Burkina Faso, Cameroon, Chad, Ethiopia, Gabon, Gambia, Guinea, Mauritania, Tanzania, Togo, and Zambia; and in South and East Asia, Cambodia, Malaysia, and Singapore. Given their contradictory mix of democratic procedures and authoritarian practices, these new authoritarian regimes have unsettled the conceptual routines of comparative politics. To make sense of the institutionalized ambiguity that characterizes electoral authoritarian regimes, scholars have adopted three alternative conceptual strategies. They have conceived those regimes either as defective democracies, hybrid regimes, or new forms of authoritarianism.

1. *Defective democracies.* Since the early days of the third wave of democratization, we have been witnessing the emergence of political regimes that fulfill the minimum conditions of electoral democracy but lack essential attributes of liberal democracy. In order to capture such deviations from best practices, authors have been attaching distinctive adjectives to the multifaceted "diminished subtypes" of democracy they observed (see Collier and Levitsky 1997). The specific labels they have chosen to describe such "democracies with adjectives" (Collier and Levitsky 1997) are meant to draw attention to specific structural deficits and weaknesses. For example, "delegative" democracies lack checks and balances (O'Donnell 1994), "illiberal" democracies fail to uphold the rule of law (Zakaria 2003), and "clientelist" democracies are weak on programmatic party politics (Kitschelt 2000). However, in the face of regimes that fail to comply even with democratic minimum norms, the notion of "diminished subtypes" of democracy loses its validity. When applied to nondemocratic contexts, rather than sharpening our grasp of democratic deficits, it weakens our sense of authoritarian realities (see also Levitsky and Way 2002; Howard and Roessler 2006).[5]

2. *Hybrid regimes.* If we describe nondemocratic regimes as instances of democracy, however deficient, we commit the methodological sin of "conceptual stretching" (Sartori 1984). Conscious of this menacing pitfall, some authors have been treating the substandard electoral regimes that inhabit the contemporary world as genuine midpoints between democracy and authoritarianism. Because these regimes combine democratic and authoritarian features, scholars locate them at the very center of the conceptual spectrum and as a result consider them to be neither democratic nor authoritarian. Concepts such as "hybrid regimes" (Diamond 2002), "semi-democracy" (Smith 2005), "semi-authoritarianism" (Ottaway 2003), "semi-dictatorship" (Brooker 2000: 252), and "the gray zone" (Carothers 2002) express the idea of genuinely mixed regimes situated in the messy middle ground between the poles of democracy and dictatorship.

3. *New authoritarianism.* A third way of dealing with the new forms of authoritarian rule is to recognize them as such, as instances of nondemocratic governance. As scholars have been introducing concepts such as "pseudodemocracy" (Diamond, Linz, and Lipset 1995: 8), "disguised dictatorship" (Brooker 2000: 228), and "competitive authoritarianism" (Levitsky and Way 2002), they have abandoned the assumption that these regimes somehow still keep touch with the liberal-democratic tradition. Quite to the contrary, they have described them as instances of nondemocratic rule that

display "the trappings but not the substance of effective democratic participation" (Marshall and Jaggers 2002: 12). They have analyzed them as regimes that practice "democracy as deception" (Joseph 1998b: 59), as they set up, to quote from John Stuart Mill, "representative institutions without representative government" (1991: 89).

Clearly, the notion of "electoral authoritarianism" that provides the guiding concept of this book inscribes itself in the latter perspective. It involves the claim that many of the new electoral regimes are neither democratic nor democratizing but plainly authoritarian, albeit in ways that depart from the forms of authoritarian rule as we know it. The notion of electoral authoritarianism takes seriously both the authoritarian quality these regimes possess and the electoral procedures they put into practice. The emphasis on authoritarianism serves to distinguish them from electoral democracies and the emphasis on elections to set them apart from "closed" autocracies. Electoral democracies lack some attributes of liberal democracy (such as checks and balances, bureaucratic integrity, and an impartial judiciary), but they do conduct free and fair elections, which electoral authoritarian regimes don't. The residual category of closed autocracies designates all nondemocratic regimes that refrain from staging multiparty elections as the official route of access to executive and legislative power.

As the incipient literature on electoral authoritarian regimes has centered its attention on the controversial borderline that separates them from electoral democracies (see Schedler 2002b), here I wish to examine the frontline that separates them from their authoritarian neighbors, grouped together in the broad category of "closed autocracies." The key question is: How distinctive are electoral authoritarian regimes within the broader "spectrum of nondemocratic regimes" (see Snyder, Chapter 13 in this volume)? Surely, the use of democratic forms and rhetoric by nondemocratic regimes is nothing new. Even before the current wave of democratization, political elections, the core institution of representative democracy, were almost universally in use. As Guy Hermet, Richard Rose, and Alain Rouquié stated in the preface to *Elections Without Choice,* as of the late 1970s elections were "held in nearly every country in the world" (1978: viii). In addition, almost all regimes, democracies and dictatorships alike, claimed to embody the principle of popular sovereignty. Yet, whereas electoral authoritarian (EA) regimes open up top positions of executive and legislative power to elections that are participatory as well as competitive in form, other types of authoritarian regimes, if they take recourse to electoral processes at all, do so in much more limited ways.

Unlike authoritarian regimes that permit limited forms of pluralism in civil society, EA regimes go a step further and open up political society (the party system) as well to limited forms of pluralism. Unlike Bonapartist regimes that orchestrate occasional plebiscites to demonstrate popular consent on constitutional matters or policy issues, EA regimes invite citizens to partake in electoral processes serving (officially) as selection devices for highest office. Unlike competitive oligarchies, as in nineteenth-century Latin America or South Africa under apartheid, EA regimes do not control elections by restricting the franchise but operate on the basis of universal franchise. Unlike traditional monarchies (as well as some military regimes like Brazil between 1964 and 1989 and Pakistan since 1999), EA regimes subject the head of government to electoral confirmation, not just the legislative assembly (or local government, as in Taiwan under the Kuomintang [KMT]). Unlike single-party regimes that organize one-party (or national front) elections, either with or without intraparty competition, EA regimes allow for organized dissidence in the form of multiparty competition.

The notion of electoral authoritarianism places its emphasis on the access to power (through popular elections), whereas conventional typologies of authoritarian rule place their emphasis on the exercise of power (except for the category of monarchies, which is defined by hereditary succession).[6] They ask about the identity of rulers and their modes of governance and legitimation. For instance, Juan Linz's seminal distinction between totalitarian and authoritarian rule (Linz 2000) revolved around the structure of power relations (monism versus pluralism), strategies of legitimation (ideologies versus mentalities), and the treatment of subjects (mobilization versus depoliticization). More recent typologies of nondemocratic rule tend to focus on the nature of the governing coalition. For instance, the widely used distinction between military regimes, single-party regimes, and personal dictatorships asks about the organizational bases of authoritarian governance (see, for example, Brooker 2000; Geddes 1999 and 2004; Huntington 1991; and Morlino 2005: Chap. 2).

As the notion of electoral authoritarianism shifts its analytical focus from the nondemocratic exercise of power to the nondemocratic access to power, questions about authoritarian governance (who rules how) do not become irrelevant; rather, they become *contingent* (and may therefore serve to differentiate various subtypes of electoral authoritarian regimes).[7] Besides, issues of access to power and exercise of power interact. On the one side, over the long run, the authoritarian exercise of power is incompatible with democratic procedures of access to power. Authoritarian rule tends to subvert the conditions of freedom democratic elections demand. On the other side, authoritarian elections cannot constrain rulers as effectively as democratic elections are supposed to constrain them. If it is not popular preferences but manipulative skills that determine election outcomes, elections will fail to serve as mechanisms of accountability. The same way authoritarian governance engenders authoritarian elections, authoritarian elections feed authoritarian governance.

The Observation of Electoral Authoritarianism

How do we recognize an electoral authoritarian regime when we see one? It seems to be easier to define the concept of electoral authoritarianism than to measure it for the purpose of cross-national comparison. As they preach democracy but practice dictatorship, electoral authoritarian regimes tend to provoke intense debates within individual countries about the "true" nature of their political system. As a simple rule, incumbents try to sell their regime as democratic (or at least as democratizing), while opposition actors denounce it as authoritarian. The more repressive, exclusionary, and fraudulent a regime, the more likely it is that disinterested observers of good faith converge in their assessments and extend certificates of authoritarianism in accordance with opposition accusations. In more messy cases, however, drawing the dividing line between electoral democracy and electoral authoritarianism may prove to be complicated and controversial, and nothing close to an "expert consensus" may emerge. Yet, if the dense knowledge of competent observers does not suffice to settle disputes over the classification of "hard cases," how shall we ever be able to classify large numbers of political regimes in valid and reliable ways?

Standard methodological advice tells us to base our measurement decisions on "observations, rather than judgments" (Przeworski et al. 2000: 55). I understand that to mean that we are to partition the complex enterprise of conceptualization and measurement into two phases. In the first stage, we are to make all the judgments necessary to select and define the empirical phenomena we admit as observational evidence, as well as to devise the coding rules that permit us to assign categories or numbers to cases. In the second stage, by contrast, we are to ban judgmental elements and limit ourselves to applying our self-made rules of codification in a mechanical fashion. The first phase is deliberative, demanding the intersubjective justification of conceptual and operational decisions; the second one is observational, demanding the transparent collection of information and the quasi-bureaucratic application of rules.

In order to establish such a functional separation between deliberation and observation, we need empirical indicators that are valid, visible, and readable. The empirical evidence we are looking for must make theoretical sense across time and space (validity); it must be open to ocular inspection (visibility); and it must be sufficiently obvious to be processed on the basis of simple rules of interpretation that transform eventual ambiguities of meaning into operational clarity (readability). Clearly, the main methodological difficulty in identifying electoral authoritarian regimes lies in the obstacles they establish to the *visibility* of their manipulative practices.

In their widely (and justly) acclaimed *Democracy and Development,* Adam Przeworski and his collaborators identify democratic regimes on the basis of three institutional attributes: (1) executive selection: the head of government is elected in popular elections; (2) legislative selection: the legislature is elected; and (3) party pluralism: there is more than one party (for a synthesis, see Przeworski et al. 2000: 28–29). Until this point, their operational definition of democracy is identical with the definition of electoral authoritarianism I proposed above. What distinguishes EA regimes from electoral democracies are not the formal properties of political elections, but their authoritarian qualities. It is not on the surface of formal electoral institutions that electoral authoritarian regimes differ from electoral democracies, but in the surrounding conditions of political freedom and legal security. Electoral authoritarian regimes, just like their democratic counterparts, hold multiparty elections for presidents and legislative assemblies. Yet, as they subject these processes to systematic authoritarian controls, they deprive them of their democratic substance. Formal institutional facts are easy to ascertain. By contrast, practices of electoral manipulation are much less accessible to public inspection.

What we can see in electoral authoritarian regimes are election results, the official distribution of votes and seats among parties and candidates. Under authoritarian conditions, however, electoral figures cannot be taken as reliable expressions of "the will of the people." Rather, they represent the product of authoritarian manipulation and popular preferences. With v standing for votes, i for the integrity of elections, and p for citizen preferences, we can write:

$$v = p \cdot i$$

Under conditions of electoral integrity ($i = 1$), election results correspond to popular preferences; under conditions of electoral manipulation ($i \neq 1$), the official distribution of votes distorts the actual distribution of citizen preferences. In the former, democratic case, the institutions and practices of electoral governance are fundamentally neutral; in the latter, authoritarian case, they are gravely redistributive.[8] The problem, for the purpose of regime classification, lies in the fact that two of the three variables in the equation are unknown. Official election figures may be a "deforming mirror" (Martin 1978: 127), unreliable and imprecise, but at least they are out there, the tangible products of some central state agency. Acts of authoritarian manipulation and patterns of popular preferences, by contrast, are shadows in the dark.

To a significant extent, electoral manipulation is an undercover activity. Some things we can see, such as the enactment of discriminatory election laws, the repression of protest marches, or the exclusion of candidates from the ballot by administrative fiat. Such manipulative efforts take place in broad daylight, mobilize agents of the central state, and invoke the language of legality and public reason for their justification. By contrast, many other authoritarian strategies of electoral control, such as the alteration of electoral lists, the purchase and intimidation of voters, or the falsification of ballots on election day, constitute more decentralized activities that involve a myriad of public and private agents trying to do their job without leaving public traces. For all the knowledge we may be able to gather, be it episodic or systematic, narrative or statistical, the hidden realm of authoritarian electioneering constitutes an impenetrable black box we can (almost) never whiten in its entirety. Only few regimes have the panoptic aspirations of the Fujimori-Montesino regime in Peru, whose comprehensive system of extortion, surveillance, and videotape recording allowed the public to inspect the black box of authoritarian maneuvering at least after the fact, once the regime had fallen. Normally, however, we will not even remotely know what nondemocratic actors are up to on the invisible backstage of electoral politics, and even if we knew everything, we could not know that we know everything. The logic of distrust that prevails under authoritarian rule would make us uphold the suspicion that the worst may be hidden from our eyes. The WYSIWYG (what you see is what you get) rule never works under authoritarianism. Political actors know that usually what they see is *not* what they get from the authoritarian regime. They know that, if they wish to survive, they must practice the ancient art of *dietrologia,* the study of politics behind the scenes.[9]

With respect to popular preferences, the third variable in our electoral authoritarian equation, we face a similar situation of partial knowledge built upon foundations of fundamental ignorance. We may learn something about popular preferences, be it through access to "local knowledge" (Geertz 1983) or through representative public opinion surveys. Yet, under authoritarian conditions, we never know to what extent citizens engage in the public falsification of their private preferences (see Kuran 1995). We do not know either to what extent their genuine private preferences are endogenous to authoritarian governance. In the absence of individual autonomy and freedom, popular attitudes are always suspected as the products of authoritarian manipulation. Authoritarian rule distorts the formation of popular preferences as well as the expression of popular preferences.

We may deal with these problems of imperfect information in two ways. We may limit ourselves to the factual realm of official election results. Knowing that we cannot take official figures as simple expressions of voter preferences, we may treat them as proxies for electoral manipulation. The weaker the opposition parties are, the stronger we take the authoritarian controls to be. Alternatively, we may expand our scope of vision and gather evidence about either electoral manipulation or popular preferences or both. If election data are available, learning about one of our unknown variables (electoral manipulation, voter preferences) should allow us to estimate the other. Similarly, we may combine information about all three variables in order to reach broad judgment about the authoritarian quality of the electoral process under scrutiny. I shall briefly discuss the "alternation rule" proposed by Adam Przeworski and colleagues (2000) as exemplifying the former alternative (the use of election data as proxies for manipulation) and Freedom House indicators of political rights as representative of the latter (the use of multiple sources of information to reach judgment on the authoritarian quality of elections).

According to the alternation rule introduced by Adam Przeworski, a regime should not be classified as democratic if it fills executive and legislative offices by elections, but the ruling party never loses elections (Przeworski et al. 2000: 27). Democracy involves the possibility of alternation in power, but without the actual experience of alternation, we cannot know whether a ruling party would be willing to give up office peacefully in the case of electoral defeat. Taking election results and, in particular, alternation in office as primary evidence of procedural integrity runs the risk of misclassifying some regimes—a risk the authors readily acknowledge. Still, the alternation rule makes sense in normative-democratic terms; offers a clear-cut, easily discernible criterion of classification; avoids the uncertainties that come along with counterfactual reasoning; and allows the analyst to stick with simple observables, rather than struggling to make sense of a myriad of diverse facts.

Przeworski and his coauthors hold that passing judgment on the authoritarian quality of elections is an elusive enterprise, as attempts "to assess the degree of repression, intimidation, or fraud . . . cannot be made in a reliable way" (2000: 24). If their skepticism is meant to indicate that our judgments on the democratic quality of elections are often controversial, at least in complex and ambiguous cases, they are right. They err if they mean to imply that disinterested election observers are generally unable to reach convergent, or at least overlapping, assessments that have a good chance of surviving public interpellations by actors as well as experts. Take, for instance, the annual reports on political rights in the world offered by Freedom House in New York since 1973. Despite its notorious penchant for methodological opacity (see Munck and Verkuilen 2002), Freedom House does a reasonable job in evaluating the democratic quality of electoral regimes.

In its assessments of political rights, Freedom House asks more questions than we need, yet still asks the right questions, in order to judge the democratic quality of electoral processes. Some items on its "political rights checklist" relate to the exercise of power rather than the access to power we are interested in here. In particular, Freedom House asks about the sovereignty, integrity, and accountability of elected decisionmakers. Yet, the questions that come first in its political rights survey concern the procedural integrity of elections: Are the chief executive and the national legislative assembly, the Freedom House survey team asks, elected "through free and fair elections"? Do citizens enjoy freedom of association, and are there "fair electoral laws, equal campaign opportunities, fair polling, and honest tabulation of votes"? In addition to electoral procedures, Freedom House considers electoral outcomes as well, as it inquires into the intensity of electoral competition: Is the political system, the survey team asks, "open to the rise and fall of . . . competing parties"? Do we observe "a significant opposition vote, de facto opposition power, and a realistic possibility for the opposition to increase its support or gain power through elections"?[10]

Freedom House formulates its normative and empirical questions at a fairly high level of abstraction. Naturally, translating them into concrete assessments of national political processes demands a good sense of judgment, in addition to empirical knowledge and moral sensitivity. Still, by evaluating procedural and substantive information with recourse to a broad range of evidence and sources, the Freedom House team is able to reach judgments on the quality of electoral processes that seem fundamentally reasonable. In particular, the qualitative evaluations of political rights that Freedom House offers in its country reports commonly assess in their opening sentence whether "citizens are able to change their government through regular elections." With no recent exception I am aware of, these summary judgments about the effectiveness of electoral processes are sound and defensible in the light of available evidence and democratic norms.

Despite their apparent validity, there are obvious methodological problems associated with using Freedom House political rights scores as a basis for classifying regimes. As mentioned above, for the particular purpose of distinguishing electoral democracies from electoral authoritarian regimes, their level of aggregation is too high, as they bundle concerns about elections (the access to power) with concerns about governance (the exercise of power). Besides, because the measurement effort is multidimensional, it is not clear how qualitative judgments on various dimensions translate into the seven-point scale Freedom House uses; nor is it clear what specific scores and differences between scores are meant to mean. For the same reason, any effort to translate the numerical scale (from one to seven) into qualitative regime categories is bound to raise suspicions of arbitrariness.

Nevertheless, because its survey questions address the core concerns that motivate our distinction between electoral democracies and electoral authoritarianism, Freedom House data serve reasonably well to identify electoral authoritarian regimes, if complemented with some basic electoral data. For example, we may (quite safely) classify as electoral authoritarian all those regimes that (1) hold multiparty elections to select the chief executive as well as a legislative assembly and (2) earn average Freedom House ratings between four and six (see Schedler 2004). Such simple rules of delimitation (which some authors in this book use as well) seem to do a reasonable job of identifying electoral authoritarian regimes.[11]

The Dynamic of Electoral Authoritarianism

Electoral authoritarian regimes set up the whole institutional landscape of representative democracy. They establish constitutions, elections, parliaments, courts, local governments, subnational legislatures, and even agencies of accountability. In addition, they permit private media, interest groups, and civic associations. Although none of these institutions are meant to constitute countervailing powers, all of them represent potential sites of dissidence and conflict. Without ignoring these multiple sites of contestation, the notion of electoral authoritarianism privileges one of them—the electoral arena. It assumes that elections constitute the central arena of struggle (see also Levitsky and Way 2002: 54).

Designating elections as the defining feature of a distinct category of nondemocratic regimes makes sense only if they are more than mere adornments of authoritarian rule. Talking about electoral authoritarianism involves the claim that elections matter, and matter a lot, even in contexts of authoritarian manipulation. Still stronger, it involves the claim that it is the intrinsic "power of elections" (Di Palma 1993: 85), more than anything else, that drives the dynamic of stability and change in such regimes. In electoral authoritarian regimes, if they are to deserve their name, elections are more than rituals of acclamation. They are *constitutive* of the political game. Even if they are marred by repression, discrimination, exclusion, or fraud, they are constitutive of the playing field, the rules, the actors, their resources, and their available strategies.

Nested Games

Even though electoral authoritarian regimes establish competitive elections as the official route of access to state power, they do not, as a matter of course, establish electoral competition as "the only game in town." At the same time they set up the electoral game (competition for votes), they introduce two symmetrical metagames: the game of authoritarian manipulation, in which ruling parties seek to control the substantive outcomes of electoral competition, and the game of institutional reform, in which opposition parties seek to dismantle nondemocratic restrictions that choke their struggle for votes. Authoritarian elections thus are not conventional games in which players compete within a given institutional framework, known, accepted, and respected by all. They are fluid, adaptive, contested games whose basic rules players try to redefine as they play the game itself. In the language proposed by George Tsebelis, they form "nested games" in which strategic interaction *within* rules goes hand in hand with strategic competition *over* rules (1990). Formal institutions do not represent stable equilibria, but temporary truces. If the substantive outcomes of the game change, or if its underlying correlations of force change, actors will strive to alter its basic rules—either to prevent or to promote more democratic outcomes. The partisan struggle for votes is embedded in a partisan struggle over the fundamental conditions of voting (see also Schedler 2002a). Because authoritarian elections constitute the game of electoral competition, perpetually put into question by the metagames of manipulation and reform, they are also constitutive of its component parts, in particular, its lead actors and their available strategies.

Citizens

By opening the peaks of state power to multiparty elections, electoral authoritarian regimes establish the primacy of democratic legitimation. They may feed themselves from various ideological sources of legitimacy: revolutionary (the creation of a new society), transcendental (divine inspiration), traditional (quasi-hereditary succession), communitarian (nation building, anti-imperialism, ethnic mobilization), charismatic (magical leadership), or substantive (material welfare, public integrity, law and order, external security). In the last instance, however, popular consent carries the day. Competitive elections recognize subjects as citizens. They endow them with "the ultimate controlling power" (Mill 1991: 97) over who shall occupy the summit of the state. By establishing multiparty elections for highest office, EA regimes institute the principle of popular consent, even as they subvert it in practice.

The institutional concessions EA regimes make to the principle of popular sovereignty endow citizens with normative as well as institutional resources. Most importantly, elections open up avenues of collective protest. They provide "focal points" that may create convergent social expectations and thus allow citizens to overcome problems of strategic coordination. Elections constitute citizens as individual carriers of political roles, but they also enable them to turn into collective actors, be it at the polls or on the streets.[12]

Opposition Parties

By admitting multiparty competition for positions of state power, EA regimes legitimate the principle of political opposition. They may still try to shape the field of opposition actors to their own liking. Some regimes create official opposition parties and even assign convenient ideological positions to them, as in Egypt under Anwar Sadat and Senegal under Léopold Senghor. Others exclude uncomfortable opposition parties and candidates at their convenience, which is a standard operating procedure in the post-Soviet regimes of Eurasia. Yet they still have to live with opposition forces that enjoy at least minimal degrees of autonomy. By the simple fact of instituting multiparty politics, they abandon ideologies of collective harmony, accept the existence of societal cleavages, and renounce a monopolistic hold on the definition of the common good. Subjecting the opposition to repressive treatment does not affect its basic legitimacy embodied in the formal institution of competitive elections. Quite to the contrary, once regimes recognize the principle of pluralism, silencing dissidence is likely to turn counterproductive; it is likely to augment the status of opposition forces, rather than diminishing it.

Because EA regimes are systems in which opposition parties (are supposed to) lose elections, electoral contests are a profoundly ambiguous affair for opposition parties. To the extent that they serve to legitimate the system and demonstrate the power and popularity of the ruling party as well as the weakness of its opponents, elections tend to demoralize and demobilize opposition forces. To the extent that they allow opposition forces to get stronger and to demonstrate that the emperor is naked, that his grip on power is based on manipulation rather than popular consent, elections tend to reinvigorate opposition parties. In any case, authoritarian elections do not provide any of the normative reasons for accepting defeat losers have under democratic conditions. They fail to display the procedural fairness and substantive uncertainty that makes democratic elections normatively acceptable, and they fail to offer the prospects of a government pro tempore losers may hope to replace after the next round of elections. What remains is a calculus of protest in which opposition actors have to weigh the uncertain pros and cons of different strategic options both inside and outside the electoral arena. Most importantly, as authoritarian rulers convoke elections, opposition forces have to decide whether to enter the game of unfree competition or to boo from the fences (participation versus boycott). Once the polls have closed and official results are published, they have to decide whether to swallow the outcome or to take their complaints to the media, the courts, the streets, or the international arena (acceptance versus protest).[13]

Ruling Parties

EA regimes may display "sultanistic tendencies," with patrimonial rulers ratifying themselves in power through periodic multiparty elections. The organizational demands of authoritarian elections, however, limit the degree of personalism they can afford. Rulers who wish to govern through controlled multiparty elections need a party (as well as a subsidiary state) to mobilize voters, and they need a state (as well as a subsidiary party) to control elections.[14] Electoral authoritarian regimes do not rest upon single parties, but on parties they rest.

Elections are ambivalent tools, as much for the ruling party as for the opposition parties. They create opportunities for distributing patronage, settling disputes, and reinforcing the ruling coalition, but they also mobilize threats of dissidence and scission. Like their opponents in the opposition camp, rulers have to take some key decisions regarding their strategic behavior in the electoral arena. Most importantly, they have to decide how to mix electoral manipulation and electoral persuasion in order to keep winning electoral contests. To what extent should they rely on authoritarian controls, and which strategies are they to pick from the variegated menu of electoral manipulation? And to what extent should they rely on the persuasion of voters, and which strategies are they to choose from the variegated menu of electoral mobilization?[15]

* * *

Authoritarian elections are creative institutions insofar as they constitute these three classes of actors (citizens, the opposition, and ruling parties) and their respective bundles of core strategies. They are not determinative, however, insofar as the actual outcomes of the conflictive interaction between the three groups is open. The nested game of authoritarian elections may facilitate gradual processes of democratization by elections, as in Senegal or Mexico. It may lead to democracy through the sudden collapse of authoritarianism, as in Peru and Serbia in 2000. It may provoke an authoritarian regression, with a breakdown of the electoral cycle through military intervention, as in Azerbaijan in 1993 and Côte d'Ivoire in 1999. It may also lead to extended periods of static warfare in which authoritarian incumbents prevail over opposition parties that neither succeed in gaining terrain nor accede to disband and abandon the unequal battle.

Under which conditions do authoritarian elections fulfill a "stabilizing" role (Martin 1978: 120), and when do they act as "subversive" forces (Schedler 2002a)? Under which conditions do government and opposition forces succeed in maintaining their coherence and act as unitary actors? Under which conditions do rulers and opposition parties adopt which kind of strategies and to what effect? When are they successful, and when do they lead to failure? How do their strategic decisions in the conflictive game of authoritarian elections shape their correlations of force? To what extent do the nature of the actors and their choices respond to the endogenous dynamics of "unfree competition" and to what extent are they molded by structural conditions, institutional factors, and external actors?

This book does not pretend to respond to these questions about the internal dynamic of EA regimes either exhaustively or conclusively. Yet, each chapter addresses one particular analytical puzzle within the larger dynamics of electoral authoritarianism. The chapters strive to explain the emergence of actors, their relations of force, their conflictive interaction, and their institutional constraints under electoral authoritarian regimes on the basis of careful cross-national comparison, covering either a specific region or a cross-regional subset of cases.

The Outline of the Book

"If I were to write a book on comparative democracies," Juan Linz writes in his introduction to the 2000 book edition of his seminal essay on totalitarian and authoritarian regimes, "it would have to include a section on failed transitions to democracy, defective or pseudodemocracies, which I would rather characterize as 'electoral authoritarian' regimes . . . where a democratic façade covers authoritarian rule" (2000: 33–34). This book, while expectant of the piece we hope Juan Linz will write at some point, offers thirteen chapters of original reflection and research on electoral authoritarian regimes.

Part 1 discusses some basic conceptual problems and measurement issues that have been haunting the emergent study of electoral authoritarian regimes. Dissolving the dichotomy of democracy and dictatorship, the category of electoral authoritarian regimes occupies an intermediate position along the continuum of political regimes. It is sandwiched between two broad concepts, electoral democracies on the democratic side and closed autocracies on the authoritarian side. As both neighboring categories are afflicted by fuzzy frontiers, issues of boundary delimitation have been dominating the conceptual debate on electoral authoritarianism. In Chapter 2, on the construction of intermediate concepts, Gerardo L. Munck frames the discussion in new terms by identifying the generic problem underlying the controversy. Conceptualizing electoral authoritarianism as an intermediate category of regimes between the poles of democracy and dictatorship, Munck argues, involves the systematic construction of measurement points grounded in explicit relations of conceptual difference and equivalence. He illustrates his methodological point by drawing upon the twin dimensions of Robert Dahl's seminal conception of democracy—participation and contestation.

If we succeed in defining generic attributes that allow us to distinguish systematically between democratic and authoritarian elections, we still face the challenge of taking our abstract criteria to the concrete, operational terrain of empirical observation. As noted above, authoritarian regimes are opaque regimes that do not lend themselves to easy observation. Much of their manipulative maneuvering takes place on the hidden backstage of politics. In Chapter 3, Jonathan Hartlyn and Jennifer McCoy discuss the systematic difficulties and paradoxes involved in the observation and evaluation of elections, be it from the perspective of participants (political parties) or observers (independent domestic or international election monitors). Specifically, the authors examine the problem of divergent and shifting normative standards, the challenge of choosing the appropriate scope of observation, the trade-off between comprehensiveness and firmness of judgment, the irritating yet inevitable impact substantive outcomes have on procedural judgments, and the frequent contamination of normative assessments by strategic calculations. Accordingly, an open mind, balanced judgment, and methodological refinement are indispensable for reaching defensible conclusions about the democratic or authoritarian nature of particular electoral processes. Despite the incremental sophistication and professionalization the business of electoral observation has experienced over almost two decades, the assessment of electoral manipulation, Hartlyn and McCoy conclude, remains "an enterprise filled with the potential for uncertainty."

Part 2 of this book studies the logic of actor formation under conditions of electoral authoritarianism. In particular, it addresses problems of strategic coordination both ruling parties and opposition parties face. In her account of subsequent elite splits within the ruling Kuomintang in Taiwan and the Institutional Revolutionary Party in Mexico, Joy Langston emphasizes the centrality of the electoral arena for generating divisions within the ruling party. Under electoral authoritarianism, dissidents within the governing coalition need not risk their lives in armed insurgency or military rebellion. Rather, they may take their chances in an effort "to beat the official . . . candidate and win the presidency via elections." Especially in critical moments of leadership succession, Langston argues, electoral contests may encourage elite ruptures as they offer low-cost exit options for discontented regime politicians.

In Chapter 5, on the dynamics of opposition coalescence in sub-Saharan Africa, Nicolas van de Walle analyzes the interplay between regime cohesion and opposition cohesion as a "tipping game" that may lead to rapid shifts from an authoritarian equilibrium, in which the regime is united and the opposition fragmented, to a democratizing situation, in which the regime disbands and the opposition gets together. In accordance with the literature, van de Walle observes "a clear correlation" between opposition cohesion and electoral victory. Yet, as he argues against the literature, the coalescence of the opposition camp appears to be "not a cause of transition but rather a consequence of a growing probability of transition." As they derive from the complex and contingent coordination of social expectations, tipping games are typically "overdetermined" processes in which multiple events, actors, and factors intervene and intermingle. The author reviews some structural and institutional factors that affect tipping dynamics: electoral systems, forms of government, previous democratic experience, ethnic fragmentation, and external pressures. As he finds, two-round majority systems in presidential elections seem to bear a "decisive effect" on the ability of opposition actors to forge effective antiregime coalitions.

Part 3 of the volume turns its attention to core conflicts and strategic choices faced by ruling parties and opposition actors on the "electoral battlefield." In Chapter 6, on the variegated practices of electoral authoritarian governance in Southeast Asia, William Case describes the region as the homeland of electoral authoritarianism. In order to reconstruct the differing degrees of effectiveness of manipulative strategies, the author introduces the distinction between "skillful" and "clumsy" manipulation. The former are expressions of strategic rationality, whereas the latter are instances of strategic miscalculation. As the author contends, the "countervailing set of historical legacies, social structures, and cultural outlooks" that characterizes Southeast Asian countries provides solid structural foundations for electoral authoritarian rule. The ambivalence of electoral authoritarianism as the modal regime type in the region is rooted in the structural contradictions of Southeast Asian societies. When these regimes come under stress, though, as in economic crises, authoritarian rulers may either respond "skillfully"—with intelligence, foresight, and empathy—or they may respond "clumsily"—with stupidity, myopia, and arrogance. As Case claims, skillful manipulation has been a recipe for regime survival, but clumsy manipulation has worked as a trigger of regime crisis—leading to democratic change in the presence of a strong opposition (as in Thailand, the Philippines, and Indonesia) or to authoritarian involution in the absence of a strong opposition (as in Burma).

In their chapter on the logic of electoral theft, Mark R. Thompson and Philipp Kuntz ask about the conditions and calculations that may drive authoritarian rulers to "steal" an election they happen to lose. Although authoritarian rulers tend to "hold elections only because they expect to win, they sometimes make mistakes" (Przeworski et al. 2000: 25). As Thompson and Kuntz argue, the incipient literature on EA regimes has been trying to explain the origins, but not the consequences, of "stunning" defeats authoritarian incumbents may suffer in presidential elections. As their comparative review of emblematic cases suggests, quitting executive power after defeat may be a painful choice for the party in power, but clinging to the presidency and trying to steal an election is a highly "risky option" too. When presidents break off the electoral game the moment they stop winning, they step into "dangerous territory." Rulers have to weigh the costs of abiding by the rules and conceding defeat against the costs of interrupting the electoral cycle and defending their grip on power in open defiance of the express will of the people. In their calculations, they have to take into account at least three aspects: the prospects of legal prosecution for abuses in power, the probable loss of economic privilege and patronage, and the eventual discontinuity of their policy programs, in case they pursued any. After revising these utility calculations, Thompson and Kuntz conclude that electoral thieves are most likely to be found at the apex of "electoral sultanism"—highly repressive and weakly institutionalized regimes in which personal rulers have too much to lose from losing an election.

In electoral authoritarian regimes, citizens are the arbiters of last instance in the electoral arena. However, the police and the military are the arbiters of last instance *over* the electoral arena. Because the nested game of authoritarian elections is inherently conflictive, the security apparatus often has the last word (or the last bullet) in deciding the grave conflicts they provoke. In Chapter 8, John F. Clark examines the "contributing conditions" of military intervention in contemporary sub-Saharan Africa. His discussion of military intervention in electoral authoritarian regimes focuses on "the all-important question of legitimacy." Authoritarian elections are standing invitations to military intervention to the extent that they create the typical conditions of military intervention: situations of political confrontation in which civilian actors "knock at the barracks," asking the military to restore social peace and political order by resolving the conflict in their favor. Clark's systematic analysis of military coups and democratic legitimacy (as measured indirectly by annual Freedom House scores of political liberties and civil rights) bears out his principal hypothesis, albeit with a twist: In sub-Saharan Africa between 1993 and 2003, backsliding regimes that held free and fair first elections while subjecting subsequent elections to authoritarian controls were most vulnerable to military coups. Stable democracies that continued their democratic trajectory after successful transitions were almost "invulnerable" to military unrest. However, military behavior in countries that underwent more limited transitions from single-party rule to electoral authoritarianism, without a democratic interlude, seemed largely determined by exogenous variables, such as economic performance and external support.

The strategies authoritarian incumbents pursue are fundamental to the topography and trajectory of electoral authoritarian regimes. Yet, rulers do not play their political games alone. If an "autocrat" is someone who holds "uncontrolled authority; an absolute, irresponsible governor; one who rules with undisputed sway,"[16] then rulers in EA regimes are not properly described as autocrats. Their authority is "essentially contested"; their power is constrained, at least to some extent, by the existence of elections; and in conducting government they have to take into account the players they empower by convoking elections: citizens and opposition actors.[17] In Chapter 9, Staffan I. Lindberg analyzes the sources and consequences of opposition behavior in sub-Saharan Africa's electoral authoritarian regimes. His comprehensive dataset, covering ninety-five executive and 125 legislative elections held between 1989 and 2003, registers whether opposition parties participate in or boycott elections and whether they acquiesce to or protest electoral outcomes. His empirical findings run counter to the widespread expectation that opposition protest drives democratization. Quite to the contrary, Lindberg concludes, it is neither boycott nor protest but opposition participation and acceptance of the outcome that are associated with "the transformation of electoral autocracies into democracies over a sequence of multiparty elections." As the author suggests, if parties withdraw and protest, they do so out of resignation, in a position of weakness. Opposition boycott and protest, it seems, are acknowledgments of defeat rather than weapons of democratization.

Part 4 of the book switches its analytical focus from the strategic interplay between rulers and opposition parties to exogenous factors, both institutional and international, that condition their correlations of force in the electoral arena. In Chapter 10, on the impact of state capacity on regime dynamics, Lucan A. Way extends the common argument, according to which "a strong state is essential for democracy," to nondemocratic rule. As he argues, a strong state is essential for authoritarianism, too. If the control of leaders over their subordinates is put into question, centralized efforts of authoritarian manipulation are likely to dissipate. Exemplifying his argument with the experiences of post-Soviet Belarus (1992–1994), Moldova (1992–1999), and Ukraine (1992–2004), the author shows how failures in establishing "control over coercive agencies and local governments" tends to frustrate authoritarian schemes designed to distort and contain electoral competition. In all three cases, alternation in government was less an indication of democratic success than a sign of authoritarian failure; rather than an expression of democratic commitment, it was a consequence of administrative incapacity. Unable to impose their authoritarian impulse on the state apparatus under their nominal command, chief executives found that they could not rely on their security forces to suppress dissidence or on local public officials to coerce voters or stuff the ballot boxes.

Just as the strength of the state bureaucracy matters for the dynamics of political regimes, the strength of the legislative assembly matters, too. In his analysis in Chapter 11 of the causal impact legislative powers have on regime trajectories, M. Steven Fish shows a striking association between weak legislatures and authoritarian governance in the post-Soviet world. His use of the Legislative Power Index, a new continuous measure of legislative strength based on expert assessments, cuts across the discussion of presidential versus parliamentary forms of government, and his empirical findings invert standard assumptions of constitutional debate. Authoritarian systems, the literature tends to assume, choose weak legislatures. The causal arrow, however, seems to go the other way round: weak legislatures produce authoritarian systems. As the author states, although "the origins of choices about the powers vested in legislatures varied across cases, the consequences of those choices did not." Post-Soviet countries that established strong legislatures at the moment of achieving their (either de jure or de facto) independence embarked on a trajectory of democratization; those that established weak legislatures bought a ticket to enduring authoritarian rule. Substantive initial differences in legislative powers translated into dramatic subsequent divergences in regime trajectories. As these findings suggest, strong legislatures tend to consolidate democracy and subvert electoral authoritarian governance, whereas weak legislatures tend to erode democracy and reproduce authoritarianism. The key causal mechanism, Fish suggests, lies in the negative incentives powerless assemblies entail for the development of political parties. Weak legislatures weaken political parties, and by doing so, they end up undermining both "horizontal" and "vertical" forms of accountability. The author illustrates his causal argument through the paired comparison of two contrasting countries: Bulgaria, a case of successful democratization driven by a strong parliament and strong parties, and Russia, a case of authoritarian regression driven by an executive unencumbered by either legislative or partisan checks.

Whereas most authors in this book embrace the domestic perspective on regime dynamics that has dominated the comparative democratization literature, Steven Levitsky and Lucan A. Way shift the explanatory focus from internal to international actors and factors. In Chapter 12, they strive to explain why democratizing pressures by international actors have borne divergent consequences in different settings. The key to success, they argue, lies in two factors that vary with relative independence of each other—linkage, "the density of economic, political, social, organizational, and communication ties," and leverage, the "vulnerability" of national governments to international pressures. If both are high, as in Latin America and Central Europe, democratization is likely to ensue. If both are low, as in parts of the Middle East, Central Asia, and East Asia, the most likely outcome is stable authoritarian rule, with or without the adornment of electoral façades. Finally, if both diverge, we may expect "mixed regimes" (electoral authoritarian regimes) to survive, at least for some time, and muddle through the mixed signals of the international environment. In this respect, the authors' argument echoes William Case's contention (itself an echo of Harry Eckstein's notion of "congruence") that ambivalent societal settings tend to sustain the political ambivalence of electoral authoritarianism.[18]

In his concluding chapter, Richard Snyder, while lauding the emerging empirical research on new forms of authoritarianism, issues a plea for broadening the agenda beyond the study of electoral authoritarian regimes. His principal concerns are threefold. First, he warns against overlooking old forms of authoritarian rule that have continuing empirical relevance. At present, a large share of the world population continues living under single-party regimes, military dictatorship, and traditional monarchies. The author also warns against obliterating the profound differences between these regimes by stuffing them in the residual conceptual box of "closed" regimes. Second, Snyder warns against limiting our attention to routes of access to power. If we place all emphasis on the electoral arena, we are neglecting the questions about the exercise of power that animated the vast literature on totalitarianism, bureaucratic authoritarianism, sultanism, and other forms of nondemocratic rule. As the author argues, old concerns about the goals and instruments of authoritarian rule and about the relationship between rulers and subjects have not lost their analytical relevance. Third, the author pleads for placing the conflictive electoral games we study in their structural context. In particular, he argues for "bringing the state back in" to the study of electoral regimes. We may ask about the consequences of electoral contests for state capacity, as elections may have state-building as well as state-subverting functions. Yet, in the first place, we should ask about the structural prerequisites of electoral contests in terms of state capacity. It makes no sense to study elections as routes of access to state power in contexts where there is nothing resembling a state. No state, no regime. Richard Snyder concludes his critical review by outlining the contours of a future agenda of research. The standard phrase summarizes the state of things pretty well: much research needs to be done on contemporary nondemocratic regimes.

Notes

Work on this chapter was made possible by research grant 36970-D from the Mexican National Council for Science and Technology (CONACYT). I wish to thank Jonathan Hartlyn, Staffan Lindberg, Jennifer McCoy, and Nicolas van de Walle for most useful comments on earlier versions.
    1. A disclaimer of originality: The metaphor of the political specter, widely used in the literature on populism and other elusive threats to public tranquility, was originally introduced by Karl Marx and Friedrich Engels in the introduction to their 1948 *Manifesto of the Communist Party.* They described the "specter of communism" as a "nursery tale" they strove to demystify with their public declaration of principles (see www.marxists.org).
    2. Actually, waves are not supposed to change the sea level. On the "third wave" of democracy, see, among others, Huntington (1991), Diamond (1999: Chap. 2), and Doorenspleet (2005). For a contrasting view that observes a gradual accretion of democracies, rather than the occurrence of waves, see Przeworski et al. (2000).
    3. Freedom House 1975 and 2005 *Annual Report on Political Rights and Civil Liberties* (www.freedomhouse.org). As the number of nation-states has increased, in particular with the disintegration of the Soviet empire in 1991, the proportions become somewhat less impressive.
    4. On the normative foundations of democratic elections and the corresponding

menu of manipulative strategies that undermine these foundations, see Schedler (2002b).

5. For a recent discussion of defective democracies, see the April 2004 issue of the journal *Democratization.*

6. On the distinction between access to power and exercise of power and its relevance to the literature on political regimes, see Mazzuca (forthcoming).

7. For instance, attention to the institutional bases of authoritarian rule (who rules) may lead us to distinguish between "party-based" EA regimes, which reproduce themselves through well-institutionalized ruling parties; "military" EA regimes, in which elections ratify military domination of politics; and "personalist" EA regimes, which concentrate state power in the hands of one individual (see also Thompson and Kuntz, Chapter 7 in this volume).

8. On neutral (impartial) versus redistributive (discriminatory) institutions, see Tsebelis (1990: 117). On the notion of electoral governance, see Mozaffar and Schedler (2002).

9. I owe the notion of *dietrologia* to Philippe Schmitter (see his corresponding entry in *Les Intraduisibles: The Dictionary of Untranslatable Terms in Politics,* www.concepts-methods.org). On the generic research problems generated by secrecy under dictatorship, see Barros (2005).

10. The quotes are from the "Political Rights and Civil Liberties Checklist" in the methodological appendix to the Freedom House 2002 survey of political rights and civil liberties (Karatnycky, Piano, and Puddington 2003: 697).

11. Of course, no codification rule is perfect, and a rigid reliance on Freedom House scores is bound to produce false positives at the lower end. Freedom House assigns double scores of four (in the realms of political rights and civil liberties) to some regimes that are not in the grip of dictators exercising centralized authoritarian controls but are under the pressure of violent rebellion, organized crime, or military unrest that call into question the authority of elected state actors. Examples are Colombia in the late 1990s and Guatemala in more recent years.

12. On the role of stolen elections in coordinating citizens and triggering protest movements, see Thompson and Kuntz (2004).

13. For a somewhat more extensive discussion of opposition choices and dilemmas, see Schedler (2002a).

14. On the organizational demands of electoral fraud, see Chapter 10 in this book.

15. On the menu of electoral manipulation, see Schedler (2002b). On the menu of electoral mobilization, along the guiding distinction between "clientelistic" and "programmatic" campaign offers, see Kitschelt (2000).

16. "Autocrat," *Oxford English Dictionary Online,* Oxford University Press, www.oed.com.

17. With apologies to W. B. Gallie (1956) for transposing his notion of "essential contestation" from the realm of ideas to the sphere of power.

18. On Eckstein's theory of congruent authority patterns, see Eckstein (1992).

Part 1

Methodological Challenges

2

Drawing Boundaries:
How to Craft Intermediate
Regime Categories

Gerardo L. Munck

The notion of convergence around a single political model, a matter of much discussion in the heady days of 1989, increasingly seems to run counter to political realities in the post–Cold War era. Thus, even as scholars have recognized the unprecedented shift toward democracy—for the first time in history it is credible to claim that more than half the countries in the world fulfill the requisites of a minimalist definition of democracy—they have also grappled with the variety of ways in which politics is practiced around the globe. One important strand of thinking has focused on the quality of democracy (O'Donnell 2004; Diamond and Morlino 2004; Munck 2004: 450–456). Another potentially fruitful literature, which serves as the point of reference for this chapter, has focused on cases that have been variously characterized as instances of semidemocracy (Case 1996), illiberal democracy (Zakaria 1997), semiauthoritarianism (Ottaway 2003), authoritarian democracy (Sakwa 1998), competitive authoritarianism (Levitsky and Way 2002), electoral authoritarianism (Schedler 2002a), or more generically, hybrid regimes (Karl 1995; Diamond 2002).

This literature on hybrid regimes seeks to exploit a key insight: a considerable number of countries seem to be neither fully democratic nor blatantly authoritarian and thus are best characterized with intermediate categories. Yet, even as this literature calls attention to the broad variety of current political regimes and exposes the limitations of concepts that are conventionally used to describe political practices, it suffers from its own problems. Methodologically, it tends to ignore standard practices that have been refined in the literature on measurement and that for some time have been used to generate large-N data sets on regimes and democracy. Substantively, it largely overlooks an established theoretical literature on democracy and political parties that offers key insights relevant to the methodological choices involved in the creation of measures that envisage intermediate categories. In short, though this literature focuses on a real world problem of great import, it has still not proposed a clear and methodologically appropriate way to generate data, let alone presented systematic data that could be used to conduct a rigorous empirical analysis.

In this chapter I seek to show how the insight at the heart of the literature on hybrid regimes might be developed by focusing on the methodological issues involved in crafting intermediate categories of political regimes. I emphasize basic issues regarding the methodology of measurement. But I also argue that new thinking about core methodological issues is called for. Specifically, the central point of this chapter is that the measurement of each regime dimension requires an appreciation of the fundamental role of equivalence/difference relationships that upsets the deeply ingrained perception that researchers must choose between measures that highlight distinctions of kind or degree. A secondary point is that more attention needs to be given to the decisions involved in the aggregation of measures of multiple regime dimensions and to how these decisions revolve around a distinct type of part/whole relationship. These are complicated matters, and it is important to be sensitive to the manner in which methodological discussions can turn into a long detour that slows progress in responding to pressing questions about politics. But it is equally important to recognize that circumventing methodological issues most likely leads to unwarranted knowledge claims. Thus, it is advisable to tackle these methodological questions head on and to build on the accomplishments of existing scholarship, drawing whenever possible on clues offered in the substantive literature as to how various methodological choices might be confronted.

Drawing Boundaries and Establishing Intermediate Categories: Some Preliminary Considerations

From a methodological perspective, a central issue raised by the recent literature on hybrid regimes concerns the identification of thresholds that establish boundaries between categories and between cases and, relatedly, the development of measures that include multiple thresholds and thus entail intermediate categories and cases. This is, of course, not a new issue in political science. After all, Aristotle's classical typology is based on a dichotomous distinction regarding the use of power (the common good versus private interest) and a tricotomous distinction regarding the number of power holders (one versus few versus many). But students of political regimes have still to address in a satisfactory way the methodological issues relevant to drawing boundaries and exploring intermediate categories.

One of the main obstacles to devising better measures of political regimes and, hence, to improving our ability to describe regimes in a systematic and nuanced manner is the widely held view that scholars face a choice between generating dichotomous and continuous measures (Collier and Adcock 1999). The oft-repeated phrase that there are distinctions "of kind" and "of degree" and that they should not be confused indicates how deeply this stark choice is ingrained in current thinking. Even self-consciously methodological discussions of measurement focus on the pros and cons of choosing dichotomous or continuous measures without ever addressing the wisdom of this dichotomous choice. Yet this supposedly critical choice is a fallacy based on a false dilemma.

This fallacy originates in a failure to grasp a deceptively simple point: the most basic decision in measurement, the drawing of a boundary that establishes an equivalence/difference relationship, underlies each and every level of measurement that could possibly be used in constructing a scale. Indeed, all measures involve, first and foremost, classifications that distinguish between cases that are relatively similar to each other and relatively different from other cases in terms of some category. Understanding this point is critical to grasping why, in fact, scholars do not have to weigh the virtues of dichotomous versus continuous measures and why, as Carl Hempel (1952: 54–57) argued, it is always preferable to have more advanced, higher level measures.

Put in different terms, measurement is quantification because it consists of assigning numbers to objects according to rules. Yet measurement is also necessarily qualitative, because each number, inasmuch as it is theoretically interpretable, can always be linked to a class of phenomena. Thus, the proper distinction to draw among scales concerns not whether the scales are qualitative (i.e., of kind) or quantitative (i.e., of degree), but rather the mathematical properties of the relationship among the numbers. Indeed, efforts to distinguish between qualitative and quantitative scales lack meaning and are based on arbitrary choices.[1] It follows that higher level measures are always preferable because they offer more information than lower level measures—even if we should not strive to "replace qualitative distinctions by quantitative ones" (Cohen and Nagel 1934: 290), because quantitative distinctions are necessarily rooted in qualitative ones, assuming that all measures are of equal validity.

With these basic points about measurement in mind, the following discussion seeks to show how this false dilemma can be overcome. It focuses on Robert Dahl's (1971: 6–7) concept of political regime, disaggregated into the twin dimensions of participation and contestation (Figure 2.1). Thus, it takes the choice of conceptual attributes used to define a political regime as a given. Moreover, the discussion is further circumscribed because it treats participation and contestation in fairly narrow terms, as involving the right of suffrage and the right to compete in elections, respectively. The point is not to offer a full assessment of how to measure political regimes but rather

Figure 2.1   Dahl's Regime Property Space: An Adaptation

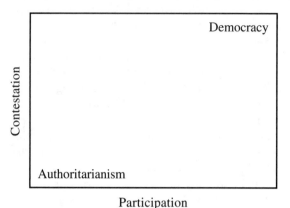

Source: Dahl (1971: 6–7).

to highlight how the introduction of thresholds, or cutoff points, generates categories that provide a foundation for increasingly more powerful scales of participation and contestation.

Disaggregate Measures: Building on Equivalence/Difference Relationships

Participation: The Right of Suffrage

The construction of a scale of participation that uses the right of suffrage as an indicator can take as its starting point a threshold that distinguishes cases that do not allow elections or do not recognize the right of suffrage from cases that allow elections and recognize the right of suffrage to some degree (see Scale 1 in Figure 2.2). Note that this is not a simple dichotomy, in that it includes information about order but is also based on the identification of an endpoint, the absence of the right of suffrage.[2] But this two-point ordinal scale with an endpoint has a stark limitation: it relies on a definition *a contrario,* and thus generates a residual category—"electoral regime"—that does not differentiate among varieties of electoral regimes. It is quite easy, however, to improve on this simple scale.

More nuanced scales can be built by adding points to this ordinal scale. One way to do so is to identify the thresholds that subdivide the category electoral regime. For example, by using universal male suffrage as a threshold, the category of electoral regime can be replaced by two, more informative categories: "male-based electoral regime" and "cross-gender electoral regime." Another way to build a more discriminating scale is to add a second endpoint,

Figure 2.2   Participation Scales

Scale 1: A two-point ordinal scale with one endpoint

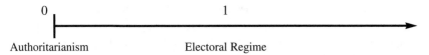

Note: 0 = no elections and no suffrage; 1 = elections are held and the right of suffrage is recognized to some degree.

Scale 2: A three-point ordinal scale with one endpoint

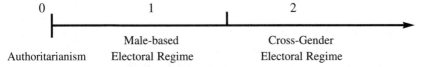

Note: 0 = no elections and no suffrage; 1 = elections are held and the right of suffrage is granted to men; 2 = elections are held and the right of suffrage is granted to all men and to women.

Scale 3: A three-point ordinal scale with two endpoints

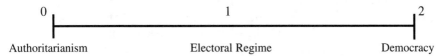

Note: 0 = no elections and no suffrage; 1 = elections are held and the right of suffrage is granted to some men and/or some women, or to all men but not to all women, or to all women but not to all men; 2 = elections are held and the right of suffrage is granted to all men and to all women.

Scale 4: A four-point ratio scale with two endpoints

Note: 0 = no elections and no suffrage; 1 = elections are held and the right of suffrage is granted to less than two groups or only to elite groups; 2 = elections are held and the right of suffrage is granted to two or more groups, one of which is a mass, nonelite group; 3 = elections are held and the right of suffrage is granted to all men and women.

the full presence of the right of suffrage.[3] In this case, the resulting scale is a closed scale, anchored at either endpoint by the categories of authoritarianism and democracy, with electoral regime serving as an intermediary category. Thus, starting with an ordinal scale with just one endpoint, improvements are made either by subdividing the category of electoral regime or by setting an upper boundary to it (see Scales 2 and 3 in Figure 2.2).

These two basic strategies—building ordinal scales with either one or two endpoints—can be pushed further by introducing more thresholds and thus developing ordinal scales that include further information. Indeed, fairly sophisticated measures can be obtained using these relatively simple strategies. But neither strategy can be used to identify the threshold that marks a boundary between authoritarian and democratic levels of participation. This boundary has a special status. Indeed, it has long figured prominently in theorizing about democratization. Thus, the need for even more powerful scales is apparent.

The task of identifying a threshold separating authoritarian from democratic levels of participation can be articulated quite easily. What is needed is a new type of scale, one that involves not just ordered categories but demands categories separated by equal intervals of distance. Or, more specifically, what is needed is the identification of a midpoint between the endpoints defined by the absence and full presence of the right of suffrage. The practical difficulties of actually identifying this threshold are quite great, however.

These difficulties can be seen in a cursory review of just a few efforts to determine at what point the extent of the right of suffrage crosses from an authoritarian to a democratic level. On the low end are proposals that this threshold should be established at 25 or 30 percent of the adult population or, more precisely, when the proportion of adult males with the right to vote reaches 50 percent (Huntington 1991: 16; Boix 2003: 66) or 60 percent (Rueschemeyer, Stephens, and Stephens 1992: 303). On the high end are suggestions that the threshold should be set at 90 percent of all adults (Dahl 1971: 232–233, 246–248).[4] In light of these disparate views and the explicit claim by some authors that their choice of threshold is arbitrary (Vanhanen 2000: 257),[5] one might legitimately wonder whether it is possible to build a scale that distinguishes authoritarian from democratic levels of participation. But we do have some useful leads for dealing with this thorny problem.

First, the literature offers some guidance concerning the most vital issue: the theoretical grounds for making a decision about the location of the threshold that distinguishes authoritarian from democratic levels of participation. What is at stake in the extension of the right of suffrage is whether the views of groups likely to have conflicting interests are included or excluded from the political process (Dahl 1971: 28–29, 246–247, 1998: 76–78; Valenzuela 1985: 28–35, 2001: 251–256). Moreover, democratic theory provides good reasons for defining the threshold separating authoritarian from democratic levels of participation in terms of the extension of the right to vote to two groups, one of which must be a mass, nonelite group. These are important insights, which can be formalized in a fairly simple coding rule (see Scale 4 in Figure 2.2).

Second, various attempts at measurement offer lessons regarding how this core insight might be further operationalized. It is important to emphasize the shortcoming of the standard approach, which is to pinpoint the key threshold in terms of a fixed percentage of citizens who enjoy the right to vote. The problem is that such a landmark is unlikely to travel well across countries, for what is at stake is not just a certain percentage of potential adult voters or male adult voters, or even the extension of the right to vote to a certain percentage of the working class.[6] Indeed, cross-national variation in the structure of societies and the relative salience of cleavages other than class will alter the precise percentage of enfranchisement that would guarantee that the right to vote has been extended to at least two groups, one of which is a mass, nonelite group. Thus, establishing equivalent indicators requires that we get beyond the commonly employed, yet deceptively simple, criterion of identifying a certain percentage of the adult population that can vote.[7]

Contestation: The Right to Compete

Measuring contestation, understood here in terms of the right to compete in elections, involves a distinct set of challenges, and responding adequately to these challenges is central to research on regimes. Contestation is the aspect of regimes that is at the heart of some of the most significant contemporary political struggles. Indeed, as formal and overt restrictions on the right of suffrage become harder to sustain politically, variation in political regimes today appears to hinge increasingly on the rules and conditions under which actors compete for access to political power (Przeworski 1991: 10; Przeworski et al. 2000: 15–16).[8]

Moving directly to the task of constructing a scale with two endpoints, it is relatively easy to anchor the scale by defining the absence and full presence of contestation. On the one hand, the absence of the right to compete in elections is indicated by the lack of elections or, alternatively, by elections in which only candidates from one party can run.[9] On the other hand, the full presence of contestation is denoted by elections in which only antisystem extremist groups are banned.[10] However, building a scale of contestation that adds further information is a complicated task.

Some important insights can be drawn from the literature, especially with regard to a criterion for establishing the halfway point between these two endpoints. As various authors have stressed, the critical threshold that distinguishes authoritarian from democratic patterns of contestation hinges not only on parties and candidates losing elections but, more precisely, on the *possibility* of all parties and candidates losing elections.[11] This point clarifies what is theoretically at stake and offers a handy way to define coding rules (see Figure 2.3). Moreover, by highlighting how measurement decisions ultimately rest on an assessment of a "nonevent"—usually framed as the possibility of an incumbent's electoral defeat that did not, in fact, transpire—it also offers a basis for distinguishing unproductive from fruitful attempts to measure contestation.[12]

An example of an unproductive proposal is one that seeks to pinpoint this key threshold in terms of the percentage of votes garnered by the winning party. Such a proposal fails because it simply does not capture the concept of interest, confusing competition with competitiveness (Sartori 1976: 218–219). In addition, such a proposal is likely to lead to frequent misclassifications, either by counting as competitive elections that are not or by counting as noncompetitive elections that are actually competitive.[13] In contrast, an example of a fruitful attempt to measure contestation is Giovanni Sartori's (1976: 192–201, 230–238, 283) distinction between (1) systems with a "hegemonic party" that permits other parties to exist but only as "second class, licensed parties," thus foreclosing the possibility of an electoral loss by the hegemonic party; and (2) a "predominant party system," in which parties other than the predominant party exist and contest elections, yet, in spite of the possibility of winning elections, fail to defeat the incumbent party.[14] Thus, this clarification of what needs to be measured helps researchers avoid dead ends and identify contributions that provide a foundation that can be built on.[15]

These important leads notwithstanding, two important challenges remain to be tackled adequately. One concerns the basis for judging whether the possibility of a loss by incumbents exists. Adam Przeworski and his collaborators (2000: 23–28) offer a useful discussion of the difficulties of making coding decisions in the absence of clear observables, and their proposed coding rule for getting around this problem—the "alternation rule"—is a valuable point of reference. But it falls short of providing

Figure 2.3   Contestation: A Four-Point Ratio Scale with Two Endpoints

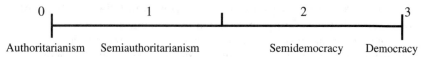

Note: 0 = no elections, or elections with only one party or candidate; 1 = elections in which more than one party or candidate runs, but not all parties and candidates face the possibility of losing; 2 = elections in which more than one party or candidate runs, and all parties and candiates face the possibility of losing; 3 = elections in which only antisystem extremist groups are banned, and all parties and candidates face the possibility of losing.

a solid basis for coding. Specifically, the proposal to use information in a retroactive manner gives more weight to the certainty of the information at hand than to the direct relevance of the information. Further work is needed to establish criteria for systematically using all available information and to weigh the reliability of this information.[16]

A second challenge concerns the development of a scale of contestation that adequately distinguishes among degrees of contestation that lie on the democratic side of the threshold separating authoritarian from democratic levels of contestation. This is a significant gap in current research. After all, existing scales either simply distinguish contested from uncontested elections (Przeworski et al. 2000: 28–29) or, if they go further, only introduce distinctions among cases with nondemocratic forms of contestation (Sartori 1976: 283; Hermet 1982: 27–29). Yet the need for such nuanced measures is suggested by the multiple ways in which contestation can be restricted short of totally preventing the possibility of an electoral loss by incumbents. Some restrictions operate through legal constraints on parties and candidates, including bans on the formation of parties or on their right to compete in elections, bans on certain classes of candidates (e.g., based on class, ethnic, or gender characteristics), and bans on specific candidates. Others manifest themselves in failures by the state to guarantee the conditions for contested elections, such as the physical safety of candidates and their right to campaign throughout the entire territory of a country. All these restrictions undercut the democratic principle that all citizens should be eligible to be both electors and candidates and, in turn, that all candidates should have the opportunity to reach voters with their message and run for office on a level playing field. Thus, the implications of these restrictions for a scale of contestation cannot be taken lightly.

The range of variation produced by these restrictions is unlikely to fit easily in the category of semidemocratic contestation (see Figure 2.3). For example, the banning of the Communist Party in Chile in the late 1940s and early 1950s was of a different scope than the banning of the Peronist Party in Argentina and of the American Popular Revolutionary Alliance (APRA) in Peru in many elections from the 1930s through the 1960s. Likewise, the assassination of presidential front-runners, such as Luis Carlos Galán in Colombia in 1989 or Luis Donaldo Colosio in Mexico in 1994, had a different impact than the assassination of party activists. To capture such distinctions, a scale with further thresholds must be constructed. Yet how such new thresholds might be best established remains largely an unexplored matter.[17]

In sum, the development of scales of participation and contestation hinges on complex methodological choices, many of which can be illuminated by an established theoretical literature and many of which remain to be addressed in future work. The tasks at hand, to be sure, are quite demanding. But the pitfalls of shortcuts, usually associated with the identification of an easily observable quantitative milestone, are also apparent. Unless the methodological choices discussed above are consciously confronted and each decision is duly justified, one of the most basic goals of the social sciences—the elaboration of theoretically meaningful and systematic descriptions—will not be fulfilled.

Aggregate Measures: Adding Part/Whole Relationships to the Picture

In addition to the construction of scales like those just discussed, measurement can involve the creation of composite measures. The distinction between disaggregate and aggregate measures is frequently overlooked, and the issues involved in generating composite measures are poorly understood. Hence, it is worth considering how, having disaggregated a concept (e.g., political regime) into distinct parts (e.g., participation and contestation) and measured these parts, one might proceed from these partial measures to generate a measure of the whole. To this end, three issues deserve consideration.

The first issue is whether it is even desirable to reduce multiple measures into one single measure. Aggregation entails a gain in parsimony that is offset by a loss of information. Thus, what is critical to assess is how great the loss is and whether it is worth incurring. That can be done by considering the underlying dimensionality of the measures that are candidates for aggregation and by assessing how closely correlated the disaggregate data are. The idea is quite simple. In terms of the example in Figure 2.4, the closer the data are aligned on the diagonal linking the bottom left corner to the top right corner of the property space, the more correlated the data are and the less a loss of

Figure 2.4   Aggregation and Dimensionality

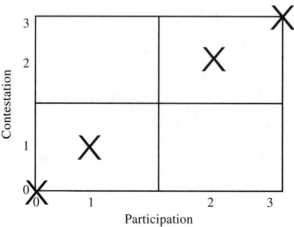

information is incurred in aggregation—in other words, the less the view of the trees will get lost in the picture of the forest.[18]

An assessment of the relationship between the dimensions of contestation and participation goes beyond the scope of this chapter. But the implications of some empirical studies deserve mention. Dahl (1971: 33–40) emphasizes the alternative paths to polyarchy countries have followed, contrasting the way in which contestation and participation were variously sequenced in England, France, and Germany. And subsequent works offer further evidence that progress along the dimensions of contestation and participation does not fit one single pattern (Higley and Gunther 1992; Dix 1994; Dogan and Higley 1998; Collier 1999). Thus, some research suggests that these dimensions are weakly correlated and that the common tendency to reduce complex data to a single aggregate measure comes at a cost. At the very least, the trade-off in pursuing parsimony should be recognized.

A second issue, if a decision to aggregate is taken, concerns the rule of aggregation that is used. This issue hinges on the way the relationship between the indicators used to measure a concept and the concept being measured is theorized. The broadest options involve considering indicators either as "effect" or "cause" indicators of the concept, that is, as indicators that are generated by or that influence the concept being measured (Bollen and Lennox 1991).[19] Moreover, if the indicators are seen as cause indicators, standard options to specify the relationship between indicators and concept include linear or nonlinear models. Thus, the decision to aggregate the measures of multiple regime dimensions opens up an inescapable set of choices that should be deliberately confronted and justified.[20]

A last issue concerns the interpretation of aggregate data, for the three inputs discussed above affect their meaning in a direct manner. The interpretation of aggregate data depends first and foremost on the initial construction of valid and interpretable scales for the disaggregate dimensions. It is also affected by the degree of correlation among the disaggregate data and complicated by the lack of a strong correlation—the lower the correlation, the less a particular aggregate score will correspond to a unique configuration at the disaggregate level. Finally, the interpretation of aggregate data hinges on the theory that is invoked to justify the choice of an aggregation rule—as a result of different rules of aggregation, the same aggregate score can correspond to different configurations at the disaggregate level. In short, aggregate data are summaries that synthesize various distinct, individually intricate inputs, and the interpretation of aggregate data requires attention to each of these inputs.

Conclusion

Abraham Kaplan (1964: 24–25) warned about "the myth of methodology," the view that "the most serious difficulties which confront behavioral sciences are 'methodological,'" and he associated this myth with an unhealthy diversion of efforts from substantive to methodological problems. This warning may, in many circumstances, be relevant, and the statement that "methodology is very far from being a sufficient condition for scientific achievement" is certainly accurate (Kaplan 1964: 24). There is plenty of methodologically sophisticated work that is substantively flat and offers superficial, trivial results. But Kaplan's (1964: 24) admonition to resist "the notion that the cultivation of methodology is . . . necessary . . . for successful scientific endeavor" goes too far. Indeed, good research depends on the marriage of methodological and substantive knowledge, and thus, one of the necessary conditions for scientific progress is the availability and proper use of adequate methodological tools.

The implications of the methodological questions addressed in this chapter are quite direct, affecting how we describe the world, the questions we choose to ask, and the way we learn about these questions. For a long time the literature on regimes and democracy has insisted that scholars analyze democratization with either dichotomous or continuous measures, and this choice has led to the development of two literatures that do not talk to each other very much. But this choice is a false dilemma that, with due attention to certain methodological issues, can be overcome. Although there is merit to the claim that the transition from an authoritarian to a democratic regime is distinctive and marks a kind of political quantum leap, acknowledging this point does not, in fact, require that democracy be treated as a dichotomous variable. Rather, the insight behind this notion of a quantum leap can be retained at the same time that we develop more nuanced measures that allow us to analyze democratization as a process consisting of multiple thresholds.

Notes

I would like to thank Richard Snyder for extensive feedback on this chapter.

1. Sartori's (1976: 273–299) strongest argument for separating distinctions of kind from distinctions of degree and for using this distinction as a basis for separating classification from quantitative measurement is that certain thresholds pinpoint discontinuous, exogenous change, whereas others identify continuous, endogenous change. As suggestive as this idea may be, no change is either entirely driven by exogenous or endogenous forces, and thus the distinction collapses.

2. Scales can establish relationships of order (e.g., 1 = low, 2 = medium, 3 = high) or relationships of distance (e.g., 2 = midpoint between 1 and 3) or involve the identification of the endpoints of a scale (e.g., 0 = absence, 1 = full presence).

3. The full presence of the right of suffrage is harder to define than the absence of the right of suffrage due to ongoing debates about who should be included in the demos and who should have the right to vote. But there is nevertheless a sound theoretical basis for defining full suffrage (Dahl 1989: Chap. 9). In other words, even

if the standards countries adopt change over time and old problems take new forms, there is still a basis for defining in abstract terms what is meant by full suffrage in a manner that will stand the test of time and will not lead to censoring at the high end of the scale.

4. Dahl (1971: 232, 248) does not explicitly state what percentage of adults with the right to vote he uses to distinguish "near polyarchies" from "non-polyarchies," the relevant threshold. Nonetheless, the exclusion of Ecuador from his list of near polyarchies seems to be based on its failure to extend the suffrage to 90 percent of all adults.

5. At times, authors propose varying thresholds. For example, Vanhanen (2000: 257; 2004: 19) uses a threshold linked with actual voter participation in elections and has set it either at 10, 15, or 20 percent of the entire population. The usual rationale for using different standards—that democratic standards regarding the right to vote change over time—reflects a relativist fallacy. Though an interesting topic for a study of changing public opinion, the issue of changing standards has no place in measurement exercises.

6. An understanding of society as divided into social classes offers a justification for taking the working class's right to vote as an indicator that divergent views, including those of mass, nonelite segments of the population, are being included (Rueschemeyer, Stephens, and Stephens 1992: 47–48, 303). But it is necessary to consider whether this model of society, which has offered a solid basis for thinking about democratization in Western Europe and Latin America, can be used without adjustment in other societies or whether ethnic, gender, linguistic, religious, or territorial identities would have to be considered on a par with class identities.

7. The problem of distinguishing authoritarian from democratic levels of participation can be solved with a dichotomous scale in which a 0 would refer to everything on one side of the threshold that distinguishes authoritarian from democratic levels of participation and a 1 would refer to everything on the other side of this threshold. Nonetheless, the value of more nuanced measures should be underscored. For example, focusing only on the democratic side of such a scale, the proposed "two-group" threshold between authoritarian and democratic levels of participation can be crossed without women having the right to vote, without minority groups enjoying the right to vote, and even with significant shares of majority groups lacking the right to vote. Therefore, it is normatively important to record systematically the progressive inclusion of different groups into the polity, and it is analytically important to construct scales that allow us to test the causes and effects of the exclusion/inclusion of different groups.

8. The extent of variation in recent times on the participation dimension, understood in narrow electoral terms, is a matter of some dispute. Certainly elections were held without the full extension of the suffrage to all adults even after the end of World War II. Moreover, a variety of formal and informal barriers to the effective use of the right to vote continue to be of relevance, especially inasmuch as they are targeted against certain classes of citizens. See, for example, Borneo and Torres Rivas (2001) on Guatemala.

9. That would correspond to what Sartori (1976: 221–230) calls no-party states and one-party states.

10. On the democratic nature of such bans, see Linz (1978: 6) and Hermet (1982: 25).

11. On this point, see Sartori (1976: 217–221), Linz (1978: 6), Hermet (1982: 26), Rouquié (1982a: 58), O'Donnell and Schmitter (1986: 57, 61), Przeworski (1991: 10), and Przeworski et al. (2000: 15–18).

12. Framing the question in terms of the possibility of an incumbent's electoral defeat amounts to equating contestation to the right of opposition. The reason for highlighting this right is that the government is seen as having an intrinsic advantage in terms of access to resources, including the power to coerce (Dahl 1966: xiv–xv), and this chapter essentially adopts this perspective. But its limitations should be noted: it is conceivable that opposition forces are stronger than the government, and thus it is important to consider potential abuses of democratic norms of competition by both the government and the opposition.

13. For example, if one adopts the criterion that elections can be considered democratic if the winning party wins less than 70 percent of the vote (Vanhanen 2000: 257), elections would be classified as democratic even if a party won election after election with 69 percent of the vote, committed blatant fraud, and never relinquished power. Likewise, such a criterion would misclassify cases of democratic elections where winners win more than 70 percent in verifiably free elections.

14. On this basis, systems that fail to meet the easy tests of whether contestation exists (i.e., no elections or no parties indicating "no contestation" versus electoral loss by an incumbent indicating "contestation") can be classified as systems with a hegemonic party, if they fall on the authoritarian side of the contestation scale, or, alternatively, as predominant party systems, if they fall on the democratic side of the scale.

15. Other valuable efforts that frame the issue in terms of the possibility of parties losing elections include Hermet (1982) and Przeworski et al. (2000: 14–29).

16. A relevant concept that is used by observers of elections is that of credible elections, as assessed by the degree to which domestic actors accept electoral results. Other useful insights can be gleaned from Hartlyn, McCoy, and Mustillo's (2003) effort to measure the "quality" of elections.

17. Beyond these blatant restrictions, further work is needed on a range of regulations that affect the conditions of entry into, and success in, the game of political competition. These regulations include thresholds for the formation and continued recognition of parties, bans on candidates that are independent of parties, and probably most importantly, the rules of party and campaign financing. Talk in the United States of a "money primary" that narrows the field of candidates before voters cast their first vote in a caucus or primary attests to the impact of money on electoral competition.

18. In the example in Figure 2.4, the data might be represented as follows (0,0; 1,1; 2,2; 3,3), indicating that the scores on one dimension perfectly predict the scores on the other dimension and thus are perfectly correlated.

19. Of course, a third possibility is that indicators are both a cause and an effect of the concept being measured.

20. Numerous scholars have seen indicators of contestation and participation as cause indicators and, more specifically, as necessary conditions (Dahl 1971: 2, 1998: 38, 84, 93, 99; Przeworski et al. 2000: 28–29; Mainwaring, Brinks, and Pérez-Liñán 2001: 41, 47–48; Valenzuela 2001: 252; Schedler 2002b). Thus, an important degree of consensus has developed regarding this issue. But it is important to emphasize that much hinges on the specific indicators used to measure contestation and participation. For example, if participation is measured in terms of the right to vote, one might consider it a necessary condition. However, if participation is measured in terms of voter turnout, the theoretical justification for considering it a necessary condition would be significantly weaker.

3

Observer Paradoxes: How to Assess Electoral Manipulation

Jonathan Hartlyn and Jennifer McCoy

Elections are the lifeblood of democracy, but not all elections are democratic. Conceptually, the threshold between electoral authoritarianism and electoral democracy, a central concern of this book, can be determined by the quality of electoral processes. Empirically, this means that actors and analysts must examine electoral processes and make judgments about their quality in ways that appear reliable and valid to others. Authoritarian regimes that hold elections may vary considerably in the extent to which they employ repression, fraud, or other forms of manipulation, and electoral processes in recently democratized countries may deteriorate over time, calling the nature of the regime into question. There are many ways in which electoral processes can be manipulated to decrease the inherent uncertainty of outcome they should provide.

In this chapter, we focus on how we know when intentional manipulation by an incumbent, a political party, or another actor occurs in elections that may or may not meet some minimal threshold of electoral integrity, and how we can judge whether that manipulation is successful in determining the outcome of a vote.[1] Widespread irregularities due to incompetence or lack of resources are often confused with malicious intent, and thus observers and candidates need tools to distinguish between the two. As such, we focus on transitional contexts of democratization and on hybrid regimes that may embody some form of electoral authoritarianism, drawing on data and case studies from Latin America. In the clearly observed presence of administrative competence and probity or, alternatively, of blatant fraud, it can be a relatively straightforward exercise to classify an electoral process as above or below some minimal threshold. Thus, we believe we can learn the most from examining cases that fall in a gray zone, where judgments about the minimal acceptability of electoral processes are highly uncertain at the outset; at the same time, there remains considerable variation across the elections we examine, which are drawn from both authoritarian and democratic regimes.

In this more muddled middle, issues regarding the observed and the unobserved, as well as differing perspectives, standards, and interests of political actors and independent observers, make the exercise of classification difficult. We begin our examination of this complexity first by considering the value of two potentially differing perspectives on elections and the question of standards. The views of the principal political parties competing in an election are crucial, for their acceptance of the process and the results unquestionably provide legitimacy to an election. Furthermore, embracing their assessment could potentially provide a mechanism for sidestepping numerous conceptual and empirical challenges surrounding standards of judgment (and we could end our chapter here). However, the views of political parties may be biased and may therefore differ from those of election observers who provide an independent assessment of the quality of the process. Observers' assessment of election quality, in turn, inevitably requires the establishment of a set of standards against which to judge an election. In exploring this issue, we reject both extreme relativist, context-sensitive standards as well as maximalist universal ones, embracing the notion that under certain circumstances flawed elections might still be deemed acceptable. We then turn to questions regarding what should be observed and explain why the scope of attention has been expanding beyond election day and the vote count.

Assessing electoral manipulation requires determining its pervasiveness and its decisiveness regarding the outcome. In the third section, we explore the types of methods employed to address the inevitable issues of limited ability to observe and incomplete information that confront all election observation exercises, and we identify four potential paradoxes. Fraud is more likely to be blatant when parties and observers are weak, but as a result we are less likely to know about it in a reliable fashion, which creates a *paradox of capacity.* And as the scope of observation expands to include a wider set of potentially critical issues, some quite distant in time from the election, in a *paradox of comprehensiveness* we may be able to make a more valid judgment about the overall electoral process, but a less certain one. Issues of capacity and scope of observation appropriately draw attention to electoral procedures. However, election outcomes may have a significant and potentially pernicious impact on what assessment is made of an electoral process. In a *paradox of procedural judgments,* parties and observers alike may be tempted, when there is a wide margin of victory, to be more flexible in their assessments of the process if they believe that possible fraud did not have an impact on the outcome.

In a final section we discuss reasons why assessments by political parties and observers might diverge. We argue that their differing assessments about electoral integrity may be driven more by their interests and the application of varying standards than their judgments regarding what they observed. Thus, in a *paradox of convergence,* when parties and observers do agree, one needs to consider that their convergence may result from a convergence of interests, rather than judgments. The conclusion considers ways in which the challenges raised by these paradoxes may be addressed.

Perspectives and Standards

In assessing electoral manipulation, analysts may consider at least two alternative perspectives, one based on the views of the major candidates and political parties and another based on the views of informed election observers. To begin with, in order to sidestep the conceptual and empirical challenges of determining the democratic quality of an electoral process, one could ask if the key relevant political actors extend legitimacy to it. An election may be considered successful if "the major parties all accept the process and respect the results" (Pastor 1998: 159).

There is a certain attractiveness to focusing on the perspective of political parties in elections in transitional or democratizing contexts. In these cases, as Robert A. Pastor (1998) underscores, authoritarian governments often seek to manipulate the electoral arena to ensure victory, and opposition forces continuously weigh deploying their last resort tool of a boycott to rob the regime and the election of legitimacy. Thus, if in these circumstances these key actors participate in the elections and accept the results, then the electoral process should be deemed successful. They are the actors most intimately involved in the electoral process and for this reason are usually the ones best informed about procedural and technical issues surrounding an election. Furthermore, compliance with the outcome and the legitimacy of the elected candidates is not fully ensured if one or more major groups reject the outcome. An electoral process can be considered a failure if the major opposition political parties boycott the elections to begin with or if all the major losing parties reject the results; intermediate outcomes short of full acceptance can also be established.

A major advantage of this perspective is that it is relatively easy to assess. It is readily apparent if parties boycott elections; similarly, based on their statements and actions after election day, it is easy to determine whether all, some, or none of the major parties accepted the results. A final advantage is that it appears to control for contextual differences and level of development or capacity differences. The parties within a given country and at a given time evaluate their specific experience according to their own criteria, not some objective measure.

However, as we elaborate further later, relying exclusively on party assessments has one principal difficulty: their perspective may not necessarily correlate with that of independent observers. These observers may be more impartial and equally or better informed, even if the risk remains that their judgments, like those of political parties, may also be affected by strategic calculations and interests.

Independent observers examine an electoral process and make a judgment about its quality. Doing so requires comparing the election to some set of standards. At the international level, there is a gradual movement toward developing a universal set of minimal standards for electoral processes. There is no consensus yet on what that might be, though some international organizations have been gradually specifying elements of a comprehensive set of standards (see International IDEA 2002; OSCE/ODIHR 2003).

Others do not necessarily reject constructing a minimum set of standards but assert that context-sensitive judgment in employing them is required, based on such factors as a country's level of development, level of state capacity, and history of democratization. They assert that elections that fall into a gray zone between clearly free and fair and clearly not, due to technical and other limitations, may still be deemed "acceptable" if it appears that both the expressed will of the people and the country's electoral law and regulations have been respected (Elklit and Svensson 1997). This is a reasonable perspective in democratizing contexts, though it does not necessarily eliminate empirical uncertainties or thorny theoretical issues, and its misapplication may have pernicious effects in subsequent elections.

The Scope of Observation

What, though, should election observers observe? When a judgment is made that an election is "free and fair," just what types of processes are being weighed and considered? The attention of voters and of the media tends naturally to be drawn to the final weeks of the campaign, to the actual process of voting on election day, the vote count, preliminary results, and the adjudication of disputes. The most blatant forms of fraud may take place on election day, through vote buying (or abstention buying), voter intimidation, ballot box stuffing or theft, or deliberate miscounting.

Observers and analysts, however, have begun extending the focus of their attention well beyond election day for two major reasons. One has to do with the increased scrutiny of election day practices by domestic and international groups and improvements in preelectoral polling and election day quick counts, forcing authoritarian incumbents to become more sophisticated in the ways in which they seek to influence electoral outcomes, often well before election day. Another has to do with the persistence or (re)emergence of patrimonial and/or hybrid regimes. The transformation of seemingly rule-bound, law-abiding politicians in the opposition into patrimonial rulers once in office, who seek to extend their rule through questionable means, is evident in some countries, as is the sometimes overlapping emergence of what may be termed "hybrid regimes," in which regime leaders elected to office through democratic elections appear prepared to extend their mandate through electoral manipulation, again often beginning well before election day.[2]

Since 1989 we have seen a clear learning curve on the part of the most serious international observer groups, with the most significant evolution being an enhanced analytical focus on critical issues that precede election day by many months (see Middlebrook 1998; International IDEA 1997, 1999; Carothers 1997). As a result, delimiting what precisely should be considered part of the electoral process becomes the new challenge. One attractive option is to equate a minimalist conceptualization of democracy, electoral democracy, with the existence of a satisfactory electoral process (Schedler 2002b). If one moves beyond this view of democracy, there is the potential of conflating broader processes of democratization—respect for human rights and the rule of law—with the electoral process, with the risk of expanding excessively the range of topics to be addressed under the rubric of electoral manipulation. Nevertheless, we recognize that the rule of law and the independence of the judicial system are major determining factors with regard to the quality of specific elements of the electoral process, particularly adjudication of disputes.

There have been several recent efforts to demarcate the key steps necessary for a democratic election. One has been to specify in a comprehensive and ideal fashion what aspects of an electoral process must be regulated by law. In a recent publication, the International Institute for Democracy and Electoral Assistance (International IDEA 2002) provides an excellent comprehensive review of issues regarding the legal framework in fifteen areas, ranging from the electoral system to the boundaries of electoral units, requirements for candidates and for voting, the nature of electoral management bodies, voter registration, media access, campaign finance and expenditure, balloting and vote tabulation, and enforcement of electoral law. As it acknowledges, it is necessary to move beyond the letter of the law to consider actual practices in a given country, though it does not specify how that might be done. Likewise, Jørgen Elklit and Palle Svensson (1997) and Elklit and Andrew Reynolds (2002) specify crucial elements required in the preelection period, on election day, and in the postelection period for an election to be considered "free" (which they consider to be most important because it is a precondition for democracy) and "fair" (applied impartially). An alternative, theoretically more ambitious approach is developed by Andreas Schedler. Building on Robert A. Dahl's conceptualization of polyarchy, he carefully specifies a seven-step chain of democratic choice, with elections being democratic if and only if each step is satisfied; "gross violation of any one condition invalidates fulfillment of all the others" (Schedler 2002b: 41).

These approaches put forward useful conceptual schemes, specifying elements that should be considered part of a democratic electoral process. Yet, they do not fully resolve dilemmas regarding how observers should weigh different areas, elements, or steps. And difficult judgment calls are still required regarding such questions as whether fragmentation of the opposition is caused primarily by manipulative, undemocratic changes in election rules and intimidation or more by decisions within the opposition movements themselves, or whether certain formal mechanisms are established primarily to ensure greater control and oversight or to implement targeted disenfranchisement.

In spite of these continuing challenges, we conclude that it is clearly insufficient and inappropriate to consider only election day and immediate post–election day issues. The types of factors that election observers focus on thus incorporate an increasingly long list of items:

- what offices are up for election and what effective powers they have
- the neutrality, professionalism, and effectiveness of the electoral authorities, including their responsiveness to legitimate party concerns
- the nature of the legal framework for the electoral process, including electoral laws and boundary demarcations; the use and abuse of state resources; procedures for ballot creation, voter education, election day procedures, and vote tabulation
- the ability of opposition forces to organize into political parties and campaign freely, without violence or intimidation
- the ability of citizens to gain information about their alternatives freely and fairly and their ability to participate in campaigns without fear of harassment or violence
- the process of voter registration and the accuracy, transparency, and availability of the voter registration lists
- the absence of voter intimidation and vote buying (or abstention buying)
- the respect for procedural fairness, party and observer monitoring, and vote secrecy on election day and for key procedures before and after, including all steps of the vote count; and the existence of impartial dispute resolution mechanisms

Significant failure on any one key factor, even one distant from election day itself, may be sufficient to deem an election undemocratic. At the same time, what is of greatest interest is whether electoral manipulation has had a decisive effect on the election outcome. Thus, the more extensively electoral manipulation is directly observed, the more proximate its relationship to ballot box outcomes, and the clearer its impact on the outcome, the easier it may be to condemn. To the extent election monitors have difficulty in directly observing manipulation or measuring its impact on the outcome, several dilemmas and potential paradoxes emerge.

Electoral Assessment and Uncertainty

As a first step in determining whether electoral manipulation has had a decisive effect on an electoral process, actors and observers must determine the pervasiveness of fraud. It is true that fraud may often not affect the outcome of an election, either because the fraudulent actions of the parties partially cancel each other out or because of its relatively small magnitude (Lehoucq 2003). In elections fraught with mutual suspicion, candidates and political parties commonly make multiple charges of fraud; even in situations where fraud is present, political parties typically overaccuse opponents of fraud, forcing observers to sort out factual instances of fraud from false charges.

The challenge for observers and political parties alike is to determine to what extent irregularities result from incompetence or a lack of resources or training, rather than from fraudulent intent, and whether fraud is localized and sporadic rather than centralized. Yet, their ability to do so may be limited by a lack of organization and resources. In what can be termed a *paradox of capacity,* most blatant fraud is more likely to occur where low capacity of parties and observers inhibits their ability to detect and deter it. In such cases, in particular if they come with administrative chaos and low technical capacity, we are unlikely to know the extent and nature of any fraud (as in the case of Haiti in 1990). That may also be the case where there is a great asymmetry between those carrying out the fraud and their opponents, with limited or no domestic or international observation (as in Mexico in 1988).

Nevertheless, in the face of blunt instruments of open fraud, even restricted access by domestic or international observers might compensate for the weakness of opposition parties and enable them to detect, denounce, or deter manipulation, as was the case in Panama in 1989 with the domestic quick count and international observers directly observing and denouncing fraud, and in Chile in 1988 with a domestic quick count helping to deter the government from manipulating the results.[3] As these examples underscore, the emergence of new techniques and improvements in communication have steadily improved scrutiny of election day practices, without thereby necessarily ensuring acceptable electoral practices.

With more resources, organization, staffing, and time and often relying on thousands of trained volunteers, domestic observer groups have typically embraced formal methodologies with so-called checklists or systematic qualitative observations to examine election day processes in a much broader and more comprehensive fashion than is possible for international groups, given their more limited size. International observer groups typically try to coordinate among themselves to ensure as comprehensive coverage as possible or to ensure that key data points for a quick count will be reported; they usually question opposition parties about their major concerns. Improved methods of transportation and communication have also facilitated mobility and response times on election day (Canton and Nevitte 1998; Middlebrook 1998).

Observation processes focused on election day, particularly if well-staffed, often permit detailed examination of election day imperfections, enhancing confidence in the judgments made. To the extent they ignore issues of legal or structural bias prior to or during the campaign, though, they may obviously miss crucial potential sources of electoral manipulation. Most problematic, of course, are election observations that are narrowly focused on election day and also short-staffed, as occurred in the atypical case of the 1990 election in the Dominican Republic (see NDI, Carter Center, and Council of Freely-Elected Heads of Government 1990).

The value of the trend toward a broader, more collaborative observation process can be illustrated through the example of the presidential elections in Peru in 2000. In this case, previously organized groups in civil society and international actors began their critical review early in the process leading up to the elections, enabling them to document serious problems prior to election day. President Alberto Fujimori manipulated legislative and judicial institutions to enable a legal decision permitting him to be reelected to serve a third term. He ensured that loyalists were named to run the electoral authorities. He carried out a systematic campaign intended to undercut his opposition, with an eye toward seeking a first round victory on 9 April 2000. International groups such as the National Democratic Institute, the Carter Center, and the Organization of American States and domestic groups such as the nongovernmental organization Transparencia and the Defensoría del Pueblo (the state ombudsman's office) played key roles in documenting and denouncing the extensive abuse of state resources, manipulation of the media and of the voter registry list, and numerous other issues (see Bernbaum, Pintor, and Sanborn 2001; NDI and Carter Center 2000b; Cooper and Legler 2001; and McClintock 2001). Actions undertaken by the incumbent administration certainly helped to eliminate the competitiveness of two opposition candidates, yet the weakness of the party system and other factors not under direct control by the regime may well also have contributed to the inability of the opposition to provide a united front against the government (Levitsky and Cameron 2003).

The ability to clearly document the serious preelectoral problems led the Carter Center and NDI, for the first time in Latin America, to condemn an election as unfair prior to its realization. At the same time, given that the opposition was still campaigning and determined to participate and that the electoral outcome was not known, they called for the government and the electoral authorities to take "extraordinary steps" to improve confidence in the process (NDI and Carter Center 2000a). Transparencia's quick count on election day (purposefully based on an oversized sample to ensure an extremely small margin of error), gave Fujimori 48.73 percent of the vote to 41.04 percent for Toledo. It was key in mobilizing pressure by foreign governments on the Peruvian government not to manipulate the vote count to enable Fujimori to cross the 50 percent threshold in order to win in the first round. However, the electoral authorities refused to provide the access necessary to ensure that the vote count in the second round would not be manipulated, even as polls indicated the race would be very tight. Ultimately, that decision led to the withdrawal of Toledo's candidacy and of nearly all major observer groups.

This electoral process shows the advantages of expanding the scope and comprehensiveness of observation. Yet, it also illustrates that the demands with regard to staffing, resources, technical expertise, and time for such an effort can be daunting. Especially where these demands are not met and also as we move farther back from election day itself, a *paradox of comprehensiveness* emerges. A narrow perspective focused on election day may permit judgment to be reached with relative confidence. However, as the scope of observation expands to include a much wider set of possible forms of manipulation, providing more valid bases for judgment, the ability to draw definitive conclusions about the impact of the added structural components—the certainty in our judgment—may decrease.

Important steps, though, are being taken to improve the capacity of groups to examine such structural conditions as equitable access to media and balance of news coverage, the use of state resources, and campaign finance. For example, the United Nations in Nicaragua in 1990, Alianza Cívica in Mexico in 1994, and Participa in Chile in the 1990s documented imbalanced news coverage of election campaigns. The Carter Center systematically coded the balance of news coverage during the presidential recall referendum in Venezuela in 2004. Use of state resources in attempts to coerce voters and buy votes (*compra y coacción*) was documented in Mexico in 1997 and 2000, and new models to measure the equity of campaign finance are being developed by Poder Ciudadano in Argentina and by Transparency International and the Carter Center.[4] Nevertheless, it remains much more difficult to measure the impact of such conditions on the outcome than it is to assess the impact of disenfranchised citizens or lost ballot boxes.

This more comprehensive approach can also lead to a dilemma for observers about whether and when to condemn an electoral process before the actual vote. Structural conditions may be so unfair that they appear obviously to affect the ability of opposition candidates to compete, campaign free of harassment, or register as a political party. Yet even with a grossly tilted playing field, political actors may choose to continue playing the game, sometimes winning at the ballot box, as in Chile in 1988, and sometimes not, as in Panama in 1989 or in Peru in 2000. In these cases, international observers often follow the lead of opposition parties, as it would appear odd to condemn a process when candidates still may want to participate.

If a crucial first step is determining the pervasiveness of the fraud, a second step is to determine whether the fraud observed is sufficient to affect the outcome. Although adherence to appropriate procedures largely determines the quality of an election, the decisiveness of a potential fraud is inevitably a function not just of its impact on these procedures but also of the election outcome, which can generate a potential *paradox of procedural judgments*. Even where significant irregularities have occurred, if they do not appear to have had an impact on the outcome, most of the actors are much more willing to accept the results, even if begrudgingly.

At what point minor legal infractions on election day should be grounds for rejecting an electoral process remains difficult to specify, even when it is clear that any carefully scrutinized election process will likely come up short. Domestic observer groups, in addition to being able to staff an effective quick count, given the high number of volunteers they are often able to send out on election day as well as their desire to be perceived as professional, neutral, and comprehensive, are likely to employ a formal methodology and checklist system regarding election day and the vote count. However, interpretation of the results is still required. Are the infractions relatively minor, perhaps due to cramped facilities or poor training, or are they so serious that many voters were unable to cast their ballots or the vote count was not effectively realized? Do they fit a consistent pattern, suggesting possible centralized coordination? Do they appear disproportionately to favor a particular party? In Mexico in 1994, for example, the Civic Alliance carried out an independent "quick count" that was within 1 percent of the official vote tabulation. At the same time, its network of over 10,000 observers, covering practically 10 percent of the country's voting stations, documented what appeared to be extensive voter secrecy irregularities (such as voters showing others their ballots or someone seeing how a citizen voted), affecting as many as 39 percent of the stations observed (Lehoucq 2003: 248). But what was needed were indications of when and to what extent these irregularities pointed to fraud. In that election, the incumbent Institutional Revolutionary Party gained reelection in a process "deemed transparent by most observers," although one of the two major opposition parties did not fully accept the fairness of the process or the validity of the outcome (Eisenstadt 2004: 48).

Haiti in 1990 demonstrates the potentially pernicious consequences of this paradox. As Henry F. Carey argues, Haiti might have been ill-served by the fact that Jean-Bertrand Aristide's large and clear victory drew so much attention to the presidential contest, overshadowing the massive flaws present in the congressional and local elections. In his view, if observer groups had been more critical of these problems, it might have helped induce improvements in subsequent elections, when the opposition was less willing to look the other way and observers emphasized more the gaps between standards and reality. Ironically, the presidential elections of 1995, which were probably managed somewhat better from an administrative perspective than those of 1990, were boycotted and their results rejected by opposition forces, unlike the situation in 1990. They also came under harsher scrutiny by outside observers. Whether there was actually more electoral manipulation in 1995 than in 1990 is not clear from the evidence (Carey 1998; see also Pastor 1995).

Political Parties and Election Observers: Judgments and Interests

We began this chapter by contrasting the perspective of the major political parties with that of independent election observers. We have reviewed some of the complexities of determining appropriate standards of judgment for countries at different levels of development, varying levels of administrative competence, and histories of democratization and the inevitable uncertainties and potential paradoxes of assessing both the pervasiveness and the decisiveness of fraud.

Given these complications, why not simply employ a perspective of legitimacy, focusing on party assessments that appear to control for the complicating factors discussed here? In our view, relying exclusively on party assessments has one principal difficulty: party judgments may not correlate with those of impartial outside observers due to party organizational weakness or strategic political calculation.

In some cases, the intrinsic weakness or inchoate nature of parties or the party system in a given country may make them inherently manipulable by the incumbent. Such manipulation is common in electoral authoritarian circumstances in which authoritarian regimes tolerate only "pseudo-oppositions" or at most "semi-oppositions" (see Chehabi and Linz 1998c).

In other cases, strategic calculation may lead political parties to condemn electoral processes more harshly than election observers. Parties may choose to boycott elections they are sure to lose in order to rob the winning candidate of legitimacy, a factor that played a role in Haiti in 1995. And if they go to elections, losing candidates or party leaders may claim fraud as the reason for their defeat, rather than admit errors in campaign message or strategy, to preserve their position within their own party, as was evident in Nicaragua in 1996 (Booth 1998; Carter Center 1997) and Mexico in 1994 (Eisenstadt 2004).

Alternatively, strategic calculations may sometimes lead parties that were the victims of fraud to assert that the results are acceptable, even as election observers provide more critical judgments of what they observed. One reason may be their organizational weakness: parties may lack the technical capacity to detect the full extent and nature of fraud that took place. Another reason may be that parties either singly or in collusion are guilty of attempts to affect the outcome, or the losing parties may be co-opted. More positively, the losing parties may decide that even though they perceive the elections as problematic, they are still a promising or a transitional step forward on the path to more democratic processes, as was the case in the transitional elections in Paraguay in 1989 (NDI 1989; Freedom House 1989) and in Haiti in 1990–1991 (Carey 1998; NDI, Carter Center, and Council of Freely-Elected Heads of Government 1990).

Thus, we believe it is necessary to assess the quality of an election (from the perspective of independent observers) in addition to its legitimacy (from the perspective of political actors). Still, in their judgment, observers may be affected, too, by their own strategic interests and calculations. Observer groups may be unduly influenced by or biased against certain party actors. They may have vested interests of their own; for example, if they have worked extensively with the electoral authorities leading up to election day, they may resist publicly acknowledging deficiencies in the process.[5] They may be unduly influenced by the foreign policy considerations of their home country or by world events.

From one election to another, observers and their reports may well weight campaign access, registration issues, or election day tabulation problems differently. In addition, their own judgment may be affected by evolving views regarding required thresholds for successful elections; as already noted, there has been a shift over time toward considering more elements of the preelectoral process, and elections earlier in the 1990s may have been judged by lower standards than more recent ones. Likewise, countries at lower levels of socioeconomic development or with few experiences with democratic elections may be held in an inconsistent fashion to lower standards, depending on competing foreign policy interests, with potentially pernicious consequences for subsequent electoral processes (regarding Haiti 1990–1991, see NDI, Carter Center, and Council of Freely-Elected Heads of Government 1990: esp. 70–71).

Both party actors and observers bring strategic concerns to electoral processes. As a consequence, in a potential *paradox of convergence,* in certain cases when they agree, it may be due more to converging interests than to shared judgments about the nature of the process.

Conclusion

Assessing electoral manipulation in democratizing contexts is an enterprise filled with the potential for uncertainty. In reviewing the evolving efforts to address this challenge, we have identified four paradoxes, and here we will briefly pose ways to address them.

The Paradox of Capacity

Where weak capacity of political parties exists, even limited domestic or international observation can help detect and deter blatant fraud, usually on election day or during the count. Assessing manipulation of structural conditions requires unrestricted and more sophisticated observer efforts. Over time, the solution has been to seek to improve election administration and enhance other elements of state, societal, and party capacity by establishing professional, nonpartisan election administration within a context of a vigorous, free media and a strong, independent judiciary and with political parties that possess both a high capacity to detect fraud and a low will to commit it.

The Paradox of Comprehensiveness

Domestic and international observers should continue developing new methodologies and techniques to evaluate media bias, state use of resources, and campaign finance inequities (even as they must also continually be on guard against potential new forms of election day fraud, such as computer vote count manipulation). In the case of gross structural unfairness, observers should coordinate with the political actors and be clear about the nature of any early condemnation; for example, if there are still opportunities to compensate for adverse structural conditions on election day, they should be noted.

The Paradox of Procedural Judgments

Observers and parties alike should resist complacency when there is a wide victory margin that obscures serious administrative deficiencies, unfair conditions, or irregularities. Observers should document the problems and encourage political parties to engage in early discussions of electoral reform. Donors should push for extra safeguards when levels of distrust are high, and they should recognize problems of sustainability that may arise if large levels of foreign funding help to make one transitional election acceptable but are not forthcoming for subsequent elections.

The Paradox of Convergence

Observers and analysts should continually assess party strategic calculations and interests, as well as their judgments, in assessing the legitimacy of an election. Observers themselves should be transparent about their own interests, competing priorities, or role in providing technical assistance or funding to the election authorities. International organizations should develop a set of minimum international standards and observer codes.[6]

Finally, it is important to note that *acceptable* elections represent a minimal threshold only; all democracies confront the continuing challenge of making their elections more just and more free and fair.

Notes

We appreciate the acute suggestions by Andreas Schedler, particularly regarding the language of paradoxes. This chapter builds on arguments advanced in Hartlyn, McCoy, and Mustillo (2003).

1. Thus, we do not analyze how to make elections that meet some minimal standard more free and fair (for one such effort, see Thompson 2002).

2. On patrimonial regimes, see Bratton and van de Walle (1997) and Hartlyn (1998); on hybrid regimes, see Diamond (2002); and on competitive authoritarian regimes, see Levitsky and Way (2002).

3. A "quick count" is a projection of results based on a statistical sample of voting stations carried out by international and/or domestic observer groups. It provides an independent assessment of results within hours of the polls closing and ideally deters fraud and bolsters confidence in the results being emitted by the electoral authorities, if they are similar.

4. Further information may be found at Poder Ciudadano (www.poderciudadano .org.ar/), Participa (www.participa.cl), Alianza Cívica (www.alianzacivica.org.mx), and Transparency International's "Global Corruption Report 2004" (www.global corruptionreport.org).

5. Haiti 1990–1991 again serves as an example, with the United Nations in the awkward role as both technical adviser for the electoral commission and as evaluators (Carey 1998).

6. The United Nations, the Carter Center, and the National Democratic Institute developed the "Principles for International Election Observation and Code of Conduct for International Election Observers," which was signed by those organizations and others on 27 October 2005 (United Nations 2005). As of early 2006, a similar consensus on the standards for judging elections has yet to be developed.

Part 2

Regime and Opposition Dynamics

4

Elite Ruptures:
When Do Ruling Parties Split?

Joy Langston

Authoritarian breakdowns and subsequent transitions to democracy have been the subject of innumerable studies that cover all regions of the world. One of the major breakthroughs of the more recent literature has been the classification of different sorts of authoritarian regimes into separate categories to better understand variation in both breakdown and transition. An important subtype of authoritarian government is the single-party state, which is notable because of its ability to withstand economic crises, promote socioeconomic change, and manage leadership and succession struggles. In this chapter I examine this special subset of single-party states to understand how one factor—elite rupture—can lead to its breakdown.

One reason given for the considerable longevity of single-party regimes is that minority factions within the party have few incentives to bring down the regime (Geddes 1999). If all members of the authoritarian coalition cooperate, all are better off because the minority faction remains part of the winning coalition (which tends to be inclusive) and the party itself continues in power. Even if the individual politician does not win a certain post, there is still the possibility in the future that he or she will be able to accede to a position that will bring benefits. However, splits within the single-party regime constitute its greatest danger; if an offshoot of the hegemonic party challenges the regime in elections and wins, the party loses the resources and institutional position that made it hegemonic in the first place (Langston 2002). How do the mechanisms of internal cohesion and discipline break down in hegemonic parties? This question is especially interesting for electoral authoritarian regimes, because elections are an always present exit vehicle that disgruntled coalition members can use to topple the hegemonic party regime. To study this issue, I examine two important cases, the Kuomintang (KMT) in Taiwan and the Institutional Revolutionary Party (PRI) in Mexico.

There were no splits in the KMT between its reestablishment on the island of Taiwan in the late 1940s and the death of its second leader in the early 1990s, nor were there any serious elite splits in the PRI between 1952 and 1987. However, in both cases, an internal party rebellion and subsequent exit from the hegemonic party did instigate further opening in the authoritarian regime and, eventually, its breakdown. Therefore, it is important to understand why the calculations of those within the minority factions changed so that an electoral exit became a reasonable strategy. I do not argue in this chapter that elite dissension is the only or even the primary cause of single-party breakdown. Other variables such as socioeconomic modernization, together with subsequent economic downturns, have been identified as long-term structural bases that made a transition possible (Magaloni 1999). I do argue that at certain moments of the regime's trajectory, divisions within the governing coalition are important triggering mechanisms and deserve to be looked at, both in their causes and consequences.

Elections and the role they play in hegemonic party states are crucial to this discussion, because without these forms of aggregate decision, regime politicians could not have found political life outside the KMT or the PRI and so would have found it far more difficult to leave the single-party regime. The costs of creating electoral institutions would have been extremely high, making ruptures either less frequent or more violent. Electoral processes, which were seen only as manipulated exercises in legitimation, in fact formed the basis for exits by regime politicians; such opportunities did not exist in other types of authoritarian regimes, which did not hold regular elections. Not only did opposition groups and parties use the elections to weaken the hold of the hegemonic party over government office, but electoral processes also strengthened minority factions within the authoritarian coalition.

In this chapter I do not consider hegemonic party regimes in African nations such as Angola, Botswana, Mozambique, Senegal, and Tanzania, or the Eastern European Leninist parties. Taiwan and Mexico are both developing states that have seen their indicators of modernization rise dramatically during the post–World War II era. They are middle-income nations with important industrial sectors and large state bureaucracies whose governments intervened heavily in industrial-led development during certain periods. They were not propped up by an external military power (although obviously Taiwan received military support) as were the regimes in the Eastern bloc, and they did not govern developmentally backward societies.

This chapter is only a first step toward understanding the role of elite splits in single-party regime transitions because I cannot examine a full range of cases here. I would need the entire universe of all single-party authoritarian governments to see, first, whether regime divisions existed in single-party states that did not undergo transitions; second, whether splits existed in all cases of single-party regime breakdown; and third, whether divisions that did occur had an effect on regime survival. Did they strengthen the electoral institutions, weaken the incumbent party's ability to win vote shares, or embolden opposition parties? In effect, I include cases of elite splits with no transition, splits with transition, and no splits with no transition but not cases of a lack of elite splits with a regime transition. Therefore, I cannot make any overarching statements about elite divisions in single-party systems. I can, however, speculate about what exogenous variables cause hegemonic party members to change their calculations. The electoral authoritarian element is important in talking about how institutions can change actors' preferences and strategies, because elections offer individual party politicians far easier access to exit options that do not require a massive organizational effort.

Giovanni Sartori defines hegemonic parties thus: "The hegemonic party neither allows for a formal nor a de facto competition for power. Other parties are permitted to exist, but as second class, licensed parties; for they are not permitted to compete with the hegemonic party in antagonistic terms and on an equal basis. Not only does alternation not occur in fact; it cannot occur, since the possibility of a rotation in power is not even envisaged" (1976: 230). A crucial aspect of most hegemonic party states is that they exist in authoritarian electoral environments in which elections are permitted but manipulated to the incumbent's advantage. Elections, held at regular intervals, served as one mechanism that constrained internal regime conflict. In the case of Taiwan, local elections kept the local leaders tied to the KMT through patron-client exchange and allowed voters to choose among different factional alternatives for local posts, while never challenging the KMT's hold over power at the national level. In Mexico, elections allowed for regular elite turnover, which in turn gave PRI politicians the hope that they would win posts in the near future, rewarding their loyalty and discipline. Over time, these unfair elections themselves not only became instruments for opposition parties to weaken the authoritarian hegemonic regime, but also became vehicles that fomented intraelite ruptures that helped end the hegemonic parties' grip on power.

* * *

In this chapter, I look at how hegemonic states maintain their unity and cohesion. I mean to examine why there were few attempts to defeat the dominant party from factions or groups within it. Then I observe how increases in electoral competition in the context of electoral authoritarianism created exit options both for national and local politicians and how these options changed the internal dynamics of regime cohesion. I also discuss the consequences of splits for both regimes.

The Dynamics of Breakdown

Barbara Geddes argues that the inclusive, co-optative nature of single-party regimes should make them the most durable type of authoritarian regime because of the strong incentives for factions to stay within the regime. In this way single-party regimes are unlike military regimes, in which officers concern themselves more with the integrity of the armed forces than with remaining in government (1999: 121–122). Contrary to personalist regimes, single-party states have built their support coalition upon a wide base that includes several classes, not simply a family or clan or ethnic group, and therefore they are better able to weather economic downturns. Elite splits, which were so important in bringing down Latin American military dictatorships, should not be the most important factor explaining the downfall of a single-party regime (see also Geddes 2003). It is in the interests of all groups within the ruling coalition, even those who are (temporarily) in the losing faction, to remain within the party. There is a fair chance they will win posts and privilege in the future, but if they leave, a high probability exists that they will win nothing in the cold outside, mostly because of the regime's iron control over the management and outcomes of electoral contests. Geddes remarks that even long-term economic crises do not have a strong effect on this type of regime and that they often survive the death of an important leader or founder (unlike personalist regimes). Geddes never clearly pinpoints an expected trigger to transition for single-party states, however, as she does for military and personalist governments, other than stating that "neither faction is better off ruling alone, and neither would voluntarily withdraw from office unless exogenous events changed the costs and benefits of cooperation" (2003: 60). In this chapter, I attempt to fill out Geddes's explanation for why hegemonic parties finally do fall.

An already existing electoral system that provides for (unfair) elections dramatically lowers the costs that dissident regime politicians must pay to defect. They do not need to construct a series of institutions that aggregate preferences and provide legitimacy to rulers—they simply have to reform what already exists. Nor do they have to ask their supporters to commit great sacrifices to evict the hegemonic party: no one has to die for his or her country. Elections, together with rising levels of electoral competition that allow regime politicians to survive outside the hegemonic party, are factors that change the calculations of coalition members. More research is needed to determine how, exactly, changing levels of electoral competition affect the cost-benefit calculations of regime actors.

Once electoral competition begins to rise and opposition parties become better organized, a focal point for the transition becomes reforms to the electoral laws and the constitution designed to remove or at least ameliorate the gross advantages of the hegemonic party in the electoral arena. These reforms, however, do not always bring down the hegemonic regime. The combination of electoral competition and electoral reforms changes the incentives for minority factions to remain within the party. The growing willingness on the part of the electorate to vote against the dominant party, as well as fairer elections that make these votes count, allows the ambitious politician within the dominant coalition to make a new cost-benefit analysis: the payoffs from remaining within the regime fall, while at the same time the benefits from competing outside of it rise. As politicians begin to leave the coalition and challenge it via elections (not mass mobilizations designed to bring down the regime immediately), the brakes on uncooperative elite behavior begin to lose their efficacy. As a result, the hegemonic party weakens from within as well as from without.

In Taiwan, during the late 1980s to early 1990s, two KMT factions at the national level (called the mainstream and nonmainstream factions) fought over the direction, endpoint, and speed of the reforms to the 1947 constitution. Beginning in the early phase of Taiwan's transition in the late 1980s, and continuing on until the mid-1990s, President Lee Teng-hui, leader of the mainstream faction (MSF), was able to exclude the more conservative group from party and government leadership positions and isolate it by using the newly formed opposition Democratic People's Party (DPP) as a negotiating partner. When many of the leaders of the nonmainstream faction (NMSF) left the KMT in the early 1990s, they formed the New Party (NP) and attracted many votes from former party brethren. However, the final nail in the KMT's now dominant status (after the erosion of its hegemony in the preceding years) was the exit of the rising KMT politician James Soong from the ruling party in 2000, when he was denied the right to compete for the party's presidential nomination. The charismatic Soong, running for an independent party in the 2000 presidential elections, split the KMT's vote. That allowed the opposition DPP's candidate to win the presidency and turn over executive power for the first time in Taiwan's postwar history to a non-KMT leader.

In the case of Mexico, elite splits were quite prevalent in the early postrevolutionary period before the formation of the hegemonic party (1917–1929) and in the first three decades of PRI rule (1929 to the early 1950s). Over time, however, the regime's leaders were able to devise both formal electoral rules and informal practices that effectively ended internal splits and created several decades of elite discipline, in which losers in nomination and appointment battles accepted their defeat without leaving the party and awaited better political opportunities. In the late 1980s, however, after six years of tremendous economic troubles, the Democratic Current (Corriente Democrática, CD), a dissident group within the PRI, was formed under the leadership of Cuauhtémoc Cárdenas, charismatic son of former president Lázaro Cárdenas (1934–1940). Representing left-wing, protectionist development programs, the group mobilized within the PRI coalition to prevent the imminent imposition of yet another fiscally conservative neoliberal economist as president of Mexico. After being pushed out of the PRI in 1987, Cárdenas came close to unseating the PRI's presidential candidate in the 1988 election, and although a new, far better organized center-left party would be created from this front, the exit of the CD was only the first spring of the river of defections that would plague the PRI for the next fifteen years.

The Construction of the Party-State

In this section, I provide a short overview of the characteristics of each party to better understand how they changed and how they differ from one another, as well as how both parties were able to control their coalition members.

The KMT

The Kuomintang was characterized as a semi-Leninist party, with a "highly structured organization" that reached into all geographic and functional arenas of Taiwanese society (Cheng 1989; Huang 1996). The party was loosely organized on the Leninist model of party cells that were inserted into the military, the government, and nominally private business, student, and professional organizations. The KMT reached into every level of government and bureaucracy and organized many societal groups to better mobilize and control them; it did not, however, have any pretensions to change the basis of the market economy, although its leaders were quite active in regulating it.

There are several reasons the KMT was so successful at maintaining the internal coherence of its elite for over four decades. First, the two leaders of Taiwan from 1949 to 1988, Chiang Kai-shek (hereafter CKS) and his son and successor, Chiang Ching-kuo (CCK), were able to block the formation of national factions, and under their largely undisputed leadership, the two Chiangs were able to manipulate and control the disparate groups within the KMT party-state. Several authors have noted that national factions were not permitted to solidify in Taiwanese politics. Apparently, CKS blamed excessive factionalism for the political and military defeat the KMT suffered on mainland China and strove to eradicate factions from the KMT on Taiwan (Bosco 1992: 164; Dickson 1998: 350).

Second, competitive elections were allowed only at the local level and became channels for the participation of native Taiwanese. National elections were outlawed under martial law, and so positions within the federal legislature and executive branches of government were not open to dispute.[1]

Candidate selection to local posts was controlled at the national level. There was serious electoral competition locally, but new opposition parties were legally prohibited from forming, and a KMT nomination was equivalent to an electoral victory. Because no national elections took place on Taiwan until 1991, there were few political-electoral outlets available to dissident KMT leaders. Politicians within the KMT party regime had to make a calculation: if they left the coalition, their only political future lay in becoming local politicians; but because new parties were illegal, they could only run as independents and never participate in national policymaking.[2] This calculation dampened elite splits.

Because the two Chiangs were considered natural leaders of their nation and party, between 1950 and 1988, political struggles revolved around lower-level bureaucratic and political posts, not the presidency or the party chair—the nation's top political posts.[3] Once the younger Chiang died in 1988, a serious breach appeared in the KMT, as groups within the party began to dispute leadership posts in both the party and the executive.

During its early years on the island, the party brought millions of mainlander Chinese and native Taiwanese into its ranks. It organized societal groups and associations from the top down, controlled their political activities, and mediated relations between the state and private interests.[4] The number of affiliates reached 15 percent of the total population in 1977 and rose to 17 percent by 1986 (Huang 1996: 114). Public officials, including members of the military, veterans, teachers, and bureaucrats, were obliged to join the party and did so in the hundreds of thousands, creating a solid electoral base for the party in local elections, in addition to the territorially based local factions.

The power and authority of the party were highly concentrated in the leadership offices: the president of the nation was also the party's chairman. Members of the Central Standing Committee (the equivalent of the National Executive Committee in the PRI) were hand-picked by the president, and the wishes of this leadership body were simply ratified during periodic party congresses (Domes 1999: 60). The party directed the operations of the bureaucrats who were subordinated to its authority. As was the case in Mexico, the legislative branch of government was beholden to the president/party leader up until the early 1990s transition, with a similar subordination of the judiciary that one saw in Mexico (Ying-Mao Kua 1996: 288).

Local elections were held under largely competitive conditions, with independent candidates permitted both to run and to win seats. However, the KMT-backed candidates won the large majority of seats. Local power brokers were co-opted by the party but not integrated fully into the party structure. Bruce J. Dickson (1998) points out that local factions were responsible for winning local elections, not the local party branches. The KMT strove to support more than one faction per electoral district and fanned the competition between them (Bosco 1992). These factions were bounded in their activities, and no cross-district consolidation was allowed. The party linked the local groups to the party by delivering selective benefits such as construction and insurance contracts. The factions themselves mobilized voters to KMT candidates through networks of patron-client relations, as well as clan and family ties. As one would expect, candidate selection for local races was highly centralized in the hands of party leaders. Local branches of the KMT sounded out party members at the base for their preferred candidates and delivered this list of possible candidates to central party headquarters, the decisionmaking body that actually nominated the candidates (Wu 2001: 105). This relative independence at the local level would become important in the 1990s as electoral competition grew.

The KMT was a well-organized, extensive, and inclusive party that organized local elections while controlling the national political game. At the national level, no elections were held, and the president and party chair could safely ignore the legislative branch, whose members were largely unchanged since the late 1940s. By controlling both the party's organization (and huge resource base—unlike the PRI, the KMT took pains to buy property and companies, making itself one of the wealthiest parties in the world) and the executive branch, the leaders of Taiwan ruled both the party and the bureaucracy with great success. Control over both government appointments and candidate selection for local elections gave the two Chiangs enormous control over their political and bureaucrat elites. Party members had few incentives to leave the organization.

The PRI

The PRI was also a highly organized party with both functional and territorial bases. The party organized branches in the capital, as well as in each of the thirty-one Mexican states, in over 2,000 municipalities, and in the hundreds of electoral districts (although these lower-level branches were often extremely weak). Leaders of the PRI, in particular President Lázaro Cárdenas (1934–1940), organized mass associations that encapsulated millions of Mexicans into one of the three sectors of the party—the workers, whose largest organization is the Mexican Confederation of Workers (Confederación de Trabajadores de México, CTM); the peasant, whose most important group is the National Confederation of Peasants (Confederación Nacional Campesina, CNC); and the popular, which is made up of professional groups, the teachers' union, and state bureaucrats.

Each president of Mexico was the unofficial leader of the party, and although there was a formal president of the National Executive Committee (CEN), this figure served at the president's pleasure. The chief executive controlled his far-flung coalition through several mechanisms, both formal and informal. Informally, he dictated who would succeed him in office and was able to impose this choice on both the party and the voters. The president appointed his party's candidates for governorships and was able to depose elected state executives if they were unable to handle the demands of state government.[5] The president chose the party's candidates for governor and senator, who were assured an automatic electoral victory in the general elections against extremely weak opposition parties. Candidates for the lower house of Congress were selected with the input of several important party bodies, including the leaders of the sectors, the governors, and cabinet ministers. However, the president vetted the final list of PRI congressional candidates. As we saw in Taiwan, the legislative branch of government was extremely weak and ratified the decisions made in the executive bureaucracy. Unlike the case of the KMT before the constitutional reform, each Mexican president served only a six-year term, at which point he was obligated to turn over power to his personally appointed successor. Elections were held every three years for local and federal legislators and mayors and every six years for the president and governors. Consecutive legislative reelection was and is prohibited, and governors and the president can never hold those same posts again.

The hegemonic party in Mexico did not control the executive or bureaucracy, and there were no commissar groups that monitored and dictated administrative behavior (Centeno 1994). The PRI became progressively less important as a decision- or policymaking unit (Garrido 1982) and was left with the responsibility of conducting campaigns, mobilizing voters, and winning elections under conditions that were highly unfair to the opposition parties. Similar to the case of Taiwan, opposition parties were allowed to exist, but their creation and activities were highly regulated by the regime; in this case, the Ministry of the Interior (Secretary of Governance). As Sartori (1976) points out, these opposition parties existed, ran campaigns, and forwarded candidates but were not permitted to win elections or expect to take over the reins of government. In many cases, the opposition parties were financed and controlled by the PRI regime.

Unlike in Taiwan, national political factions were allowed to exist during the hegemonic period. Most *camarillas* (currents or wings) were based on loyalty toward the leader of the faction, not on ideological or policy goals. Membership in the factions was extremely fluid: if one leader became politically immobilized, members were tacitly permitted to cast about for a new group to help them attain higher political positions. One group within the party-regime solidified into something more than a *camarilla* and became outwardly active and vocal in mobilizing opposition to then-president Miguel de la Madrid's (1982–1988) choice of successor (Bruhn 1997; Garrido 1993; Langston 2002).

The PRI governors, although politically beholden to the president, did by and large control state and local politics. Governors placed most of their state party leaders, decided the candidacies of many PRI mayors, and had authority over their state assemblies. State-level factions existed and formed mostly around former governors and politicians who had moved to the national arenas but maintained an interest in state politics. There was not a strong separation between state and national politics, as we saw in Taiwan; ambitious state politicians moved from the local political arena to national politics, and many national party and bureaucratic leaders were sent back to their respective states as governors (Díaz-Cayeros and Langston 2003). Governors were unable to create state political dynasties because the president of Mexico determined who would succeed them. However, state factions existed under hegemonic conditions, and they would become far more important and independent in a context of growing electoral competition.

In Mexico, as in Taiwan (although for different reasons), elections were one of the mechanisms that allowed the hegemonic regime to remain in power for several decades. The constitutional prohibition of consecutive reelection eliminated long-term legislative careers and forced politicians to search out new posts after the end of their three- or six-year terms in office. To win either an elective or appointed position within government, PRI politicians were forced to hitch their political wagon to a powerful factional leader, who in turn owed his future to the current president. However, losing out on a nomination in the present did not constitute the end of one's political career; by remaining loyal and disciplined, one could return to the nomination ring in the next electoral cycle and attempt to win another post.

Internal Ruptures: Causes and Consequences

In both the KMT and the PRI, despite differences in their institutional and electoral contexts, internal ruptures resulted from two related phenomena: succession crises and growing electoral competition. By looking at these ruptures, we can better understand when hegemonic party systems weaken and then break down. Electoral processes change not just the calculations of opposition forces and voters but also the cost-benefit analysis of minority factions within the ruling coalition. One sees changes in the calculations of the "out" faction in both the Taiwanese and Mexican cases: it was no longer more beneficial to take the hit in the current round with the probability of winning a prize in the next. The likelihood of the minority faction ascending to power in the near future was low enough that the future benefits derived from supporting the regime were no longer high enough to forestall a rupture. The costs of maintaining a loyal and disciplined posture also grew dramatically.

Splits Within the KMT

There were, in the case of Taiwan's KMT, two important moments of regime rupture, one well-managed by then–party chair and president Lee (1989–2000), and the other badly fumbled by the same president, which led to the defeat of the KMT in the second direct presidential election of 2000.[6] After the death of CCK in the late 1980s, for the first time open and active factions began working within the KMT.[7] Yun-han Chu (2001: 271) and Michael Ying-Mao Kua (1996: 294) argue that the first split within the hegemonic party was caused by differences over the direction and pace of constitutional reform, struggles over national identity, and control of the party apparatus. CCK, before his death, had both continued the process of Taiwanization of the KMT (bringing leaders born to Taiwanese families into the KMT) and had appointed a Taiwanese-born politician, Lee Teng-hui, as his successor. The opposition DPP had loudly proclaimed the KMT an imposed foreign force (of mainland Chinese) and had called for the independence of Taiwan from China.[8] President/KMT Party Chair Lee refused to repress these calls for independence and so the "struggle over democratic reform and redistribution of power from mainlander elite to native Taiwanese was mixed with the international problem of Taiwan's status as a nation and its relation with mainland China" (Tien and Chu 1996: 1144). President Lee also pushed for quick and profound constitutional reform to allow direct elections for the two legislative bodies, provide for the direct election of the president, and decriminalize calls for independence.

Two factions within the KMT formed around these three divisive issues, the mainstream faction, tied to President Lee, and the nonmainstream faction, tied to mainlander KMT leaders who feared the growing power of the opposition DPP and wanted to maintain martial law.[9] President Lee had initially been weak within the party and so used the constitutional reforms and negotiations with the DPP to weaken his enemies within the KMT. The DPP found itself in the happy position of equilibrium. Most of its more radical demands for political reform were taken up by Lee: direct election of the executive, renewal of direct elections for the Legislative Yuan and National Assembly, and respect for political rights.

By 1993, it became clear that Lee had outmaneuvered the NMSF and its leadership, so several of the leaders of the NMSF decided to jump ship, leave the KMT, and form a new party, called just that—the New Party. Strangely enough, once the NP was formed by what was seen as more recalcitrant KMT members, its leaders began to advocate changes that threatened certain prerogatives of the KMT, such as the new law passed with the support of the DPP that forced public officials to declare their net financial worth. Hung-mao Tien and Yun-han Chu (1996: 1159) write that the NP redefined partisan competition and caused a series of electoral problems for the now dominant KMT in the Legislative Yuan (whose representatives would now be elected every four years, but not concurrently with the president). The popular vote of the KMT fell below the 50 percent mark for the first time in the mid-1990s, and the party was able to maintain its seat majority only through its inspired use of the single, nontransferable vote system. In the first direct elections for president in 1996, two former KMT politicians challenged Lee but were unable to unseat him (Tien and Chu 1996: 1162). The NP hereafter became a secondary party, unable to compete successfully for executive or legislative posts, in large part because it was unable to overcome its foundation as a party for mainlanders on Taiwan.

The consequence of this first split was to drive the negotiations with the opposition to reform the constitution, revoke martial law, and democratize electoral institutions, all in the course of five years. Although the rupture did not bring down the KMT-led regime, it did speed up the process of opening considerably.

The second split within the KMT had more far-reaching effects and contributed directly to its defeat and removal from executive office for the first time since CKS arrived in Taiwan in the late 1940s. The combination of electoral competition and the lack of acceptable rules for selecting the party's presidential nominee led to the Soong split and KMT's electoral debacle of 2000. In part because of his struggles with the NMSF, President Lee had pushed, together with the opposition DPP, to transform Taiwan's form of government from an authoritarian, semiparliamentary regime to a democratic, semipresidential type (Chu 2001: 272).[10] In doing so, he had strengthened his hand against the NMSF and against the local factions by drawing the focus of electoral activity to the national, executive level.

As Chu persuasively argues (2001: 272–275), President Lee was unable to resist the temptation of imposing his successor on his party, and because of the importance of the executive office in the altered constitutional landscape, the struggle became a winner-take-all game within the KMT. In the Taiwanese case, with the incursion of money and media in politics, the importance of candidate-centered campaigning, especially in national executive races, had grown dramatically (Liu 1999). Soong, a former governor of the province of Taiwan for the KMT, whose voting constituency was the same as that for the presidency, was perfectly poised to run and win.[11] Soong had no way to compete for the right to run for the KMT and so he left the party, ran under an independent label (he formed a personalist party after the 2000 elections), and almost won the presidency, coming in second place to the DPP candidate. The KMT's candidate and Lee ally came in a poor third. The Soong split had cost the former hegemonic (and later dominant) party its control over government. The rise of successional politics, together with the growth of an opposition party, led to an important rupture within the governing party that aided and abetted the reform of the constitution and electoral system. The second split within the KMT, also caused by successional conflict, ended fifty years of KMT control.

Splits Within the PRI

There have been two important types of internal ruptures in the PRI since the late 1980s: one that resulted from the inherently unstable nature of the succession process, in which one hand-picked president of Mexico chose his designated replacement, and the other due to increasing exit options offered by more fair elections for all levels of candidacies, from mayors to governors. The split of a left-wing group within the PRI in 1987, which was not preceded by strong increases in electoral competition, was made possible by the fact that presidential elections allowed internal struggles to grow into regime challenges, once the minority faction's payoff structure had been transformed. Without this electoral outlet, the internal regime dissidents would not have had any vehicle to challenge the majority faction within the PRI-regime. The costs of exiting an authoritarian coalition are far lower when electoral institutions already exist.

The 1987 rupture by Cuauhtémoc Cárdenas has been well documented (Bruhn 1997; Garrido 1993; Langston 2002), and the main outlines are the following: a group of former regime leaders (and others who had never reached the pinnacle of government) were largely frozen out of power and had little hope of future advancement due to the changing nature of the regime's economic development program (Hernández-Rodríguez 1992; Lustig 1998). This small group of PRI politicians chose to mobilize openly to democratize the mysterious presidential succession process, thereby breaking a central informal rule of Mexican political behavior.

The leaders of this small group of dissidents began working within the party to open up the presidential succession process and influence the presidential candidate chosen by then-president Miguel de la Madrid (1982–1988). They knew that if Carlos Salinas de Gortari, secretary of planning and budget, were to win, the developmental turn to the right begun by de la Madrid would only deepen. It was not just that Salinas and his supporters would extend and intensify de la Madrid's reforms; a Salinas win would mean the end of any political hopes for those politicians who were tied to more protectionist factions. The benefits from remaining loyal to the system were falling dramatically, making an exit a more reasonable option.

The regime's political leaders responded with a typical mixture of threats and selective benefits to keep the members of the CD within the regime. Some leaders of the regime have stated that they did not take the threat of a regime rupture by the CD or its possible electoral consequences very seriously.[12] However, that was a serious miscalculation: the leader of the CD, Cuauhtémoc Cárdenas, ran for president under the Democratic

Front (an alliance of many small leftist parties) in 1988 and came extremely close to defeating Salinas de Gortari.[13]

We can compare, at least in the case of Mexico, elite ruptures that did not cause regime breakdowns with those that did. The early elite ruptures within the party were caused by the temptation to beat the official PRI candidate and win the presidency via elections (instead of the now close to suicidal military rebellions). In the 1930s, the very youth of the regime and lack of experience meant that minority payoffs had not yet been clarified: it still appeared that the hegemonic party could be defeated in fair elections. Also, minority groups were allowed to mobilize openly within the party to drum up support for their favored candidate. Finally, it was possible in the first half of the 1940s to legally form a personalist party with which to challenge the PRI. During the late 1940s and 1950s, PRI leaders removed all these enabling factors. Another important difference between the early splits and those in the 1980s and 1990s is that, because no real party opposition existed that could compete with the ruling party, regime challengers had to create party organizations that could not only campaign on an equal basis with the hegemon, but also protect their votes in the polling stations, which proved an impossible task.

Over time, these challenges were stifled, and after the 1952 rupture of General Henríquez Guzmán, no other PRI politician left the party to challenge it in presidential elections until 1987. The ability of the regime to manage elections, control their outcomes, and deliver both selective and collective benefits to the Mexican people, especially economic growth and increasing public services, assured the party of continued electoral victories. Because of the lack of competition at the ballot box, it made little sense for minority factions to attempt to bring down the Leviathan in elections.[14]

These incentives changed in the 1980s. By the latter half of the decade, a segment of the protectionist wing of the party realized that if another neoliberal presidential candidate were chosen, it would be difficult to turn back the tide of pro-market economic policies. Waiting out another six-year term for a better political moment to promote an interventionist economic program was seen as a losing proposition. The leaders of this protectionist wing of the PRI, Cuauhtémoc Cárdenas and Porfirio Muñoz Ledo, calculated that they could mobilize support within the ruling coalition to force President de la Madrid to put a less ideologically driven candidate in the presidency. This strategy failed when it became apparent that the PRI would brook no organized voice to dispute the president's informal right to place his chosen candidate. The leaders of the CD were backed into a dichotomous decision: either they stopped their campaign to open up the nomination decision, or they left the party. They left the PRI, ran against its candidate in the 1988 elections, and came close to dislodging the PRI from the presidency in a surprise electoral showing that is disputed to this day.

The consequences of the 1987 rift and the subsequent 1988 elections were profound; first, it became clear that the Mexican voters were ready to depose the sixty-year-old PRI in elections. The two *sexenios* (six-year terms) of terrible economic performance had taken their toll. Second, the split created a viable center-left party that not only survived but also continued to win elections, despite the attacks by the Salinas administration. Third, the PRI regime, led by Salinas, was forced to adopt a new strategy of negotiating far-reaching electoral reforms with the center-right National Action Party (PAN) designed to make the elections more fair and transparent and, at the same time, to create credible electoral outcomes, in order to keep mass protests against dirty elections from creating conditions of political chaos. It is impossible to know what would have occurred if the CD's leaders had not left the regime to lead the electoral challenge of 1988; one could argue the PAN would have continued to push for electoral reforms, and Mexican voters would have eventually rejected the PRI's presidential candidate. Nevertheless, given its long-term reverberations throughout the system, this split clearly contributed to the eventual defeat of the PRI in 2000.

The second type of intraregime rupture was less spectacular than the 1987–1988 split but no less insidious in its effects on regime coherence. From the end of the 1980s until midway through the *sexenio* of PANista Vicente Fox (2000–2006), over thirty PRI politicians (most of whom have based their political careers at the state, not the federal, level) left the hegemonic party and ran under another partisan banner in gubernatorial elections.[15] When electoral competition is close to nonexistent, there are few incentives for ambitious politicians to leave the regime, even if they do not receive selective benefits such as nominations to important elected posts. However, elections under fairer and more competitive conditions change the calculus of discipline for an individual politician, even if he or she does not enjoy the support of a *camarilla* or a group such as the CD. An individual can compete under an opposition party banner and hope to win the elected post, especially for local executive races such as the gubernatorial and mayoral contests. (This chapter has concentrated on opposition party attempts to win national office, but it is important to note that the local stage offered far more opportunities than the presidential race for disgruntled PRI politicians to split from the party.)

The consequences of this type of electorally driven split are important. Ambitious office seekers within the PRI who were denied the right to compete under the party's valuable label now had options. In executive races, the campaigns tend to be more candidate-centered (although the party label still matters), giving these politicians more opportunity to win elected posts from outside the PRI. First, the PRI eventually lost several states to formerly PRI candidates, and in many instances, these states had little history of opposition activity, organization, or possibilities.[16] A second consequence of these state-level splits was the signaling effect they had at the national level. As opposition candidates were elected and governed states, voters gained an opportunity to judge the governing abilities of non-PRI politicians. As Beatriz Magaloni argues (1999), once voters were able to make some evaluations based on performance in executive positions, they were more likely to vote against the hegemonic party. The state splits also had effects on the PRI and its internal practices. In the presidential succession of 1999, Ernesto Zedillo was well aware of the possibility that one of the ambitious politicians within his own coalition could exit the PRI if he were not permitted to compete openly for the presidential nomination under somewhat fair conditions. The nomination fiascoes in several states had proved that PRI politicians were willing to exit the coalition and were able to defeat it in elections. The decades-old prerogative of each president to designate his successor ended in 1999 with the institution of the first presidential primary in the PRI's history.

Conclusion

In this chapter I have examined how two hegemonic parties split and the consequences it has for regime breakdown in electoral authoritarian regimes. Elections in an authoritarian environment play a large role in these ruptures because they lower the costs for minority factions within the authoritarian coalition of leaving the regime and continuing a political career. This fact, together with the focal point that elections constitute for opposition forces, allows a slow evolutionary exit and soft landing for these regimes.

Electoral processes had once played an important role in maintaining single-party regime stability. In Taiwan, regular local elections kept native Taiwanese leaders tied to the national KMT through patron-client exchange, and in Mexico they offered elite politicians a chance to cycle through elected and appointed positions, allowing losers in current nomination battles to hope they would reenter the game. However, elections also created opportunities for both opposition and minority factions to improve their future payoffs. Many of the opposition demands in Taiwan involved creating more electoral space, for example, through renewed national elections in which formerly illegal parties could exist and compete with the hegemon. Once parties could vie to place representatives in the Legislative Yuan, KMT factions used this opportunity as an exit option to increase political payoffs. Much the same occurred in Mexico. When it became apparent that the leaders of the leftist group within the PRI had no future within the party because of a major shift in development strategy, national elections offered the group a viable option to leave the party and continue to compete politically. One should not exaggerate the group's electoral possibilities in 1987 when they left the PRI, however; the PRI enjoyed the benefits of unfair electoral rules, complete control over the electoral institutions, and an extreme resource advantage. Yet, elections offered voters a very low-cost way of demonstrating their frustration with the hegemonic regimes by allowing them individually to register their unfavorable opinion without fear of consequence. In this way, elections not only offered voters and opposition parties a way to bring down the regime but also gave dissident regime groups an exit vehicle.

Elite ruptures have played an important role (although they are not the only factors) in the breakdown of hegemonic regimes. In the case of Taiwan, the conflict between the mainstream and nonmainstream factions drove the president of Taiwan to negotiate democratic reforms with the newly formed opposition party and weakened the party's relation with its local factions, who were increasingly able to sell their electoral services to the highest (party) bidder. Democratic reforms alone did not explain the loss of the presidency in 2000, however. Splits within the former hegemonic party were needed as well. In 1999, a charismatic KMT politician who was not a close ally of President Lee Teng-hui was unable to participate in an open way for the presidential nomination and ran as an independent, splitting the KMT's vote.

In the case of Mexico, the rupture of the CD from the PRI in 1987 provoked a set of profound electoral reforms and the creation of a viable center-left party. These changes ushered in the age of electoral transformation of the Mexican political scene, as opposition parties focused on defeating the PRI in more fair and transparent elections. This new electoral environment eventually allowed local and state PRI politicians to defy the hegemon and win under another party's label. In both hegemonic regimes, ruptures did play a role in their eventual defeats in the hands of opposition parties in duly constituted elections. Part of the explanation of how these types of authoritarian regimes break down revolves around how electoral institutions and processes change the calculations of ambitious politicians within the authoritarian coalition.

Notes

1. National elections were held on mainland China in 1947 for representatives to the two bodies of the federal legislature, the Legislative Yuan and the National Assembly. The Legislative Yuan functioned as a unicameral congress, and the National Assembly selected the nation's president and reformed the 1947 Constitution. When the KMT was forced to flee to the island of Taiwan, it insisted it was the true government of all China and that one day it would return to govern the mainland. Under the argument that the 1947 legislature represented all China and that

any elections held only on Taiwan were unrepresentative of mainlanders, the KMT refused to call new elections (on Taiwan) for the Legislative Yuan or the National Assembly. These two bodies continued in office from the late 1940s until the early 1990s: it was the Taiwanese version of the Long Parliament. By the late 1960s, the original representatives began to die or retire, and so the KMT allowed by-elections to be called that only elected a few representatives at a time. It was not until 1991 that the second Legislative Yuan was elected.

2. Two co-opted satellite parties existed under the KMT regime but won very few seats. New parties were prohibited from forming under martial law. When the DPP organized as a party in 1986, it was still illegal, and many hard-liners within the KMT wanted the president and party chair CCK to repress the movement, which he refused to do. Martial law was revoked a few years later.

3. Because the National Assembly chose the president and because that body had originally been elected in the 1940s, there was no hope that it would ever choose a non-KMT executive. Therefore, the opposition DPP pushed for direct election of the president.

4. The KMT was particularly strong in the Veterans' Association and students' groups. But it helped organize industrial associations and professional societies as well (Ying-Mao Kua 1996: 289). See Cheng (1989: 477) for more on the party's organization.

5. Mexico has a federalist, presidential form of government with a bicameral legislature and thirty-one states and one federal district. Since the 1977 electoral reforms, the electoral system allows for both majority and proportional representation. As of now, there are 500 federal deputies, 300 of whom are elected in majority districts and 200 elected from five regional districts in closed proportional representation lists. The Senate has undergone several reforms since 1988, and now elects sixty-four senators from closed, two-person ballots in each state, as well as a first minority senator (the first name in the two-person ballot from the party that comes in second place in the state). In addition, thirty-two more senators are placed from a closed proportional representation list from a nationwide district.

6. Direct presidential elections were instituted in Taiwan only in 1996. New elections for the National Assembly were held before the 1996 presidential elections.

7. Different groups have been identified within the KMT, but they were not considered important. See Domes (1999: 60) and Dickson (1998: 354).

8. Calling for Taiwanese independence implicitly meant that the Republic of China would renounce its claim to political authority on mainland China, and thus it was a recognition of international reality that old-time Chinese mainlanders on Taiwan would never accept.

9. Tien and Chu (1996: 1145) remark that the NMSF did not want to change the 1947 Constitution (written on the mainland) because it was tacitly admitting to the end of hopes of returning to govern China. The NMSF also did not want the direct election of the president. The MSF, on the other hand, pushed for democratic reforms to the Constitution (see Chu 2001: 271).

10. Although constitutionally the National Assembly chose a president every four years, in practice, because CKS and CCK had governed the nation and controlled the National Assembly, the nation resembled a strong, executive-based regime with a weak legislature. With the inception of direct elections for the president, along with new elections for both the Legislative Yuan and National Assembly (with only one of its two responsibilities intact, that of reforming the constitution), Taiwan now approached a presidentialist form of government.

11. That was one of the oddities of the Taiwanese political system. Because officially the KMT represented all of China, the government of the island of Taiwan

was simply one more region in China. However, in practice, the governor of Taiwan (once he was directly elected, which was another of the constitutional reforms negotiated by the KMT and the DPP in the early 1990s) was a shadow president and could gain enormous popularity with Taiwanese voters if he chose to run for president. President Lee, once he realized this problem, changed the constitution so that the provincial governor of Taiwan is no longer an elected position.

12. Author interview with the president of the CEN during this period, Jorge de la Vega Domínguez, March 1996.

13. Two major factors help explain the Mexican voters' willingness for the first time to vote en masse against a PRI presidential candidate; first, the staggering series of economic downturns that had slapped the Mexican economy between 1976 and 1988, and second, the dismal crisis management by public officials in the Federal District in the aftermath of the 1985 earthquake.

14. Juan Molinar argues (1991) that the PRI was so dominant by the late 1950s that it decided to reform the electoral system to allow opposition parties to win a maximum of twenty seats each in the lower house through a modified PR system.

15. The author has compiled a database of all gubernatorial candidates for the three major parties, PRI, PAN, and PRD, and their professional backgrounds from 1989 to 2003.

16. For example, the states of Zacatecas, Tlaxcala, Nayarit, and Baja California Sur.

5

Tipping Games: When Do Opposition Parties Coalesce?

Nicolas van de Walle

Opposition cohesion is often described as a prerequisite for successful regime transitions. As long as the incumbent strongman is able to keep the opposition divided, it is argued, his hold on power is safe.[1] A relatively unpopular ruler can use incumbency advantages to maintain the upper hand, notably through state patronage and intimidation. In such cases, even relatively free and fair elections need not represent a threat to the incumbent—he can usually manufacture a victory with a plurality of the vote, as the opposition divides its support across numerous candidates.

Meanwhile, divided oppositions expend energy and political capital in internal squabbles. They criticize each other publicly as much as the incumbent and the ruling party and inevitably lose some legitimacy in the process. In regime transition narratives, the unification of the opposition under a single banner invariably is presented as a watershed in the ousting of the incumbent, just as divisions within the opposition are invariably mentioned to explain the ability of the president to retain power. Thus, in descriptions of the democracy movement in Zambia in the early 1990s, the making of a grand opposition coalition uniting business and labor under the Movement for Multiparty Democracy (MMD) banner has been described in nearly heroic terms (Rakner 2004; Rakner and Svåsand 2004; Burnell 2001). The survival of the Moi regime in Kenya throughout the 1990s, however, was widely blamed on the inability of the opposition to unite. This dynamic was particularly evident in the 1992 elections (Throup and Hornsby 1998), when President Daniel arap Moi was able to retain the presidency after garnering only 36 percent of the vote, despite intimidation during the campaign and some fraud on election day. Three different opposition candidates each managed at least 17 percent of the vote. Clearly, had the opposition overcome its disunity, it might have booted Moi out of power. Opposition politicians were widely blamed in these cases for putting their personal interests above the cause of democracy.

These two narratives are paradigmatic: key political alliances are almost invariably part of the story in any electoral victory. The ability of incumbents to keep key supporters in the presidential fold helps to determine whether they retain power, whereas defections to the opposition often presage electoral defeat. There have not been many cases of opposition victories over incumbents in sub-Saharan Africa since 1990: by my count (see Table 5.1), out of the ninety-two presidential elections that took place between 1990 and 2004, electoral turnovers occurred thirteen times. In addition, there are five cases of an electoral victory by an opposition candidate in which no incumbent was defeated. The best example of the latter is perhaps Kenya, once again: in the 2002 elections, the opposition, now united around Mwai Kibaki, defeated Moi's handpicked successor, Uhuru Kenyatta (Anderson 2003). Moi had chosen to respect the constitution and not run for another term.

There appears to be a clear correlation between cohesion and electoral victory. The issue of causation is far less clear, however. Do broad opposition coalitions bring about victory? Or do opposition candidates gain supporters as the prospects of victory approach? Unfortunately, the information necessary to disentangle these two alternatives is not easily available in systematic form. Nonetheless, in this chapter I investigate the circumstances that influence the degree of opposition cohesion in electoral autocracies and its relationship to electoral outcomes.

I start by defining the universe of states that is my focus here—electoral autocracies or hybrid regimes (Diamond 2002). Arguably, for reasons that will become clear, opposition cohesion is even more important to transitions in such regimes, defined as regimes that combine relatively competitive multiparty elections with low levels of executive accountability and various political practices associated with authoritarian rule. As has been acknowledged by a number of scholars (e.g., Diamond 2002; Schedler 2002a, 2002b), these are inherently ambiguous regimes, in which incumbents derive key advantages in the political game by resorting to a "menu of manipulation," but oppositions nonetheless have a chance to advance to power through the ballot box. It is important to problematize the degree of democracy in the political system, in order to show that opposition cohesion is more likely to occur in more democratic political systems. I then examine transitions as a "tipping game," in which opposition cohesion is not a cause of transition but rather a consequence of a growing probability of transition due to a number of interrelated factors. I argue that the particular dynamics of political transitions can be understood to result from strategic behavior on the part of key political actors playing out a tipping game in which they wish to be on the winning side. In the second half of

Table 5.1 Opposition Victories in Presidential Elections, Sub-Saharan Africa, 1991–2002

Country	Year	Winner	Winner's Vote Share	Second Candidate's Vote Share	Freedom House Score
Benin	1991	Nicéphore Soglo	36.2	27.2	5
Benin	1991	Nicéphore Soglo	67.5	32.5	5
Benin	1996	Nicéphore Soglo	35.7	33.9	4
Benin	1996	Mathieu Kérékou	52.5	47.5	4
Burundi	1993	Melchior Ndadaye	65.7	32.9	14
Cape Verde	1991	Antonio Mascarenhas	73.4	26.6	5
Cape Verde	2001	Pedro Verona Pires	46.5	45.8	3
Cape Verde	2001	Pedro Verona Pires	49.4	49.4	3
Central African Republic	1993	Angé-Felix Patassé	37.3	21.7	7
Congo-Brazzaville	1992	Pascal Lissouba	35.9	20.3	6
Congo-Brazzaville	1992	Pascal Lissouba	61.3	38.7	6
Ghana	2000	John Kufuor	48.4	44.8	5
Ghana	2000	John Kufuor	57.4	42.6	5
Guinea-Bissau	1999	Kumba Yala	38.8	23.4	8
Guinea-Bissau	2000	Kumba Yala	72	28	8
Kenya	2002	Mwai Kibaki	62.2	31.3	6
Madagascar	1992	Albert Zafy	45.9	28.6	8
Madagascar	1992	Albert Zafy	66.7	33.3	8
Madagascar	1996	Didier Ratsiraka	36.6	23.4	6
Madagascar	1996	Didier Ratsiraka	50.7	49.3	6
Madagascar	2001	Marc Ravalomanana	51.5	35.9	6
Mali	1992	Alpha Konaré	45	14.1	5
Mali	1992	Alpha Konaré	69	31	5
Malawi	1994	Bakili Muluzi	47.2	33.5	5
Niger	1993	Tandja Mamadou	34.3	26.6	8
Niger	1993	Tandja Mamadou	54.4	45.6	8
Senegal	2000	Abdou Diouf	41.3	30.1	7
Senegal	2000	Abdoulaye Wade	58.5	41.5	7
Zambia	1991	Frederick Chiluba	75.8	24.2	5

Source: Author's database.

Notes: In elections with runoff systems, both first- and second-round results are reported. Freedom House scores indicate civil rights and political liberties; the range of possible scores is 2 (most democratic) to 14 (least democratic).

the chapter, I examine the structural factors that may condition the likelihood of opposition cohesion. I consider political institutions, historical and cultural factors, ethnic pluralism, socioeconomic development, and international influences. The discussion is largely based on a data set of ninety-two presidential elections in sub-Saharan Africa, but the implications can be generalized beyond that region.

How Electoral, How Authoritarian?

This discussion has so far assumed that multiparty elections are the defining events of political transitions. But that is not always the case. On the one hand, in a number of cases, regime transitions are precipitated by military intervention or some form of extra-electoral action. Thus, in Mali, a pro-democracy military coup spelled the end of the Traoré regime. It might have survived the street protests and diplomatic pressures, much like Robert Mugabe has in Zimbabwe (Compagnon 2000), or Lansana Conte has in Guinea, if relatively junior officers had not conspired so effectively against it (Camara 2000). In Congo (Quantin 1997) and Benin (Decalo 1998; Heilbrunn 1993; Banégas 1997), a national conference pushed the president out of office in favor of an interim government and elections, in what local observers labeled a "civilian coup." In these cases, the founding election followed an interregnum and came well after the old regime had fallen. A temporary government organized the elections, and the different candidates and parties competing for seats rarely enjoyed the advantages of a typical incumbent, even if the interim government may have played favorites.

Before the regime fell, elections were either so unfair as to preclude an opposition victory, or they were nonexistent. In many cases, it was precisely the fact the elections were unwinnable that led the opposition to favor extralegal means to gain power. Here it is possible to argue that the key factors were the numerous defections suffered by the president in the preceding weeks that tipped the balance toward the opposition. In Benin, President Mathieu Kérékou's regime progressively lost domestic support throughout 1989–1991 because of simply disastrous economic performance and the explicit refusal of the major donors—including France—to support the regime without changes. The National Conference was the final event, but the fall of the government seemed inevitable long before it fell. In Mali, economic collapse in the early 1990s led to prolonged student and civil service protests against the regime. The regime's legitimacy having collapsed, top senior officers in the army did not rise to President Moussa Traoré's defense when junior officers seized the presidential palace, and his two-decade-old regime was removed without virtually anyone willing to stand up for it (Vengroff 1993; Thiriot 1999). But clearly, the decisiveness of the military action that removed the Traoré regime was not predicated on the breadth of support for it. The Malian army turned out to have democratic proclivities and organized elections, which introduced the current multiparty democratic regime. There are just as many instances in which the military intervened successfully in an antidemocratic manner, despite little popular support and no obvious political alliance behind it. The military coup in Algeria that prevented the victory of the Islamic Salvation Front (FIS) at the polls in December 1991 is an example, as is the December 1999

coup in Côte d'Ivoire by General Robert Gueï. The latter attempted to legitimize his rule with suspect elections a year later, but the absence of domestic
support, plus intense international pressure, eventually forced him to acknowledge the electoral victory of Laurent Gbagbo, himself an ethnic entrepreneur
with little respect for democratic norms (Contamin and Losch 2000).

   In this chapter I am nonetheless primarily interested in countries in
which the opposition political actors compete in elections that they generally consider imperfect but winnable. I hypothesize that existing levels of
democracy condition the ability of opposition actors to coalesce. Zimbabwe
from 1995 to 2005 offers an example of opposition cohesion despite very
high levels of repression. But Zimbabwe stands out as a relative exception,
and it seems intuitively clear that the ability of the opposition to coalesce
and eventually win an election is in large part a function of the degree of
democracy that exists within the system. That is not easy to test quantita-
tively without knowing much more about the dynamics within the opposition. Nonetheless, a crude test is possible: in a data set of ninety-two direct
presidential elections in Africa between 1990 and 2004, I collected data on
the share of the vote received by the leading opposition candidate, since the
higher this score, the more likely the opposition is united. In fact, that number is significantly correlated ($p = -0.44$) with the Freedom House scores
of political rights and civil liberties.[2] Since some authoritarian leaders tolerate reasonably high scores by the leading opposition candidate in elec-
· tions that they have no intention of losing, it is a remarkably high correlation. Clearly, the more democratic the country, the higher the share of the
vote going to the opposition's top candidate.

   In some countries, no matter how popular the opposition is, it will not
win an election because fraud, intimidation, and gerrymandering (for parliamentary regimes) will rob it of the victory. In Chad, for instance, the
Idriss Deby regime has countenanced regular elections since the early
1990s in order to assuage donor demands for governance improvements.
Deby has even allowed the opposition to force him into a runoff (in 1996).
But the regime has used a combination of electoral manipulation, intimidation, and violence—political assassinations have been common—as well as
co-optation of key elements of the opposition to dominate the political
game (Buijtenhuijs 1998). Various structural factors militate against opposition cohesion: Chad is a huge, sparsely populated country, with very low
levels of literacy and poor communications systems. There is little experience of legislative politics, and the party system is volatile and weakly
institutionalized. Religious, regional, and ethnic differences divide politicians and their parties. But Deby has masterfully used the carrot and the
stick to worsen the effects of these structural dynamics.

   Andreas Schedler (2002a) may well be correct in his assessment that in
all electoral autocracies, each election that is conducted provides a medium

to long-term boost to the opposition and delegitimizes autocratic rule, but nonetheless a clear distinction exists between "gray regimes" and pure electoral autocracies such as Chad or Togo under Gnassingbe Eyadema, where an opposition victory is simply inconceivable. In the "gray regimes," the presumption exists that the opposition could possibly win despite incumbency advantages; in other words, it may secure such a decisive majority that incumbents cannot secure an official victory. In such states, constitutional legitimacy has some weight, and governments cannot steal elections too blatantly. Thus, President Ibrahim Babangida's best efforts were not enough to prevent the electoral victory of Moshood Abiola in the 1993 elections in Nigeria, for instance. In Madagascar's December 2001 elections, similarly, incumbent president Didier Ratsiraka appears to have tried various forms of fraud to deny a simple majority electoral victory to his rival, Marc Ravalomanana, in order to force a second round, which he hoped to win in some manner. Although distinguishing between these regimes is difficult, the distinction is still meaningful.

Thus, opposition cohesion and the possibility of an electoral victory over an incumbent are functions of the level of democracy in countries that convene multiparty elections. At the risk of stating the obvious, electoral fraud almost invariably benefits incumbents; thus the greater the amount of electoral fraud, the less likely a transition, even if oppositions are united. The perfect illustration is Zimbabwe, in which a relatively united opposition is unable to remove President Mugabe from power because his core coalition remains intact, most notably the military and internal security apparatus (Compagnon 2000). The link between the level of democracy and the prospects for the opposition are well captured in Table 5.1, which provides information on the eighteen cases in which the opposition managed to win a presidential election. The Freedom House scores show that all of these elections have taken place in states that are "partly free" or "free," with the exception of the victory of Melchior Ndadaye in Burundi, a tragically pyrrhic victory since he was assassinated in a military coup less than a year later. In addition, the table shows that eleven of the seventeen cases were decided in two-round majority voting systems, which suggests that this electoral system facilitates opposition cohesion, a theme I return to below.

Transitions as Tipping Games

Regime transitions and the ouster of an incumbent ruler in an electoral autocracy are often overdetermined processes. Several factors appear to play a central role. For this reason, scholarly debates continue in the "transitology" field about the relative explanatory power of different factors, from international pressures to economic pressures, external shocks, elite fragmentation, and opposition cohesion. Usually, a compelling case can be made for each factor.

Some explanatory factors are clearly exogenous. For instance, leaders' actions cannot influence weather patterns or the international price of raw commodities, yet prolonged drought or a worsening in the international terms of trade can negatively affect the domestic economy, with consequences for the popularity and stability of the regime in place. Similarly, positive shocks can benefit governments. Analysts typically emphasize negative shocks, but recent history provides plenty of examples of windfall revenue increases coming to governments because of a sudden jump in oil or coffee prices.

Of course, the actions of government also affect the economy. Thus, unpopular governments may be tempted to engage in excessive borrowing or unsustainable monetary policies to buy support with public expenditures in the short term, though that will eventually undermine macrostability. Indeed, politicians have notoriously short time horizons and may be tempted to pursue unsustainable policies to buy time in reaction to exogenous factors. Thus, the quality of Nigerian economic policymaking decreased sharply after the oil price declines in the 1990s. A number of governments all over the world have reacted to economic shocks with unsustainable international borrowing, sometimes causing considerable damage to long-term economic prospects.

But many of the factors shaping the dynamics of a regime transition are not so clearly exogenous. To be sure, the behavior of political actors, both within the governing majority and within the opposition, can be partly explained by stubborn ideological or ethnic factors. In Cameroon, as well as in many other countries, for instance, the army has been ethnically shaped over many years by the regime; since his arrival in power, Paul Biya has made sure the officer corps is predominantly Beti and southern. The loyalty of top officers to the regime is strengthened by various links of kith and kin, as well as their rational calculation that Biya's fall would result in the probable loss of a number of advantages from which they benefit. In the early 1990s, democratization in Burundi was brutally ended by the Tutsi officer corps, which simply could not countenance the loss of power and privileges that elections and the emergence of a Hutu-dominated government implied. Dan Posner (2004) and others may be right to say that ethnic identity and conflict are constructed, but once they are constructed, their logic pervades economic and political institutions and can be considered as fixed in the short and medium terms.

At the same time, the behavior of political actors is often highly contingent: self-interested and rational actors respond to events in a context of substantial information asymmetries and uncertainty. Even in ethnically or ideologically polarized political situations, institutional actors are likely to support a stable regime but less likely to back one that is tottering or obviously unstable. Political actors want to be on the right side of history. Their support for a regime is in part self-serving, and they are more likely to withdraw support if the regime's survival seems in doubt. Their main difficulty is gauging correctly the regime's chances of survival, which is typically difficult in a political environment without an effective press, poorly institutionalized parties, and little transparency.

Defecting from the regime is risky, moreover, for if the incumbent manages to stay in power, then defectors will pay a substantial penalty. In some cases, if the defector is correct in his assessment that the regime is doomed but defects too early, the penalty will be exacted before the incumbent actually falls. That is why highly unpopular and bankrupt regimes take so long to fall. To the bitter end, the regime manages to retain some support from would-be defectors who do not want to defect too soon. Once it is clear that the incumbent's fate is sealed, however, things can move very fast—numerous actors defect as quickly as they can to derive the benefits of defection.

Political transitions thus constitute highly contingent political processes, in which actors act strategically in a context of information asymmetries. The dynamics of opposition groups and the degree to which they coalesce can be viewed as a tipping game. Political transitions can be understood as the rapid movement from one power equilibrium to another, in the course of which a majority of political forces moves from one coalition to another. The incumbent had a winning majority but loses it, thanks to defections of key elements to the opposition.

I would like to argue that tipping, or "cascades" (Laitin 1998), represent a useful heuristic to understand these dynamics in electoral autocracies. First, in mature democracies, politics are considerably less autonomous of voters and their preferences. It would be inconceivable for the socialist and communist-dominated trade unions in a country like France to switch their support to a right-wing party, and even if they did, their members would be unlikely to follow suit. Ideological divisions and long-standing cleavages shape the actions of politicians, who seek the support of voters within a fairly narrow and well-established political space in which economic and social policies dominate. In most multiparty systems that have emerged out of the third wave of democratization, however, political cleavages are not well-set, and identity politics typically trump ideology. Voting is often closely tied to region, ethnicity, language, or religion. As a result, political alliances are more fluid and changing, and individual politicians have a greater degree of autonomy in the deals and alliances they make to gain political power. I recognize that the previous statement is not equally true in all countries and may change over time, and below I examine the impact of variance on this issue for the likelihood of opposition coalescence. But as a general statement comparing the electoral autocracy with the typical mature democracy, the statement can be viewed as relatively unproblematic. Tipping dynamics are essentially elite processes that seem more likely to take place in political systems in which party platforms do not sharply polarize the party system and, as a result, the relationships among politicians and across parties are more fluid.

Second, elections are not the entire show in the electoral autocracies with which we are concerned. Because elections are highly imperfect, with fraud before and during election day, and because the incumbent uses various underhanded tactics to try to win the election, elite deal making is an important dimension of politics. The decisions of key politicians weigh heavily on electoral outcomes and their legitimacy.

How do these tipping dynamics take place? In some circumstances, a single actor can tip the balance away from the incumbent regime. The defection of an important ethnic leader, who in effect represents a sizable segment of the national electorate, may be the signal that the incumbent's fate is sealed and encourage a cascade of other defections. In Benin, for instance, the victory of Nicéphore Soglo in 1991 hinged on his ability to convince other opposition candidates, whom he had defeated in the first round, to support him. One key ally proved to be Adrien Houngbedji, who would be rewarded with the position of speaker of the parliament. Yet, four years later, it was the latter's open support for Kérékou, once again following the first round (in which he had come in third with 19.7 percent of the votes) that would ensure the defeat of President Soglo. Kérékou would name Houngbedji his first prime minister.

More typically, no single actor can claim this leverage, or it is impossible to know in advance which actor will tip the balance in this manner. Then the key dimension of a tipping game is a problem of coordination: the survival of the regime depends on the support of actors A, B, C, and D. It is probably the case that the regime only needs the support of two of them to survive. Thus, any of the four need to be sure that at least two of the others are defecting before they will choose to defect. A will defect from the regime, if A believes that at least two of the other actors are also defecting. The probability of defection is a closely guarded secret, since it will be severely punished by the regime if it manages to survive or does not fall immediately, so it is very hard for A to know the intentions of the other key actors, and similarly, it is in A's interest to conceal his preferences. True, there may be a special reward to those actors who defect first and early, since they may be rewarded with a prominent position in the successor regime, but early defection is particularly risky.

Much the same dynamic takes place within the declared opposition. There also, problems of coordination are paramount. As long as the incumbent appears unassailable, opposition cohesion is less likely. Individual

opposition leaders gain an advantage from maintaining their own autonomy, deriving notoriety and perhaps material advantage as leaders of a specific region, ethnic group, or social class. As such leaders, they can negotiate with the incumbent ruler, who will have more of an incentive to deal
with them than if they were secondary leaders in a larger opposition alliance.
Perhaps each would like to lead the opposition alliance, even if its defeat was
assured, but deciding whom that will be poses classic prisoners' dilemma situations—each prefers the secondary gains of being a minor opposition leader
to the larger but far more uncertain gain associated with being the leader of
the opposition.

These calculations and collective action dilemmas change somewhat as
the ruler becomes less popular and the regime begins to totter. On the one
hand, the bickering over who gets to lead the transition becomes more acer-
bic as the fruits of victory become more tangible. But on the other hand, the
incentives to strike a side deal with the regime go down as its future seems
less assured and the gains from becoming even a lieutenant in the successor
regime seem more certain. Overall, opposition cohesion becomes more
likely when an opposition victory appears more likely. Of course, this cohesion may not last long. The "united front" that wrested power from the
autocratic incumbent may fall apart after the election, when a new executive emerges and bickering over how to share power becomes inevitable.
But in the run-up to victory, it is not unusual to see a cohesive opposition.

We often see the phenomenon of regional or ethnic leaders sitting on
the fence, not entirely of the regime yet not of the opposition either and
willing to join the governing coalition, albeit temporarily, in exchange for
various material and other benefits. Again, the tipping dynamic is charac-
teristic: the movement of one actor away from the regime, or from the
fence to the opposition, may be decisive in shifting perceptions about the
viability of the regime.

It is indeed striking how often the new leadership following a transition
is made up of politicians who were neither radically opposed to the old
order nor prominent in it. Far more typical is the emergence of political
actors during the transition who may have played secondary roles within
the regime before defecting, or who moved back and forth between regime
and opposition throughout their careers. Thus, in Senegal, Abdoulaye Wade
and some of his closest lieutenants in the Senegalese Democratic Party
(PDS) had served in governments under Abdou Diouf at different points in
the 1980s and 1990s, and Wade's victory in 2000 was in part due to key
defections from the Diouf regime. In Eastern Europe in the 1990s, a surprisingly large proportion of the politicians that emerged from elections to participate or lead governing cabinets could not be described as hard-core opponents of communist rule but typically had not been dissidents either. Instead,
they were men and women who had "gone along to get along" with the
region's communist order.

If I have discussed opposition cohesion and regime defections together, it is because they are usually part of the same general dynamic. Thus, in Zambia, most of the components of the united opposition were elements of the United National Independence Party (UNIP) regime until the end of the 1980s (Burnell 2001; Rakner 2004). In sum, the key dynamic of the Zambia transition was not the unity of the opposition, but rather the inability of Kenneth Kaunda to maintain the integrity of his ruling coalition. The defection of the labor movement from the presidential majority was as important to the victory of the MMD as the fact that the union movement then became part of a bigger alliance. Opposition cohesion and incumbent fragmentation often mirror each other and cannot be understood separately. Opposition cohesion is a necessary but not a sufficient condition for a regime transition. It is only when defections in the regime swell the opposition and it manages to unite that the conditions for a transition are met.

Clearly, it is important to distinguish the unity of the opposition from its breadth. The opposition can be reasonably united but not nearly substantial enough to challenge incumbents. In Côte d'Ivoire throughout much of the 1990s, Laurent Gbagbo was the undisputed leader of a united, albeit relatively inconsequential opposition, challenging the still united regime of Félix Houphouet-Boigny, but unable to threaten it. There are few such cases because it is difficult for the opposition to maintain its unity in the face of such pressures. In stable electoral autocracies like Togo, Tanzania, or Uganda, the ruling party has weathered the political liberalization of the 1990s without a significant threat to its hegemony, so opposition cohesion does not much matter (on Uganda, see Furley 2000). In these cases, the government invariably combines the carrot and the stick to undermine opposition resolve. Using state resources, incumbents can encourage defections from the main opposition coalition and promote its fissiparous tendencies. State funding for political parties can constitute one particularly insidious form of bribery in an economic setting in which the financing of political activities is problematic. The promise of an important office for politicians who join the presidential majority is another. On the stick side, various forms of intimidation, from temporary arrests to murder, all feature on the "menu of manipulation."

The opposition may remain cohesive, even as it is reduced to a core of politicians whose political identities are so marked in opposition to the regime that they are less easily able to rejoin the presidential majority. Thus, in Cameroon, Paul Biya managed to reestablish his hold on power in the 1990s, following a period in which it appeared extremely shaky. The opposition was led throughout by John Fru Ndi and his party, the Social Democratic Front (SDF). Though at one point a relatively broad multiethnic alliance, the SDF has slowly but surely been reduced to a core of support in Douala and western parts of the country. Many SDF supporters and fellow travelers have rejoined the presidential majority, and Fru Ndi is now perhaps the only major politician left in the SDF opposition (Eboko 1999; Takougang 2003). Much the same could be said of Gabon or Togo.

In sum, this first part of the chapter has advanced two propositions about opposition cohesion. First, I have argued that transition episodes are characterized by tipping dynamics, which help to explain their pace and rhythm. The likelihood of opposition cohesion is largely determined by perceptions regarding the prospects for opposition victory. Second, such tipping dynamics are more likely to characterize electoral autocracies, in which elections are rigged enough to favor incumbents but not so thoroughly that they will always necessarily win. The remaining sections of this chapter briefly investigate the factors that can affect these tipping dynamics.

Structural Conditions

Political Institutions

What institutional factors affect the ability of the opposition to coalesce? That is a huge topic, but it is possible to make two rough points, one relating to electoral systems, the other to systems of government. First, some electoral systems privilege coalition building more than others. For example, as suggested by the data presented above, two-round majority voting systems clearly facilitate opposition unity. Parties can forge reciprocal agreements that each will support the candidates of their political partner whenever they emerge on top following the first round. These pacts work well in both presidential and parliamentary elections. Thus, in Senegal in the 2000 elections, Wade emerged from the first round in second place with 30.1 percent of the vote, behind the incumbent president Abdou Diouf, who garnered 41.3 percent of the vote. In a first-past-the-post system, these results would have meant the victory of the incumbent. In Senegal, despite a bitterly disputed first round of voting, Wade was able to bargain for the support of Moustapha Niasse. This longtime Diouf associate had recently left the Socialist Party (PS) to form his own party and had come in third in the first round, with 16.8 percent of the vote. Sensing the likelihood of an opposition victory, Niasse forged a deal with Wade and publicly backed him. Wade won the runoff with 58 percent of the vote and named Niasse prime minister in his first government. One might mention that the first round's fourth-place candidate, Djibo Ka, another mainstay of PS governments in the 1980s and early 1990s, chose to endorse Diouf for the second round, mistakenly believing the socialist president would survive.

I have already alluded to a remarkably similar story of interround negotiation taking place in Benin. There as well, the incumbent won the first round before losing in the majoritarian runoff (see Table 5.1). The point is that the two-round majority system is ideal for such wheeling and dealing. Candidates can use the first round to gauge their level of support, often determined by ethno-regional factors, and then bargain for a good deal for themselves with the candidate they calculate will win in the second round.

The two-round majority system is thus relatively favorable to challengers. Nonetheless, manipulation of the process by incumbents can often trump this pro-challenger dimension. In Gabon throughout the 1990s, for instance, President Omar Bongo made sure to win a majority in the first round and thus avoid the dangers of a second round. Much of Francophone Africa has used some version of the two-round system since independence, a clear case of the historical influence of France, the colonial power, since this has been the system in France's Fifth Republic. For his part, however, Paul Biya in Cameroon changed the constitution away from the French model before allowing the country to return to multiparty rule in the 1990s; he preferred a one-round plurality system, which is much more favorable to the incumbent. It allowed him to sneak through the highly fraudulent 1992 elections with an official score of 39.9 percent of the vote.

Second, when assessing institutional factors, we can also ask whether opposition coalitions are more likely in presidential or parliamentary regimes. This question is difficult to answer because, outside the old established democracies, there appears to be a negative correlation between the power of the president and the degree of democracy in the system. Typically, electoral autocracies concentrate power in the hands of a president, whereas parliamentary regimes are more democratic than fully presidential ones.[3] So, in practice, it is hard to tell whether it is the presidential form that undermines opposition cohesion or the fact that the regime is not democratic.

In the universe of African cases, the most democratic countries tend to be the few parliamentary countries: Botswana, Mauritius, and South Africa stand out in this respect. Interestingly, only Mauritius has a history of coalition building and electoral turnover; both Botswana and postapartheid South Africa have been dominant-party regimes in which oppositions have never won an election.

Having said that, the characteristics of presidentialism do affect the likelihood of cohesion. It is well established that presidentialism results in weaker political parties and less institutionalized party systems (Mainwaring and Scully 1995; Carey 2002; van de Walle 2003). It is possible to hypothesize that party discipline and party system stability facilitates the kind of deal making that is central to coalition building, so one would think presidential systems would be less conducive to opposition cohesion. As suggested by the Senegalese case described above, however, it is easier to make deals around a presidential election, which need not involve many individual parliamentary constituencies but can be forged by a couple of men based in the capital.

History and Culture

Again, constraints of space prevent a complete discussion, but two specific points can be made. First, past experiences with democratic forms of government and, in particular, a history of elections, favors the opposition in electoral autocracies. If the country has gone through past democratic episodes, the opposition can rely on past experiences with political parties. That may be why political parties appear considerably stronger and party systems more institutionalized in Latin America (Mainwaring and Scully 1995) or Eastern Europe, for instance, than in Africa (van de Walle 2003). In the former, the opposition is likely to be stronger and more skillful, thanks to the experience gained in previous episodes.

Second, in earlier research (Bienen and van de Walle 1991), I showed that there were systematic regional differences in the length of tenure of world leaders.[4] Only 5 percent of Latin American leaders remained in power after eight full years in office, whereas in Africa and the Middle East, 30 percent of leaders remained in power. Thus, leaders in Latin America tend to stay in power for shorter periods of time. There are strikingly few leaders in Latin American history who stayed in power for a decade or more. Only eighteen of the more than 1,000 Latin American leaders in office from political independence in the early nineteenth century to the late twentieth century have been in power as long as fourteen years. In Africa, however, even thoroughly mediocre leaders with a weak grasp on power, like Samuel Doe in Liberia, routinely stay in power a decade. These differences are not easily explained and are not explained by the level of democracy, the likelihood of military intervention, or whether the system is presidential or parliamentary. Instead, they appear related in complex ways to a region's political culture.

In many cases, tenures are set by institutional mechanisms such as term limits, which have existed in many Latin American countries, even in nondemocratic times. But such institutional mechanisms are clearly endogenous responses to culturally mediated demands to shorten leaders' tenure. If so, it makes sense to think that similar dynamics may exist to assist opposition cohesion in order to limit presidential tenures. This is clearly hypothetical, but if the perception exists that a president's time in power is limited and likely to end soon, opposition leaders are more likely to unite to force the issue. If, however, the president's tenure seems legitimate and unquestioned, then the tipping mechanisms described above are likely to militate against successful opposition cohesion.

Certainly, there are striking differences across regions in the turnover rates in recent converts to multiparty politics. The low rates of turnover in Africa's newly democratic systems contrast with higher rates in other regions. Some of these differences may be related to institutional factors, and perhaps African incumbents benefit from more advantages than those in other regions, but it can also be hypothesized that regional political culture is more tolerant of long incumbency. Certainly, a number of Africanist scholars (Schatzberg 2001; Chabal and Daloz 1999) believe that there is a distinctive African political culture that is paternalistic and conservative.

Ethnic Pluralism

Ethnic fragmentation and other forms of cultural pluralism make cohesion more difficult. Situations of ethnic diversity and polarization probably increase the costs of coalition building and provide a built-in advantage to incumbents, who can more easily build cross-ethnic coalitions with the assistance of state resources (Moestrup 1999; Crook 1997). There is some evidence that ethnic fragmentation results in larger government cabinets; such deal making is costly and often beyond the means of opposition parties. True, parties can forge deals involving the cabinet positions each member of the coalition will receive in the case of victory, but unless victory seems assured, such deals are harder to sustain, and it is easier for the incumbent to match opposition promises. Again, until defections and a loss of credibility have tipped the victory toward the opposition, ethnic fragmentation will favor the government.

Socioeconomic Development

A positive correlation exists between economic development and the likelihood of opposition cohesion. Economic development and urbanization, too, are associated with higher levels of party-systemic institutionalism. In richer countries, municipal and provincial governments provide offices for opposition parties, even when they do not control national government. In poor countries, subnational administrations are far more likely to be financially as well as politically dependent on the center, even in nominally democratic systems. Having a regional or municipal seat provides offices for party officials and patronage possibilities for the party rank and file, which is enormously helpful to opposition parties without evident means of finance.

If that is true, then it also follows that parties are stronger in richer countries, even if the country has no long experience of democracy (of course, richer countries tend to have stronger party systems because they have longer experiences of multiparty electoral politics). Strong parties and institutionalized party systems probably facilitate coalition building. In sum, there is a positive correlation between opposition cohesion and economic development.

International Factors

Finally, at least two international factors appear to affect the likelihood of opposition cohesion. First, the presence of external pressures for democracy increases the costs faced by the incumbent of trying to steal an election and thus provides support for the opposition. Nonetheless, the case of Zimbabwe suggests that autocratic leaders can withstand considerable external pressure, so the importance of this factor should not be exaggerated.

A second international factor is financing for parties from expatriate communities. Little or no data exist on these financial flows, but anecdotal evidence suggests that expatriate communities can provide financial support to opposition parties, constituting a significant resource and strengthening the ability of these parties to compete effectively.

In both instances, it is assumed once again that a stronger opposition is more likely to win, and that as a result, it is more likely to be able to coalesce successfully.

Conclusion

The discussion above has been illustrative and suggestive rather then definitive. It is clearly important to develop better measures of the concepts discussed here and better data that would allow more formal tests of the hypothesis I have formulated. Nonetheless, several patterns appear highly suggestive. First, I have been able to show that opposition cohesion is positively correlated with opposition electoral victory and, in turn, with the level of democracy in a country. Second, I have argued that cohesion is often the consequence of victory, rather than its cause. Clearly, a finer grade analysis of specific country cases is necessary to demonstrate this argument more conclusively. Finally, my analysis has shown that a number of factors can influence the likelihood of opposition cohesion. Most strikingly, the nature of the electoral system has a decisive effect. A large proportion of the cases of successful electoral turnover have taken place in political systems with two-round majority systems, which appear to favor the opposition's ability to forge coalitions.

Notes

1. The overwhelming majority of incumbent presidents in these illiberal electoral systems are men, so I will use the male pronoun throughout.

2. In two-round voting systems, only the second round was used. The correlation coefficient is negative because higher Freedom House scores indicate lower levels of democracy.

3. In Chapter 11 in this book, M. Steven Fish makes a similar argument vis-à-vis the regimes in Eastern Europe and the former Soviet states.

4. The study was based on 2,256 leaders from over 100 independent countries since the beginning of the nineteenth century.

Part 3

The Electoral Battlefield

6

Manipulative Skills: How Do Rulers Control the Electoral Arena?

William Case

Southeast Asia presents a great storehouse of historical and contemporary electoral authoritarianism. Despite the region's seeming diversity of politics that inspires such wonder among first-time observers, six of its ten countries have experience with electoral authoritarianism, advancing this regime as its modal type. Indeed, having been introduced in Singapore during the late 1960s, in Malaysia and Indonesia during the early 1970s, in Thailand and the Philippines a decade later, and at least briefly in Burma in 1990, this type of regime has had a far longer run in Southeast Asia than in other parts of the world more usually scrutinized by theorists of democratic transitions.

I begin this chapter by briefly recounting the historical and sociocultural moorings of electoral authoritarian regimes in Southeast Asia. Next, I trace the ways in which these regimes, despite their deep roots, can be tested, usually when voters grow so alienated by economic crises and unevenly borne sacrifices that they use electoral openness to challenge the government concertedly. Finally, I turn to some Southeast Asian case studies, which demonstrate that when under strain, the persistence of electoral authoritarian regimes turns crucially on the level of skill by which their controls are recalibrated by rulers.

Countervailing Legacies and Skillful Manipulations

Electoral authoritarianism has grown up in Southeast Asia among countervailing sets of historical legacies, social structures, and cultural outlooks, which created pressure for both authoritarian and democratic politics. Through intense colonization by Western powers—or strong demonstration effects in the nominally uncolonized kingdom of Thailand—Southeast Asia was exposed to viceregal state apparatuses geared to administrative efficiencies and resource extraction (Diamond 1989: 10–14). But by this same colonial experience, many countries in Southeast Asia also gained democratic "tutelage," ushering in local elections and multiparty systems (Weiner 1987: 3–34).

In addition, through colonial-era labor markets and cross-regional recruitment, Southeast Asia formed plural societies, again posing mixed implications for regime outcomes. On one side, disparate ethnic and religious affiliations have encouraged vertical loyalties and mass-level rivalries, hence militating against democratic modes of behavior. But these affiliations have also increased social complexity, making authoritarian controls more difficult to enforce. Similar contrariness is found in the region's cultural outlooks. Area specialists dwell on steep patterns of hierarchy, peaking in the "big men" and *jao pho* (godfathers) of Thailand, "bosses" and caciques in the Philippines, and traditional *bapakism* (patriarchy) on Java. Equally, however, mass publics in Southeast Asia have demonstrated political assertiveness, ranging from subtle forms of everyday resistance to peasant rebellions, student uprisings, separatist movements, and religious terrorism.

In more recent decades, the electoral authoritarianism that rests upon these countervailing legacies and structures has been strengthened across large parts of Southeast Asia by late but rapid industrialization. On one side, this expansion has given rise to business entrepreneurs, new urban middle classes, and ranks of industrial workers. But the strategies by which industrialization has been pursued, involving statist interventions in local markets and waves of foreign investment in export sectors, have dampened, though not extinguished, participatory outlooks. In brief, entrepreneurs have remained dependent on state promotion and protection; middle classes have been becalmed by the "performance legitimacy" that they find in careerism and consumerism; and workforces have been scattered across free-trade zones, ethnically divided, unequally compensated, and stratified by gender.

Accordingly, many governments in Southeast Asia, far from dissembling over their electoral authoritarianism, began openly to celebrate it. With growing confidence, national leaders like Lee Kuan Yew, Mahathir Mohamad, and Suharto unveiled new notions of "Asian democracy," suitably underpinned by the region's distinctive forms of "Asian capitalism" and "shared" communitarian values. In this understanding, elections might be regularly held and contested by opposition parties. Because of their tight calibration of competitiveness, however, governments were unlikely to lose. Indeed, national leaders declared that, under Asian democracy, elections were not intended to produce turnovers but instead to provide feedback, registering fluctuations in support so that governments might adjust their policy course but never leave office.

Electoral authoritarianism came under pressure, however, when industrial performance dissolved suddenly in crisis, dissipated gradually through long periods of stagnancy, or simply appeared threatened by changes in top government position holders or policies. A pernicious dynamic set in, one in which a prior pattern of different social groups making absolute (if uneven) gains mutated into one wherein fortunes have varied inversely, with rulers protecting the social positions and prerogatives of their favorites, leaving the public to face new hardships. Under these conditions, the new classes wrought by industrialization have finally been activated, with mild discontentment over patronage and corrupt practices hardening into grievances over social injustice. They may also be galvanized by the availability of competing mentalities—for example, Islamism's promise of great probity in public life and neoliberalism's insistence on full transparency, both of which, though from different angles, confront electoral authoritarianism with strongly reformist demands. In this situation, mass publics have sometimes discovered the democratic facets of their historical and sociocultural milieu, and they have begun to look upon elections, however much competitiveness may be calibrated, as the aperture through which change might be brought about.

When electoral authoritarianism is tested in this way, much depends on the ways in which the ruler, while waiting for the economy to recover and societal grievances to abate, recalibrates electoral competitiveness. If new manipulations are skillfully introduced and sequenced, they may tamp down opposition, tiding over the government and the regime that it operates. But if manipulations are carried out clumsily, they may heighten opposition, creating the conditions in which the government and the regime may finally be changed. Figure 6.1 illustrates some simple trajectories.

At this point, how are we to know when manipulations are skillful or clumsy except in an ex post facto way, reading back from the persistence or change of an electoral authoritarian regime? And where these regimes do persist, how do we know that the skillfulness of the ruler's manipulations matters more than the opposition's weakness? First, regarding the success or failure of manipulations, I focus on what James Mahoney has characterized as "choice points" (Mahoney 2001: 6–7), cast here as moments in which the fortunes of rulers and mass publics vary inversely, activating citizens in

Figure 6.1   Trajectories of Electoral Authoritarianism

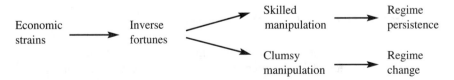

ways that require rulers to recalibrate electoral competitiveness. Where new manipulations are skillful, they appear measured and appropriately ordered. Inverse distributions between rulers and mass publics are thus softened or hidden, and adjustments in institutional and procedural functioning are stealthily carried out. Media access, for example, may be more subtly skewed, and the size and composition of electoral districts may be quietly but more grievously distorted.

By contrast, a loss of skillfulness shows either in gross and erratic manipulations or quite inflexible postures. Little is done to alleviate inverse distributions. And with societal grievances thus left uncontained, increasingly harried rulers may react by removing and then fitfully reapplying media controls, promising and then postponing elections, and closing assemblies only to reopen them in new guises. Rulers may also react clumsily by refusing to make adjustments at all, quickly bringing societal grievances to the boil. Thus the notions of skillfulness and clumsiness give us some capacity to predict when electoral authoritarianism will aid a government in keeping its grip and when a regime is on the slippery slope.

Second, the extent to which an electoral authoritarian regime's persistence results from the ruler's skillfulness or the opposition's weakness must be examined empirically. In Malaysia, for example, the ready availability of ethnic and religious sentiments contribute mightily to the mobilizing capacity of opposition parties, especially during periods of economic strain. In this case, then, where the opposition has been able to mount serious challenges, the persistence of electoral authoritarianism can reasonably be attributed to the overriding skillfulness of the ruler's manipulations. In neighboring Singapore, however, causal weighting is less clear, given the opposition's organizational frailties. But even here, it can be shown that strains in the city-state's economy cause protest votes to rise. As rulers reach such choice points, they have responded by softening inverse distributions while recalibrating electoral competitiveness.

In what follows, I simply enumerate the many kinds of manipulations resorted to by rulers in Southeast Asia. Then, I present some brief comparisons of cases in which rulers, facing choice points tinged with economic crisis, stagnancy, or uncertainty, have displayed different amounts of skill while confronting oppositions of varying strength. In this section I aim to clarify the links between the strategies of manipulation pursued by rulers and the functioning of electoral authoritarian regimes.

Calibrating Electoral Competitiveness

The complex historical and sociocultural amalgams that prevail in Southeast Asia form the bedrock atop which rulers erect their electoral authoritarian regimes. They can select from what Andreas Schedler (2002b) has called a "menu of manipulation" to perpetuate their grip on state power, at the same time fostering plausible contestation and hence a patina of legitimacy for the interminable tenures they imagine. Students of other parts of the developing world may be struck by the extensiveness of the menu on offer in Southeast Asia and the seeming crudeness of some of its items. But the lengthy periods of mass-level acquiescence upon which such a menu depends might be ascribed to Southeast Asia's comparative record of industrialization and prosperity, with electoral authoritarianism's slight democratic content often alloyed by performance legitimacy. Guided by Schedler's framework, then, let us survey the kinds of manipulations to which rulers have resorted in the Southeast Asian setting.

Restricting Civil Liberties

In trying to control elections, Schedler (2002b: 43–44) observes that rulers begin early, constraining the formation of preferences by imposing limits on civil liberties. Thus, under Southeast Asia's electoral authoritarian regimes, communication through print and electronic media has typically been muted by sundry legal controls, licensing requirements, and patterns of government or ruling party ownership. In Singapore, for example, all news dailies are owned by Singapore Press Holdings, which, in turn, is controlled by nominees of the Ministry of Information and the Arts (Ooi 1998: 392). Similarly, in Malaysia, most major English-language and vernacular newspapers are owned either by New Straits Times Press Holdings, long linked to the country's dominant political party, the United Malays National Organization (UMNO), or to Huaren Holdings, controlled by the Malaysian Chinese Association (MCA), UMNO's junior coalition partner. During periods of electoral authoritarianism in Thailand, bureaucratic and military agencies have operated all radio and television stations. In Burma, only one news daily is permitted today, the government-owned *New Light of Myanmar.* Unlicensed use of the Internet, photocopiers, and fax machines, meanwhile, attract harsh punishments.

The compliance of individual editors and reporters has also been encouraged in less formal ways. In Singapore, proscribed topics are loosely demarcated by "'OB' (out-of-bounds) markers" (Case 2004: 116–117), sometimes enforced through crippling lawsuits. In Malaysia, editors who displease top UMNO politicians are summarily removed. In the Philippines under Ferdinand Marcos, newspapers that opposed the president were confiscated (Wurfel 1988: 123), even when prominent families owned them. And in Indonesia under Suharto, a period of rule designated as the New Order, a "telephone culture" (*budaya telepon*) prevailed, whereby security officials phoned "advice" to editors about news items that were best omitted.

Freedom of assembly has also been limited in the region, with civil society organizations and social movements subjected to sundry controls.

Under Singapore's Societies Act, nongovernmental organizations (NGOs) have been barred from any political activity unless they are officially registered for the purpose. Students in Malaysia who join political protests are threatened under the University and University Colleges Act with loss of scholarships or expulsion. Further, in both Singapore and Malaysia the governments make use of their respective Internal Security Acts, enshrining a colonial-era principle whereby activists can be detained indefinitely without trial. In New Order Indonesia, the Ormas (*organisasi massa,* or mass organizations) law of 1985 required all civil society organizations to subscribe to a hazy mentality of *Pancasila* (Five Principles), incorporating it into their constitutions or bylaws as their "sole ideological foundation" (*asas tunggal*). In this way, the public remained politically inert, suspended in an official doctrine of "floating mass," except during political campaigns. And in Marcos's Philippines, left-wing leaders and labor organizers were simply "disappeared," a process known, curiously, as "salvaging."

Reserved Positions and Domains

While constraining the formation of preferences, rulers may also insulate key nodes of state power from voters, thereby staking out reserve positions and domains (Schedler 2002b: 42). Under Thailand's 1991 constitution, the military retained a majority of senate seats for its own appointees, enabling it to exercise veto power over legislation and no-confidence motions that might be passed by an elected lower house. The president of the senate also served as the president of both houses, and prime ministers and cabinet ministers need not have been elected at all. Indeed, the military sought expressly "to prevent politicians from getting into the cabinet" (Maisrikrod 1992: 22), instead recruiting top military officers and civil servants.

In New Order Indonesia too, Suharto nearly established his presidency as a reserve position, rendering it quite unaccountable to parliament or voters. As head of the Control Board (Dewan Pembina) of Golkar (Functional Groups), the government's electoral vehicle, Suharto personally selected his candidates for parliament (the People's Representative Council). He also vetted the candidates of opposition parties. In the year after elections were duly won by Golkar, those in the People's Representative Council doubled as members of an electoral college (the People's Consultative Assembly), which, padded with additional Suharto appointees, reappointed Suharto to the presidency, usually by acclamation. One gets a sense of the extent to which Suharto avoided accountability by the way in which he then set policy, usually though presidential decrees (*keppres*) and presidential instructions (*inpres*).

After establishing reserve positions, rulers in Southeast Asia have also lengthened their reserve domains, burrowing deeply into state agencies and enterprises. Under electoral authoritarianism in Thailand, the military kept close ties with the powerful Interior Ministry, enabling it to carry over many abusive practices from earlier periods of hard authoritarianism, conceptualized by Fred Riggs (1966) as a "bureaucratic polity." In Indonesia, Suharto regularly assigned large numbers of military officers to bureaucratic posts, a practice sanctioned by doctrines of *kekaryaan* (temporary transfers) and *dwi-fungsi* (dual function), traceable to the struggle for independence against the Dutch in which local politicians were seen to have wavered. In turn, civilian elements of the bureaucracy were bound to the government through their compulsory membership in the Civil Servants Corp of the Republic of Indonesia, encouraging an explicit ethos of "monoloyalty."

In Singapore and Malaysia, prime ministerial posts have functioned less obviously as reserve positions. The constitutions of these countries require that their respective national leaders be elected members of parliament. Even so, Singapore's former prime minister, Lee Kuan Yew, serves today as the unelected yet highly influential "mentor minister," and in Malaysia, persons who have failed in their electoral bids have gained ministerial posts through executive appointments to an otherwise ceremonial senate. Furthermore, these countries' rulers make use of the bureaucracy in ways that bolster their reelection prospects, tapping the apparatus for the patronage and campaign resources that invest their positions with a de facto reserve quality.

Thus, in Singapore, close links have been forged between the ruling People's Action Party (PAP) and a "partisan bureaucracy," with elites circulating quite freely across top positions in bureaucratic agencies, government-linked corporations, and the security forces. In Malaysia too, boundaries between UMNO and the bureaucracy have been blurred, with party members regularly appropriating state contracts, loans, and privatized assets. UMNO also makes use of civil servants, state facilities, and funding during election campaigns, and it relies upon postal ballots cast by the military to top up returns and enlarge its majorities.

Exclusion and Fragmentation

Rulers who operate electoral authoritarian regimes try also to exclude or fragment opposition parties, seeking to restrict voters' "range of choice" (Schedler 2002b: 43). In Southeast Asia, then, governments have arbitrarily deregistered parties and disqualified candidates, actions usually supported by pliable election commissions. More innovative, though, was Singapore's technique of weakening the opposition by designating most parliamentary districts as group representation constituencies. Under these idiosyncratic rules, all political parties are required to form interethnic slates of as many as six candidates that encompass the country's major communities, greatly straining the scant organizational resources of the opposition. A clear measure of the extent to which the opposition has in consequence been weakened involves the government attempting to revive it in hopes of sharpening up parliamentary debate. It thus recruits "nonconstituency MPs" from among the opposition's best performing—though suitably housebroken—losers and "nominated MPs" from business firms and compliant NGOs. Neither cohort, however, is given full voting powers.

In Malaysia too, parliamentary districts have been severely distorted through malapportionment and gerrymandering. Traditionally, UMNO has found most of its support among rural Malays. Accordingly, the party long perpetuated imbalances whereby rural districts averaged half as many voters as the urban ones in which ethnic Chinese support for the opposition was strong (Gomez 1998: 267). However, with Islamists in the Pan-Islamic Party of Malaysia (PAS) having in recent years made deep inroads into the rural heartland and Chinese voters recoiling in turn toward the government, UMNO has resorted to ever more intricate forms of gerrymandering, now diluting many heavily Malay districts with ethnic Chinese. Opposition parties have also been excluded through ever shorter campaign periods, in recent elections barely a week, as well as tight limits on their meetings and speechmaking.

Malaysia's government has also fueled suspicions between PAS and ethnic Chinese in the opposition, precipitating three-way contests that enable the government to snatch decisive pluralities through a first-past-the-post system. In other cases, it has encouraged party hopping, persuading opposition candidates who have managed to win office to defect. Indeed, UMNO has accumulated patronage resources with which to absorb whole parties into its ruling coalition, the Barisan Nasional (National Front), gaining a capacity for co-optation and rapid adaptation that James V. Jesudason (1996) has conceptualized as an unshakeable "syncretic state."

Under electoral authoritarianism in Thailand, the military penetrated the leadership of some opposition parties, effectively manipulating party appeals in order to polarize the opposition more widely. In the Philippines under Marcos, the New Society Movement (Kilusang Bagong Lipunan, KBL) absorbed the once venerable Nationalists, along with a number of civil society organizations. At the same time, "nuisance candidates" were routinely fielded against genuine ones, confusing voters "in order to decimate the ranks of the opposition" (Leones and Moraleda 1998: 330). And in New Order Indonesia, the government invoked the "fusion" (*fusi*) law in 1973, whereby only two opposition parties were permitted to form—the first uncomfortably aggregating nationalist and Christian groups and the other discordant streams of Islam. The regime intervened deeply in the internal dealings and candidate selection of its licensed competitors and even pressured them to designate themselves publicly not as opposition parties, but more innocuously as "electoral participant organizations" (*organisasi peserta pemilu,* OPPs). And although Golkar was free to use the bureaucratic apparatus to reach out to villages across the archipelago, these parties were prohibited from organizing branch structures below the district level, denying them the rural areas in which most votes in Indonesia were to be found.

Disenfranchisement

In addition to excluding and fragmenting opposition parties, rulers may also disenfranchise their supporters. To be sure, rulers in Southeast Asia have stopped well short of formally excluding whole ethnic communities, classes, and genders. But they invoke more subtle techniques: the malapportionment of constituencies in Malaysia mentioned above, for example, nearly halved the weight of votes historically cast for the opposition by town-dwelling Chinese. Finer-grained disenfranchisement seems also to have been carried out in Malaysia through manipulations of the electoral rolls, with voters often appearing at polling stations only to find their names inexplicably shifted to other districts or dropped from the list altogether. At the same time, "phantom" and "transfer" voters appear, equipped with aliases, fake identity cards, and false addresses. Similarly, in Thailand and the Philippines, officials have manipulated residence-based electoral rolls, secretly shifting voters across constituency boundaries or even "deliberately striking out . . . names from the official list [that have been] identified with the opposition" (Leones and Moraleda 1998: 330).

Vote Buying

Mass publics that avoid disenfranchisement may next be confronted by government efforts to buy their votes. In Malaysia, vote-buying techniques have been comparatively sophisticated, with government candidates approaching villagers with land titles or on-the-spot "development grants" for new clinics, paved roads, or mosques. In Thailand, vote buying has traditionally been cruder yet equally well-institutionalized, effectively carried out through two "rounds": an early application of "carpeting," marked by candidate "donations," entertainments, and feasts, followed on the eve of the election by "dog-barking night," during which "canvassers" distribute money so intensively that even the sleep of village dogs is said to be disturbed (Anusorn 1998: 436–438). Meanwhile, Thailand's Interior Ministry, responsible for overseeing elections until an independent commission was set up in 1998, habitually ignored these activities by canvassers for government candidates yet closely policed those of the opposition. In funding the purchase of votes, the government loosened monetary policy during the month before elections, abruptly increasing cash in circulation (Anusorn 1998: 436–438), eroding the central bank's independence, and distorting macroeconomic fundamentals. In the Philippines, practiced canvassers have also engaged heavily in vote buying and then enforced the terms by insisting that voters trace their completed ballots onto carbon paper that could afterward be examined. And in New Order Indonesia, during a three-week campaign for elections held every five years, the citizens who had long been confined to a "floating mass" posture were suddenly treated to a *pesta demokrasi* (festival of democracy), a form of vote buying in which the government sponsored rock concerts, celebrity appearances, and sundry giveaways.

Intimidation

Where vote buying fails to sway mass sentiments, governments operating electoral authoritarian regimes may turn next to various forms of intimidation. In Singapore and Malaysia, ballots are numbered and contain counterfoils, raising suspicions among citizens that their votes may not be secret (Ooi 1998: 384). The use of ever-smaller counting centers suggests too that the preferences of particular residential areas can readily be identified. In addition, as we will see, Singapore's government has threatened to cut off state funding for public housing upgrades in those districts where opposition candidates win. In Malaysia, after the opposition PAS won at the state level in Terengganu in 1997, the government halted the payment of petroleum royalties upon which administration in the oil-rich state had come to depend.

In adopting more aggressive techniques, rulers may deploy intelligence agencies or thugs who threaten opposition candidates and their supporters. In Malaysia, the Police Special Branch closely monitors mass-level attitudes, and members of the dominant party's youth group, UMNO Youth, have sometimes harassed opposition campaigners. In the last years of New Order Indonesia, the special forces (Kopassus) abducted members of an unregistered opposition party, and Pancasila Youth (Pemuda Pancasila), affiliated with Golkar, clashed regularly with rival student groups. In Burma, "fear of military intelligence is pervasive and effectively intimidates all who care for the well-being of their families . . . nobody dares to support any opposition parties openly" (Khin and Smith 1998: 120). Violence has also typically raged in local electoral contests throughout Thailand and the Philippines.

Electoral Fraud

Finally, rulers may seek to control elections through outright fraudulence, which, as Schedler (2002b: 44) observes, can take place at any stage in the electoral process, "from voter registration to the tally of ballots." Among our Southeast Asian cases, the range of techniques—many of which coincide with the practices elaborated above—is perhaps most fully articulated in the Philippines. Here, one finds the *hakot* (flying voter), moving stealthily from one precinct to another in order to cast multiple ballots. Through "chains" of voters known as *lanzadera,* members deposit a ballot that has been prepared for them in advance and then leave the booth with the fresh ballot they have been given in order that it too might be prepared and passed on to the next link. And at the end of the process, *dagdag-bawas* (add-subtract) may take place, with election officials blatantly padding and shaving the totals to produce the desired outcomes.

In Malaysia, too, as noted above, what is known locally as phantom and transfer voting has regularly taken place. In Thailand, multiple voting, ballot box stuffing, and false counting and reporting have been common, especially in rural areas. And in New Order Indonesia, the final vote count was performed by the secretive General Election Committee, located within the Interior Ministry and presided over by Suharto (Eklof 1999: 92–93). With no independent poll monitoring permitted, speculation abounded that the committee sought to forge government margins of 65 to 70 percent, overwhelming majorities, yet discreet and credible. And in the Philippines, as we will see, Marcos capped an electoral process riddled with abuses by crassly trying to steal a presidential election, pressuring Commission on Elections (COMELEC) workers not only to adjust the tally but to fabricate his victory.

Perpetuating and Transforming Electoral Authoritarianism

So far, we have seen that in Southeast Asia, rulers have put together a lengthy menu of manipulation. But when electoral authoritarian regimes come under pressure from economic strains and social inequalities, rulers confront choice points wherein they must decide whether to recalibrate electoral competitiveness. If their manipulations are skillful, their regime will persist. But where they are clumsy, citizens may be shaken from their historical and sociocultural moorings and use elections, however limited their competitiveness, to begin to demand change. Let us turn to our Southeast Asian case studies, then, in order to chart these variable outcomes.

The Persistence of Electoral Authoritarianism: Singapore and Malaysia

Although rulers in Singapore have periodically confronted societal grievances, they have responded with skillful manipulations of procedures. During the 1980s, social tensions mounted between the city-state's English-educated Chinese, who held middle-class positions in the state bureaucracy, professions, and foreign-owned firms, and vernacular-educated Chinese, who remained mired in small business, factory employment, and low-grade services. A few opposition candidates, led by the Workers' Party, were elected to parliament. The government responded by using libel suits to force opposition candidates into bankruptcy, which was grounds for their disqualification. It also made deeper use of re-delineation, intricately gerrymandering or even disbanding districts that it viewed as recalcitrant, while gradually introducing the group representation constituencies mentioned above. And as the opposition in parliament was proportionately diminished, the government began to replace it with nominated MPs and so-called feedback units through which citizens were invited to register their discontent.

During the early 1990s, societal grievances began to roil anew over the government's inflexible commitments to globalization and "meritocracy," made manifest in richly rewarded coteries of foreign and Singaporean executives alongside local workers facing increases in transportation and health care costs. The opposition, calculating that much of the electorate was irked by yet still valued the government, encouraged a safe protest vote, adopting a "by-election" strategy whereby it contested in just under half of the country's constituencies. In this way, during the 1991 election, the opposition made its best showing ever by ensuring beforehand that it could not win. However, the prime minister, Goh Chok Tong, fearing a "freak" outcome in which the opposition gained power, responded by giving parliamentarians additional roles as town councilors, directly overseeing in their districts the public housing blocks in which most Singaporeans live. Thus, while campaigning for the next election, held in 1997, Goh warned that where opposition candidates won, the government would withhold resources, ensuring that the housing under their care "will become slums." Accordingly, with scope for a safe protest vote negated, the government recovered in the 1997 election much of the standing that it had traditionally enjoyed.

Shortly afterward, though, Singapore was swept by the Asian economic crisis of 1997–1998, interrupting more than a decade of absolute gains. In this situation, the public encountered severe hardships, with the government lowering wages and employer contributions to the national pension fund. The government also responded by reducing the salaries of its ministers—a measure unveiled with much fanfare—shrewdly avoiding societal grievances over inversely varying fortunes. And it pledged to restore citizens' retirement benefits as soon as the economy had recovered. Hence, in contrast to other countries in the region where elections were held during this period, Singapore's government again increased its majorities in 2001, with "voters . . . [choosing] to stick with the [PAP] that had brought them prosperity and security" (Mauzy and Milne 2002: 152).

In Malaysia, the government has confronted more complex societal grievances, first involving ethnic rivalries between Malays and Chinese and, more recently, religious differences between moderate and revivalist Muslims. The government initially responded with clumsy manipulations. In 1990, a general election was held in the wake of an economic recession that eroded patronage flows, sparking factional battles in the UMNO, the emergence of a new Malay splinter party, and defections from the ruling coalition. The opposition was then energized by this new party, mediating electoral agreements between the Islamist PAS on one side and Chinese and other ethnic minorities on the other. Yet, regaining its mastery in manipulation, the government soon stemmed defections from UMNO by more fully exploiting its strategic domains in the bureaucracy, canceling the state contracts and calling in the bank loans of those politicians now opposing it. It also reenergized broader Malay loyalties through fraudulence, the most memorable example of which involved its labeling the leader of the splinter party as a Christian, falsely portraying the ethnic headgear he had donned while campaigning as bearing the sign of the cross (Case 1993: 200). Thus, by supplementing its existing techniques with the tactical use of reserve domains and fraudulence, the government won the 1990 election at the federal level, even if by a reduced majority and the loss of a state assembly to PAS.

In the aftermath of the economic crisis of 1997–1998, however, the government was confronted once more by similar, though more serious societal grievances, renewing factionalism in UMNO, spawning another splinter party, and encouraging even greater cooperation between the revivalist PAS and Chinese in opposition. In brief, after a decade in which rapid industrialization had enabled the government to nurture a coterie of Malay tycoons and a wider community of small contractors, patronage resources suddenly dried up. And in rushing to prop up the most favored tycoons, the government arranged bailouts, with the prime minister's son emerging as one of the most conspicuous beneficiaries (Haggard 2003: 167–171). What is more, in scouring for funds, the government drew deeply upon the national pension fund, a program to which, as in Singapore, workers are obliged to contribute. Thus the fortunes of favored elites and the public varied inversely, finally catalyzing societal grievances into demands for change.

Thus, when elections were held in 1999, the opposition parties, their cooperation encouraged by a range of civil society organizations, displayed new potency. The government responded by again making full use of its reserve domains, purging the media and central bank of those whose loyalties it doubted while arranging a generous pay raise for ordinary civil servants. It also resorted to intimidation, warning through the media that the opposition parties could not manage the country's delicate communal balance and casting the activists who supported them as expressly committed to violence. And for good measure, a variety of dirty tricks were deployed, such as the furtive distribution around Kuala Lumpur of videotapes that underscored the government's claims that a key opposition figure, the former deputy prime minister, Anwar Ibrahim, had committed sexual misconduct. Moving deeply through the menu of manipulation, then, the government retained its extraordinary parliamentary majority in the 1999 election, even as its popular vote total fell from roughly 65 to 55 percent, its worst electoral showing in three decades.

However, as the government prepared for its most recent election in 2004, the inverse variations in fortunes between rulers and the public softened. The economy gathered pace, and Prime Minister Mahathir Mohamad forced his finance minister from office, promptly diminishing the stakes of the many tycoons that the latter had favored. Soon afterward, Mahathir gave way to his deputy, Abdullah Badawi, who in turn cancelled some dubious megaprojects and ordered a few high-profile arrests on charges of corruption. Further, taking no chances, the government calibrated elections more tightly by redrawing districts yet again and then imposed more stringent controls on campaigning. Thus, as the opposition assumed an increasingly Islamist fervor, moderate Muslims and ethnic Chinese redoubled their support for the government. Under these circumstances, the government won the 2004 election with vastly increased majorities, signifying the reequilibration of its electoral authoritarian regime.

The Demise of Electoral Authoritarianism: Thailand, the Philippines, Indonesia, and Burma

In Thailand, the military seized power in 1991, resenting its loss of patronage to a civilian government that had been democratically elected three years before. It then revived a local variant of the electoral authoritarianism that it had last practiced during the mid-1980s. While promising to hold elections, the military converted the prime ministership into an unelected and hence reserve position—even though it pledged not to fill this position itself. It also retained control of the senate, and it paved the way for its delegates to enter the lower house directly by helping to form a new party vehicle, Samakki Tham (Justice Unity Party).

With the economic boom continuing, Samakki Tham won the March 1992 election. Soon afterward, though, the military made plainer its abiding interest in patronage. As Samakki Tham began to organize a governing coalition, it embraced many of the same politicians whose corruption the military had earlier cited as justifying the coup. Even more recklessly, the military reneged on its promise of civilian governance, with its commander, General Suchinda Kraprayoon, pushing Samakki Tham aside in order to seize the prime ministership for himself. And though he took care to retain some technocratic ministers, the government became a vivid example of military collusion with corrupt politicians, prompting the middle class to fret over downward pressures on foreign investment, equity valuations, and tourist markets.

Thus, as the military manipulated procedures clumsily and sowed doubts over prosperity, the public's grievances swelled into more assertive opposition, cumulating finally in protests in the streets of Bangkok. And when the military reacted with great violence, sparking a confrontation known as "Black May," Thailand's king intervened, nudging the military from power and preparing for another election at year's end. A new civilian government then emerged under the "angelic" Democrat Party, an outcome widely regarded as completing Thailand's transition from electoral authoritarianism to democracy.

In the Philippines, Marcos declared martial law in 1972, dismantling the country's two-party system and shutting down Congress. Nonetheless, during the martial law period, Marcos held two elections for the Batasang Pambansa (an assembly supplanting the Congress), a presidential election in 1981, two rounds of local elections, and five national referenda. He also tried to forge a dominant party, the KBL, through which to wage these contests, while centralizing patronage in his presidential office.

But Marcos appeared to practice electoral authoritarianism only grudgingly, more at the behest of the US government than out of any real estimation of this regime type's intrinsic resilience and legitimating capacities. He thus manipulated its procedures carelessly—scheduling elections irregularly, capriciously removing opposition candidates, intimidating voters, and flagrantly manipulating vote counts. During the 1978 Batasang election, for example, in countering a challenge led by Senator Benigno Aquino, the government "resort[ed] to clumsy illegal methods, like literally threatening to shoot [COMELEC] pollwatchers" (Kerkvliet 1996: 158). And in an extraordinarily inept action, Aquino was himself assassinated in 1983, apparently by elements in the military.

At the same time, Marcos's "outlandish" corruption, vastly enriching his family members and new coteries of business elites, began to vary inversely with the fortunes of the Philippine people. When the economy succumbed to the oil shock of 1979 and the "cronyist" dealings triggered a financial crisis in the early 1980s, the government hurriedly printed money with which to sway the Batasang election in 1984. Amid this economic stagnancy, hardship grew steadily worse among the urban poor and in coconut-, rice-, and sugar-growing areas (Wurfel 1988: 292).

Then, in a "snap" presidential election held in 1986, one that Marcos had been pressed by the US government to call, a majority voted against him. A stunned Marcos tried to steal the election but was this time exposed by COMELEC workers. In this situation, just as the public in Thailand had been galvanized by the military's seizure of the prime ministership, resulting in Black May, so now were they inflamed by Marcos's efforts to extend his presidency, producing another upsurge labeled famously as "People Power." Marcos tried next to revert to hard authoritarianism, issuing an order on television that the military "attack, demolish and exterminate 'the rebels'" (quoted in Wurfel 1988: 303). But he soon ceded power to Aquino's widow, Corazon, completing the progress that within the Southeast Asian record comes closest to democratization by election.

In Burma during the 1980s, the military deepened the country's economic stagnancy when, through inept agricultural reforms and a "sweeping demonetization" of the national currency, it triggered rapid inflation and widespread unemployment. In these conditions, the high living enjoyed by generals and top officials, sustained by "special shops, rations, [and] corruption" (Steinberg 2001: 24), contrasted sharply with the hardships endured by mass publics. Demonstrations took place around the country, culminating in popular protests—a "people's revolution" (p. 3)—in 1988.

Confronted finally by the inefficiencies of hard authoritarianism, the military pledged to hold elections in 1990, marking a sharp swing from hard to electoral authoritarianism. Its motivations, however, were unchanged. Put simply, it sought to replicate the techniques that it observed in New Order Indonesia, "where electoral politics . . . supported, rather than undermined, a leading role for the military in government" (Taylor 1996: 178). But the government, unschooled in this regime type, manipulated procedures clumsily. It clamped down tightly on the opposition's media access and campaign activities and then blocked the candidacy of Aung Sang Suu Kyi, leader of the most popular opposition party, the National League for Democracy (NLD). But the government then held elections that were otherwise remarkably fair, calculating that the formation of its own vehicle, the National Unity Party (NUP), abetted by a single-member district system, would produce the many pluralities across the country that would renew its tenure.

The military remained unaware of the depth of societal grievances, however. Thus, with opposition sentiments inflamed and electoral competitiveness thrown open, the military's "plan backfired" (Khin and Smith 1998: 134). The NUP captured only 10 percent of the popular vote, while the NLD gained 60 percent, winning even in districts that contained military cantonments. In this way, the first-past-the-post system, far from benefiting the government, now magnified the opposition NLD's totals into more than 80 percent of the assembly seats. The military reacted by repudiating the elections and emasculating the opposition, jailing most NLD leaders. And it reverted to a hard authoritarian regime, whatever its costs.

The electoral authoritarianism of New Order Indonesia—the variant to which Burma's rulers had aspired—appeared to be well-institutionalized, having persisted for nearly three decades. But the vast social inequalities that had set in, although perhaps tolerable in a context of rapid industrialization, helped to fuel opposition during the crisis of 1997–1998. Suharto's family members and top cronies worked to preserve their corporate assets. Meanwhile, the subsidies on staples consumed by mass publics were reduced, in part at the urging of the International Monetary Fund. And when security forces resorted to violence, shooting four student protesters dead at Trisakti University, the Jakarta riots erupted, involving murderous attacks on the city's Chinese community and widespread looting.

Seeking to convert protesters into voters, Suharto offered to hold more competitive elections. But given his long record of inflexibility, he failed to gain public trust. Student protesters spurned his offer, continuing their mobilization against him. Suharto, confronted now by his regime's brittleness, made no effort to impose hard authoritarianism. Instead, he ceded power to his vice president, B. J. Habibie, who, in trying to win popular favor as a reformer, agreed swiftly to begin a democratic transition.

* * *

To summarize, when their economies came under strain, rulers in Singapore and Malaysia responded with skillful recalibrations of electoral competitiveness. Most notably, they softened the inverse distributions between rulers and mass publics. They also maintained tight limits on civil liberties and deftly redrew districts. Societal grievances in these cases, then, never flared up in opposition victories and popular upsurges.

By contrast, in Thailand, the Philippines, and Burma, rulers did little to remedy inversely varying fortunes. They also manipulated institutions and procedures clumsily. When economic strains set in, the citizens grew active, with opposition parties strongly contesting elections. And governments, displeased by the electoral results they obtained, reacted erratically again, either by rashly seizing the prime ministership, as in Thailand, grossly falsifying the tally, as in the Philippines, or repudiating elections outright, as in Burma. Moreover, in Thailand and the Philippines, these manipulations triggered popular protests and democratic transitions. In Burma, the military reverted to hard authoritarianism, notwithstanding its inefficiencies. Finally, in New Order Indonesia, the ruler erred the other way, responding not erratically but inflexibly. Hazy assurances of greater electoral competitiveness, then, led just as swiftly to popular upsurge and regime change. Figure 6.2 charts these variable outcomes.

Conclusion

Anchored in historical and sociocultural legacies and structures, electoral authoritarianism has emerged in Southeast Asia as the modal regime type.

Figure 6.2   Change and Persistence of Electoral Authoritarianism Under Economic Crisis

	Strong Opposition	Weak Opposition
Skilled Manipulation	Authoritarian persistence (Malaysia)	Authoritarian persistence (Singapore)
Clumsy Manipulation	Democratic change (Thailand, Philippines, Indonesia)	Authoritarian change (Burma)

Thus, in controlling elections, rulers have been able to draw upon the menu of manipulation, one made lengthy in the region by the rapid industrialization that can plug deficits in democracy with performance legitimacy.

However, where industrialization and prosperity dissolve in crisis, dissipate through stagnancy, or otherwise appear threatened by changes in political personnel or public policies, mass publics may come to perceive elections, despite their tightly calibrated competitiveness, as the apertures through which change might begin. It is under these conditions that the strategic rationality of manipulation becomes central. If rulers respond with skillful manipulation—softening inverse distributions while adjusting institutions—they can perpetuate the electoral authoritarianism that in turn prolongs their tenure. If they react clumsily, however—either through erratic adjustments or utter inflexibility—the public may sweep past the controls on elections. To be sure, rulers may then cling tenaciously to power, reverting to hard authoritarianism rather than acquiescing to democratic transitions, but the clumsiness of this final feint appears only to inflame the public even more.

7

After Defeat:
When Do Rulers Steal Elections?

Mark R. Thompson and Philipp Kuntz

An obvious, one could say definitional danger confronting electoral authoritarian regimes is an unexpected electoral outcome that poses an existen-
tial threat to nondemocratic rule. This is the well-known "stunning elections" phenomenon, in which a suddenly mobilized opposition inflicts a
surprising defeat on the nondemocratic regime.[1] Of course, an opposition
victory may be hard to prove, given the less than democratic circumstances
under which the vote has taken place. But if regime opponents can substan-
tiate their claims with credible evidence (for example, through independent vote counting or critical comments by foreign election observers), a
severe crisis can arise nonetheless.

The occurrence of stunning elections is to a substantial degree contingent upon the incumbents' decisionmaking. Had they possessed better
knowledge of their own weaknesses and the opposition's strengths, rulers
would not have announced polls in the first place or at least would have
taken more precautions when holding them. Elections that were not
intended to endanger incumbents' hold on power can call the entire system
of electoral authoritarianism into question. After the election, the steps
taken by the regime again become crucial. Having suffered defeat, incumbents are forced to make a decision that profoundly shapes their countries'
political future. They have to choose between openly acknowledging the
opposition victory or blatantly stealing the election (by manipulating the
final vote count or annulling the entire balloting).

Scholars of electoral authoritarianism have concentrated on the conditions under which regimes lose control over electoral outcomes. They have,
however, only touched on the issue of what happens once it becomes obvious that the opposition is winning an election. It has been argued that the
regime is likely either to manipulate the results and repress the opposition
or to accept defeat and withdraw from power. If power is retained through

a stolen election, the strategy of attempting to legitimize authoritarian rule through elections has been (at least temporarily) discredited. If the regime accepts defeat, it is assumed that democratization will begin.[2] Branches A and B in Figure 7.1 indicate these two possible outcomes of electoral defeat.

This binary model does not exhaust all possible outcomes, however. It turns out to be incomplete in at least two respects. First, it does not consider the possibility of the authoritarian leadership stealing an election, only to be ousted through opposition street protests. As several cases have shown, such an outcome is unexceptional: from 2000 to 2005, postelectoral movements have toppled unyielding autocrats in Serbia (2000), Côte d'Ivoire (2000), Madagascar (2002), Georgia (2003), and Ukraine (2004). Branch C in Figure 7.1 points to this possibility. Second, once we take into account elections or referenda in which national power is not directly at stake ("limited elections"), the possibility emerges for incumbents to acknowledge defeat in order to hold onto power. In several countries this option has been taken, and authoritarian regimes have successfully reconsolidated their power thereafter, such as in Iran (1997) and Zimbabwe (2000).

If stealing an election does not guarantee the incumbent's hold on power—if that option is risky—the question arises why leaders often pursue this strategy nonetheless. In the case of limited elections, the decision to steal is all the more puzzling because accepting defeat may even be beneficial for authoritarian incumbents. Given their repeated occurrence and

Figure 7.1   Three Possible Consequences of Electoral Defeat

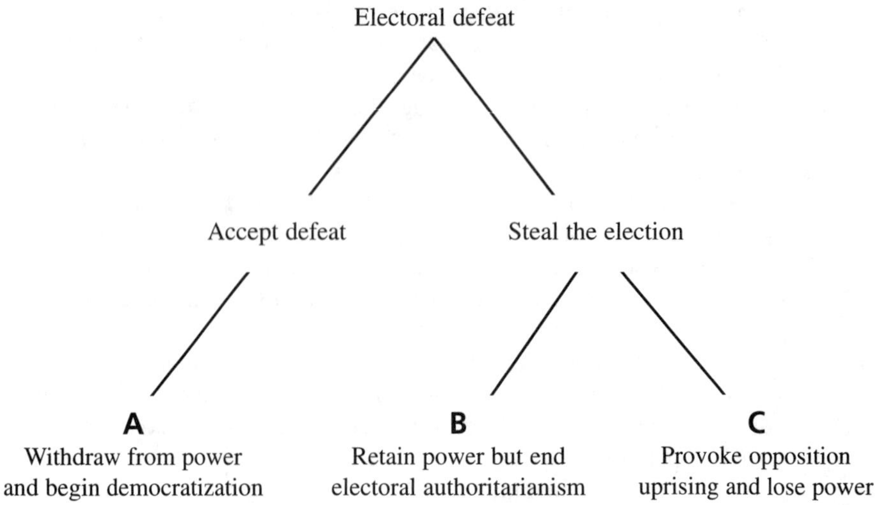

Electoral defeat

Accept defeat   Steal the election

A   **B**   **C**
Withdraw from power   Retain power but end   Provoke opposition
and begin democratization   electoral authoritarianism   uprising and lose power

significance in recent international politics, it is remarkable that such post-electoral choices have been neglected by comparativists. No systematic attempts have been made to explain why some autocrats hand over power after electoral defeat, whereas others stubbornly defy the will of the voters.

Incumbent strategies under electoral authoritarianism have been depicted as oscillating between opening and closure (Schedler 2002a). The focus has been on the degree and nature of manipulation efforts in the pre-election phase, a matter that would be better understood as crisis prevention rather than crisis management. Yet stunning defeats themselves constitute an essential part of this alternation between concession and repression in electoral authoritarianism and thus deserve further study.

Although an exploratory effort, this chapter attempts to shed light on the strategic logic of stolen elections. First we analyze the risks faced by those committing electoral theft. After that, we offer reasons why some autocrats nonetheless prefer to steal. We confine ourselves to instances of "full elections," that is, polls in which the ultimate positions of state power are at stake. A quite different logic applies to "limited" opposition victories, with these cases meriting a study of their own.

The Risks of Stealing

Invalidating an opposition victory in order to hold onto power entails great risks because authoritarian survival is by no means guaranteed. Stolen elections have an enormous impact on central political actors. The group most directly affected by a reversed electoral outcome is the opposition and its supporters. The fact that they were able to triumph over their authoritarian adversaries at the ballot box encourages citizens to defend their victory through mass action. Attempts to rob them of their votes causes widespread outrage and as a consequence contributes to the general willingness to protest. Organizational capacities, built up for the electoral campaign, also help to facilitate the mobilization of the populace. In sum, nullifying an opposition victory may trigger a mass upheaval. Rulers may have tremendous difficulty containing the popular outrage, last but not least, because elite cohesion is likely to be undermined in the wake of stolen elections as well.[3]

This constellation turns the annulment of an opposition victory into an extremely dangerous game. If authoritarian survival cannot be taken for granted, the regime must fear being held responsible for its blatant act of manipulation. A crackdown on postelectoral protests that ultimately fails would provide an additional reason for victorious societal forces to put the former incumbents on trial. The cases of Madagascar (2002) and Ukraine (2004) illustrate these dangers.

By early 2002, Madagascar was split by a contested presidential election. Didier Ratsiraka, the acting president, demanded a runoff, but his challenger, Marc Ravalomanana, claimed to have won the first round of voting outright. After Ravalomanana's auto-proclamation in Antananarivo, Ratsiraka tried to enforce his will through a blockade of the capital. It was only after weeks of fighting that Ratsiraka's last strongholds were conquered by pro-Ravalomanana troops. Ratsiraka's policy of obstruction bore the primary responsibility for this civil strife that claimed dozens of lives and left the Malagasy economy devastated. In connection with these events, several high-ranking figures of the ancien régime have been imprisoned or tried in absentia since Ratsiraka and his family fled the country in July 2002.[4]

Attempts to prevent an opposition victory in the 2004 presidential race in Ukraine proved equally risky. Through drastic manipulation on election day, the regime of outgoing president Leonid Kuchma tried to reverse the results of the runoff poll. However, opposition candidate Viktor Yushchenko refused to concede defeat and called his supporters onto the streets. Supporters of Prime Minister Viktor Yanukovich, the winner according to official results, responded by threatening the secession of Ukraine's Russian-speaking regions. Although regime loyalists stopped short of staging an unconstitutional referendum on autonomy, their moves did not remain without consequences. After the triumph of the "orange revolution," Yushchenko announced that he would hold liable those who had pursued a strategy of splitting up the country.[5] Moreover, the massive manipulation of the poll itself has not been forgotten. Ukraine's new rulers have indicated they will launch an investigation into electoral fraud, and the mysterious death of two members of the old regime elite appears to be linked to worries about such an inquiry.[6] The eventual opposition victory reminded many of the risk they had taken by engaging in vote rigging and trying to turn the tide in the ensuing crisis through illegal means.

Of course, it remains a matter of perception whether these potential repercussions influence the choice forced upon a ruler after a stunning defeat. Is protest likely to emerge at all, and if so, can it be contained? When the Serbian president Slobodan Milosevic decided to have a number of communal election results annulled in November 1996, he reckoned with an apathetic citizenry not prepared to take action against him (Pavlović 2001: 87–88). An astonishing show of civil disobedience, enduring through the winter months, proved him wrong. However, it is not simply local (and therefore "limited") elections in which autocratic regimes have underestimated the opposition's potential for mass mobilization. A similar misperception seems to have influenced the Ukrainian leadership at the moment the most important political office, the presidency, was about to be lost.[7] The Ukrainian case also suggests that authoritarian incumbents miscalculate with respect to the support they can draw from powerful international allies. During the election campaign, Russian president Vladimir Putin very publicly took the side of Yanukovich, the regime candidate. Ukrainian power holders might have erroneously concluded that Russian support would enable them to prevail over postelectoral opposition protests.

But even when (rightly or wrongly) considering themselves capable of surviving the immediate crisis, incumbents know that they will suffer from a loss of domestic and international legitimacy for years to come. The cases of Burma (1990), Algeria (1992), and Nigeria (1993) are telling in this respect. In Lesotho, the stealing of the 1970 balloting by the Basotho National Party (BNP) produced a particularly long-lasting legacy. In the first free and fair elections twenty-three years later the BNP was severely punished by the electorate for having interrupted the process of democratization two decades before (Ajulu 1995: 15–16).

In a world in which more and more autocrats try to maintain a democratic façade, stealing an opposition victory amounts to a particularly gross violation of the electoral process. Since the costs of repression are likely to be high, looking at the possible benefits of stealing becomes an important part of explaining autocratic obstinacy in the face of electoral defeat.[8]

Motivations for Stealing

In this section, we explore three major reasons for stealing elections by looking at the benefit side of the equation: legal, economic, and political factors can all motivate this behavior. Although it is helpful analytically to distinguish between these factors, all three often "hang together," as we will show in the next section. Finally, there are "soft" factors (ideological and psychological) involved in the strategic calculation of whether to steal an election (also discussed below) that can be distinguished from the "hard" reasons that will be considered first.

Fear of Legal Consequences

Probably the most important single factor motivating electoral theft is the fear of criminal prosecution. Often there seems to be no other choice than to rig the elections, given the severe abuses of office that have been committed. Most commonly, rulers will worry about charges of corruption, illegal enrichment, or the violent repression of political opponents once power has been lost. Regime decisionmaking after several stunning elections seems to have been strongly guided by such considerations. Four cases exemplify this point: the Philippines (1986), Serbia (2000), Georgia (2003), and Ukraine (2004).

In the Philippines, the 1986 "snap" presidential elections were stolen in a brazen fashion. Bribery was widespread, and opposition candidates and poll watchers were violently intimidated, resulting in dozens of deaths. But when these methods failed to produce the desired pro-regime result, the count was manipulated by the Commission on Elections (COMELEC) in such an obvious fashion that it led to a spectacular walkout by computer operators calculating the tally (Thompson 1995: Chap. 8). Undoubtedly, one of Ferdinand Marcos's main motivations for cheating was his fear that he and his family would face trial for their "politics of plunder" (Aquino 1987). It may well be that given the compromised reputation of the Philippine judiciary (one Supreme Court judge had notoriously held Imelda Marcos's umbrella like a doting servant during a public appearance), Marcos was less concerned about domestic courts should he one day lose power. Marcos had himself once been an influential attorney and as a politician had long been known as a master manipulator in a land in which "lawyer-politicians" played a leading role in the Philippine elite.[9] After the assassination of Senator Benigno Aquino in 1983, however, the opposition began holding mock trials as a form of public protest, in which Marcos was accused of massive corruption and the murder of thousands of political opponents. In addition, several prominent former judges joined the anti-Marcos movements.[10] But in hindsight, Marcos's apparent confidence in his ability to manipulate the judiciary in the Philippines has been at least partially confirmed by a long-running corruption trial that brought a conviction against his wife in the early 1990s but has left her out on bail during a series of appeals since then.[11]

Marcos, however, had good reason to fear legal action in the United States. A human rights case had already been filed against him (involving the death of two Filipino American labor leaders active in anti-Marcos exile politics).[12] In the last three years of his life in US exile after being overthrown by "people power," Marcos was preoccupied with an indictment from a Manhattan court charging he had illegally acquired US properties through stolen Filipino government funds.[13] In a class action suit for 10,000 human rights victims in the Philippines, a US lawyer won a multi-billion-dollar settlement in a US court.[14] The (justifiable) fear of facing prosecution in the United States helps to explain why Marcos complained so bitterly when a US helicopter flew him to Hawaii (he claimed he was kidnapped). Although surrounded by tens of thousands of protesters who later stormed the presidential palace, he apparently preferred staying in the Philippines (probably through retreat to his home province, Ilocos Norte) to going to the United States, where he would be safe from angry demonstrators but not from legal action (Thompson 1995: Chap. 8).

As in the case of Marcos, the fear of prosecution had a strong international dimension for Slobodan Milosevic, who had been an indicted war criminal since May 1999. But concerns also stemmed form the very nature of the regime, which the Serbian strongman established in the late 1980s.

Not only were corruption and other illegal activities an inevitable concomitant of the ruling clique's plundering of the state, but rather, the functioning of the whole political system was based on an extensive clientelistic network with numerous links to Serbia's underworld. Especially since the Kosovo war in 1999, this "criminalized state" increased its open repression of the opposition. Acts of political violence became more common, ranging from assaults on young civil society activists to the (successful or attempted) elimination of well-known opposition figures. As a consequence, even without the indictment in The Hague, Milosevic had every reason to cling to power after he had lost the Yugoslav presidential contest in September 2000. When the regime collapsed in a popular uprising two weeks later, his son Marko left the country immediately, out of fear of being arrested or even falling victim to acts of revenge; in the meantime, Milosevic's wife has gone into exile as well after having been charged with involvement in the assassination of an opposition politician.[15]

Fear of prosecution for extensive corruption may also explain regime intransigence after an election spun out of control in Georgia in November 2003. President Eduard Shevardnadze was brought down through a bloodless revolution after the main opposition party claimed it had been robbed of its victory in the parliamentary elections. To be sure, Georgian oppositionists never experienced the same degree of oppression as their counterparts in the Philippines or Serbia. Shevardnadze also can claim some credit for having allowed relatively far-reaching political freedoms, especially when compared with other countries in the Commonwealth of Independent States. But the former Soviet foreign minister never turned into a democrat, and corruption soared to new heights under his rule. Shevardnadze's government has been described by the International Crisis Group as operating "at three levels: a formal legal system, including state structures that performed according to a constitution that concentrated power in the executive; a hidden level that mixed personal relationships and feudal allegiances; and a third level, less visible yet and closely linked to organized crime."[16] After the "rose revolution," Shevardnadze did not leave the country, and his successor has promised to spare him from standing trial. But some observers expect Shevardnadze to choose exile as criminal investigations proceed, which are likely to uncover the details and the extent of corruption at the highest levels of government.[17] It is plausible to assume that the former president has favored electoral fraud to prevent such a situation from arising in the first place.

Preventing an opposition victory also became a matter of survival for the Ukrainian regime, especially for outgoing president Leonid Kuchma, because of grave abuses of power. Prime Minister Yanukovich had been chosen as a loyal successor who was supposed to protect the retired president from criminal inquiries. In addition, there had been attempts before the election to pass a law granting immunity to former presidents.[18] Among the many charges Kuchma could face, the killing of independent journalist Georgy Gongadze stands out. In what came to be known as "Kuchma-Gate," tapes leaked to the opposition at the end of 2000 linked the president himself to the Gongadze murder. Under Kuchma, the case was never properly prosecuted, although investigations were resumed after the change of power in Kiev.[19] The new authorities have also announced their intention to probe obvious cases of corruption, such as the privatization of the Kryvorizhstal steel plant. In that case, a consortium around Kuchma's son-in-law appears to have benefited from illegal interference by state officials.[20] Many more examples could be cited in order to demonstrate what was at stake for Kuchma and the Ukrainian oligarchs when the opposition seemed to be heading for victory.

Economic Motivations

In all the cases just discussed, the prospect of losing economic privileges and patronage contributed to the stealing of elections (in fact, concerns about criminal prosecution often arise from the way in which ruling elites enrich themselves). In the Philippines, maintaining a system that has been aptly called "crony capitalism" required that Marcos stay in office. Cronyism under Marcos was a kind of subcontracting of corruption that relied on his wielding state power to provide monopolies for private accumulation. Cronies came to dominate all areas of the economy.[21] Each crony had his respective fiefdom: there was a "sugar king," a "banana king," a "drug king," and so on. "According to the buttons on the intercom system at Malacañang Palace, Ferdinand Marcos was simply 'the King.'"[22] Undoubtedly, Serbia, Georgia, and Ukraine were also turned into highly profitable enterprises by their respective ruling elites. However, in order to document the worldwide reach of the stolen elections phenomenon, we now turn our attention to two examples from the African continent.

One African case that supports the claim that economic motives make regimes less likely to surrender power is the failed democratic transition in Nigeria in 1993. Shortly after a palace coup in 1985, General Ibrahim Babangida had pledged a return to civilian rule. Founding elections were promised as the final act of a transition program. However, the implementation of this program was delayed several times. Although his is usually viewed as just another military regime, "Babangida ruled in an increasingly arbitrary and autocratic fashion, personalizing authority to a degree unprecedented in Nigerian experience" (Lewis 1994: 329). Under his reign the already extensive clientelistic networks expanded further, with "elite corruption soar[ing] to new heights" (Campbell 1994: 189). When elections were finally held in June 1993, a real transfer of power was not intended. As soon as it turned out that the winner was not the candidate favored by the Babangida clique, the announcement of the results was blocked, and a few days later the entire poll was annulled. A number of reasons have been cited in order to explicate the abrogation of the transition process, but to a substantial degree it can be understood as an attempt to preserve the vast privileges that Nigeria's elite within and outside the military had enjoyed.[23]

In the already mentioned case of Madagascar, long-term ruler Didier Ratsiraka had been ousted through a democratic revolution in 1991–1992, but the weakness of his competitors allowed him to return to power through elections in 1997 and to establish a "neopatrimonial regime" (Marcus and Razafindrakoto 2003). Of particular importance was his decentralization program, which in reality meant a shifting of power and wealth to his followers in the coastal provinces. His family also benefited tremendously from Ratsiraka holding office. According to some sources, it was the businesswoman Sophie Ratsiraka who convinced her sixty-five-year-old father to run once more for president in December 2001.[24] With the surprising performance of Marc Ravalomanana, not merely a public office but a widespread network of patronage was put at risk.

Political Motives

Political motives are often closely related to legal and economic reasons for stealing, as shown above. Without political power, legal dangers cannot be avoided, nor can economic interests be protected. But there is also an independent political reason for electoral theft: to accept defeat and surrender power may involve losing all chances of regaining high public office and retaining influence. That holds especially true for highly personalistic dictatorships. In a more institutionalized authoritarian regime, by contrast, the loss of office may prove temporary, with a strong political party having a reasonable chance of improving its electoral prospects and winning future polls.

Two examples of reasonably well-institutionalized authoritarian regimes that conceded defeat in elections are Nicaragua and Poland. In February 1990, the Nicaraguan Sandinistas lost presidential and legislative elections to the US-backed National Opposition Union alliance and quickly conceded defeat.[25] Sandinista rule had been more authoritarian than totalitarian. Despite an undisputed Leninist faction, Sandinista leadership was on the whole collective and constrained. Well-documented regime repression did not eliminate limited pluralism. Also typical of authoritarianism, the regime was guided more by a vague mentality than a comprehensive ideology. In addition, there were limits on mass mobilization by the regime.[26] Facing eroding domestic support and a continuing US-supported "contra" military campaign, the Sandinistas chose to surrender power to the opposition, led by presidential candidate Violeta de Barrios Chamorro. As a relatively well-institutionalized party-regime, they were able to protect many of their interests through a complex power-sharing arrangement negotiated with the opposition. They maintained many of their party-movement organizations intact and participated in highly competitive elections in 1996 and 2001.[27]

Institutional interests in an authoritarian communist regime also help explain why the Polish regime conceded defeat after unexpectedly losing an election. The bureaucratic-communist leadership did not step in to prevent the formation of a Solidarity-dominated government after losing polls in June 1989.[28] Not only were the prospects of keeping their grip on power slim after years of unabated state-society conflict and the changed geopolitical context after Mikhail Gorbachev's rise to power, but also surrendering was acceptable to the members of the nomenclature because there were limits to what they would lose personally. They had sufficient institutional interests as members of the Communist Party that they could even hope to stay active in politics. And indeed, only a few years later former communists celebrated a remarkable comeback in both parliamentary and presidential elections (Zubek 1995). In both Nicaragua and Poland, institutionalized authoritarian regimes conceded electoral defeat because they were able to defend many of their parties' vital interests even after surrendering power.

By contrast, in the highly personalistic Marcos dictatorship in the Philippines, the ruling party was too weak to provide a basis for future political contestation. Marcos had created the Kilusang Bagong Lipunan (New Society Movement, KBL) political party to compete in pseudo-elections held during the martial law period beginning in 1978. But it was little more than a patronage network established by the president to compete in electoral exercises and dominate a powerless parliament (Batasang Pambansa). In the run-up to the 1986 polls, Marcos largely abandoned the KBL as an electoral vehicle (it was already plagued by a wave of defections), turning instead to leading cronies and the military to intimidate voters and manipulate the voting result (Thompson 1995: Chaps. 4 and 8). The KBL had no independent political standing that might have given it credibility in the post-Marcos era. Not unexpectedly, the KBL was quickly marginalized after the fall of the Marcos regime.

Compared to the KBL, the Socialist Party of Serbia (SPS) certainly played a much more important political role. Founded as a merger of two former communist organizations, it had inherited a wealth of resources and important organizational capacities. The SPS continued to participate in polls after the fall of the Milosevic regime (gaining more than 7 percent of the seats in the December 2003 parliamentary elections). From 1990 to 2000, however, the party was completely dominated by a single person, Slobodan Milosevic. When presidential elections were lost on 24 September 2000, no dissenters were left who might have challenged Milosevic's decision to steal the election in order to defend the collective interests of the party.

Electoral Sultanism and Stolen Elections

As noted above, legal, economic, and political motives for stealing can be distinguished for analytical reasons. In practice, however, they are often deeply intertwined, suggesting an aggregate explanation for stolen elections. It can be derived from the supposition that regimes organized around a "personalistic and arbitrary leadership" (denoting "sultanism") are less likely to hand over power willingly than more institutionalized authoritarian regimes.[29] The reason lies in the loss of personalized privileges a sultanistic ruler and his clique must expect (and the criminal prosecution they fear) because of their extreme corruption and chronic abuse of power. The rulers presiding over more institutionalized regimes, however, are better positioned to defend their key interests when they are not in power and thus much less reluctant to leave office.

This general explanation for regime intransigence can be fruitfully transferred to the more specific situation of authoritarians challenged by lost elections. We have explicitly applied the argument already when looking at the political motivations behind stolen elections. Members of the ruling parties of the rather institutionalized regimes in Poland and Nicaragua saw a political future for themselves after regime change. The highly personalized rule of Marcos in the Philippines, by contrast, left room only for a weakly organized ruling party, with the consequence that it could offer no political vehicle for the post-Marcos period. The Marcos regime also comes closest to the sultanistic model (Thompson 1998), but it can be argued that in many other cases (like Serbia, Madagascar, Georgia, or Ukraine) a similar constellation of personalized interests prevailed, pointing to the importance of at least sultanistic tendencies.[30] In many countries where electoral authoritarian rulers tried to reverse opposition victories through blatant fraud, they, their family members, and friends were heavily involved in the plundering of the state. Often, this personal enrichment had been accompanied by serious human rights abuses. As a result, the loss of elections puts these personal pecuniary and safety interests at stake, making the voluntary withdrawal of these regimes unlikely.

But can the concept of sultanism really be applied to the—per definition—more institutionalized electoral authoritarian regimes? At first glance, it may seem to be a strange combination, almost a contradiction in terms. According to the ideal type formulated by Juan J. Linz, Alfred Stepan, and Houchang Chehabi, sultanistic regimes are characterized by arbitrary political decisionmaking and a complete lack of the rule of law.[31] Unlike in electoral authoritarianism, formal institutional constraints play a negligible role under sultanistic rule. In such classical sultanism, opposition parties cannot participate in polls without compromising their credibility because the electoral process is little more than a farce. As a result, moderate antiregime groups are generally smaller and weaker than radical ones with nondemocratic aims. Under electoral authoritarianism, the problem with pro-democracy forces is a different one: usually there are too many moderate groups aiming to participate in semicompetitive polls. By failing to form a united front, they often deprive themselves of the chance to overthrow the authoritarian regime via elections.

Yet, the cases presented here demonstrate that sultanistic tendencies can exist alongside meaningful, albeit less than fully democratic, institutions. When arbitrary behavior increasingly eroded regime support in the Philippines, Serbia, Madagascar, Georgia, or Ukraine, the opposition could capitalize electorally on the growing dissatisfaction because in all these countries formal-democratic institutions existed that allowed this strategy to be pursued.[32] In other, "full-blown" sultanistic regimes that lacked minimally institutionalized electoral procedures, the decay of the regime resulted in the strengthening of the radical opposition instead (such as Iran under the shah or Nicaragua under Somoza). In "electoral sultanism," moderates can fight the regime through electoral competition, although (needless to say) not in the democratic sense of the word. Once control over the elections is lost, rulers resort to the ultimate kind of fraud: reversing the outcome. The alternative option of stepping down is extremely painful for electoral sultans because of the lack of an institutionalized ruling party, the loss of economic privileges, and the prospects of criminal prosecution.

It should be noted, however, that these reasons do not always add up to a sufficient condition for regime defiance. A challenge to the account just offered is the example of Kenya's long-term head of state, Daniel arap Moi. His regime possessed those sultanistic tendencies we described as hindering a smooth transition elsewhere. But when his handpicked successor lost the presidential race in December 2002, Moi did not make the slightest attempt to reverse the outcome. If he had hoped that by conceding defeat and thereby allowing for a smooth transition, he would not be tried for past abuses of power, that calculation appears to have been correct.[33] Besides these hopes for a safe exit, other reports indicate that already before the elections Moi had recognized he could not rely on the military in case of an annulled opposition victory (Holmquist 2003: 202). That realization may also have kept him from reversing the outcome.

Other Reasons for Stealing Elections

Political, legal, and economic considerations account for the decision to steal an election in many cases. Taken together, these motivations often derive from the regime's electoral sultanism. However, the struggle for personal survival is not necessarily part of the explanation for stolen elections. There may be other, "softer" factors that rule out the acceptance of an opposition victory by power holders, such as ideological commitment or psychological motivations.

Ideological commitment can refer both to the beliefs held by the rulers themselves and the political principles held by their rivals. Polish communists had already lost faith in their ideology when they were confronted with the disastrous result of the balloting in 1989. Indeed, having consented to semicompetitive elections in the first place signaled that the communist elite no longer believed in its monopoly of truth. In other cases, rulers may be convinced that political adversaries must be prevented form realizing their political goals. In Algeria, for instance, concern over the future of the secular state was a major reason for the military oligarchy to cancel the second round of the parliamentary elections in January 1992, which would have undoubtedly been won by the Islamic Salvation Front.[34]

Psychological benefits also cannot be excluded a priori as explanatory factors for unyielding dictators. Over the years, Slobodan Milosevic and his wife (as his closest political adviser) seem to have developed the conviction that they were the only ones entitled to preside over the Serbian state. That, too, forms part of the explanation for their obstinacy when they were confronted with an electoral debacle.[35] Such motives may seem trivial, and they may be hard to prove, but nonetheless they may exist and be important.

To give another example (one in which ideological and psychological motivations very much coincide), the current president of Zimbabwe, Robert Mugabe, also appears to be guided by the belief in a historical mission. So far, Mugabe has not been forced to steal an opposition victory blatantly. When in 2000 he lost a referendum on constitutional changes, he could accept defeat because his power was not put at stake through this poll. However, he reacted with determination and, above all, force to prepare the playing ground for the upcoming parliamentary elections. Before the presidential contest two years later, he even gave a speech in which he declared "war" on his opponents. That gives a hint at how Mugabe would have reacted (or will react) in case of a more serious electoral defeat.[36]

Conclusion

The terrain that authoritarian regimes enter after electoral defeats has been roughly surveyed but not yet well mapped. We know that it is dangerous territory for electoral authoritarians, but paths that may emerge from this crisis situation and how authoritarians react to electoral defeat require further exploration. In this brief discussion, we have, first, shown that there are other outcomes than the two options explored in the literature on electoral authoritarianism: (A) accepting defeat and surrendering power, or (B) stealing an election and retaining office. There is also the possibility of (C) regimes stealing elections but losing power after failing to effectively repress popular protest. In other cases (not discussed here extensively), nondemocratic rulers could accept defeat but still maintain ultimate political power due to the limited scope of elections.

We then offered explanations for why full elections (elections for the most powerful offices and institutions in a country) are stolen. We coined the term *electoral sultanism* to stress the importance of personalistic interests in explaining electoral theft. The threat lost elections pose to these interests can account for attempts to blatantly manipulate the results. Parallel to that was the argument that regimes with stronger institutional interests are more likely to concede that the opposition has won because former regime actors—who are still party members—are better able to defend vital interests outside of power.

The cases considered here imply that the degree of personalism is more important than whether the regime is electoral or fully closed authoritarian in determining how it behaves in the face of electoral defeat. Poland's communists presiding over an out-and-out authoritarian regime responded by quickly giving up power. In contrast, popular uprisings were required to force stubborn personalistic rulers out of office in Serbia and Madagascar, despite the much more competitive political environments that had persisted in these countries for years. That reveals how deceptive the appearances of regular electoralism often are. Electoral authoritarian rulers, highly "practiced" in the art of manipulation, are just as likely to falsify lost elections as fully authoritarian ones. Again, it becomes very clear that these "hybrid" regimes are not a halfway house on the way toward democracy.[37]

But the argument also shows that previous research on regime types can and should be integrated into the relatively new analysis of electoral authoritarianism.[38] With so many cases of electoral authoritarianism worldwide, further distinctions will improve the understanding of this phenomenon. The subtype of electoral sultanism, derived from the analysis of stolen elections, may contribute to this effort.

Notes

1. Samuel P. Huntington, who applied this concept to authoritarian regimes generally, was probably the first to point out its recurring nature (see Huntington 1991).

2. See especially Schedler (2002a: 112–113). Schedler also implies a third possibility by pointing at the introduction of "corrective post-electoral safeguards." Huntington (1991) considers stunning opposition victories as contributing to democratization. He thus neglects cases in which the regime steals the election and attempts to repress the opposition.

3. We elaborate these causal mechanisms in Thompson and Kuntz (2004).

4. UN Integrated Regional Information Networks, "Madagascar: Former President Sentenced to Five Years in Prison" (17 December 2003), and "Madagascar: Former Prime Minister Sentenced to Hard Labour" (26 December 2003), www.

irinnews.org (accessed 15 February 2004).

5. Associated Press, "Excerpts from AP's Yushchenko Interview" (16 December 2004).

6. Askold Krushelnycky, "Kiev Old Guard Try a Final Coup," *Times Online* (2 January 2005), www.timesonline.co.uk/article/0,,2089-1423187,00.html (accessed 11 January 2005).

7. Stephen Mulvey, "Kuchma Scrambles to Secure Future," *BBC News Online* (2 December 2004), news.bbc.co.uk/1/hi/world/europe/4061883.stm (accessed 7 January 2005).

8. Or, to put it in Dahlian terms, we also need to look at "costs of tolerance" (Dahl 1971).

9. Our thanks go to Paul Hutchroft for the phrase "lawyer-politician." Sterling Seagrave writes: "Among his peers [Marcos] had a reputation for ruthlessness that frightened even the corrupt old lions in Congress" (1988: 162).

10. Most prominently, Claudio Teehankee and Cecelia Munoz Palma (see Tate 1999).

11. Kristina Luz, "Dictators Beware," *Asiaweek* (13 October 1995), www.asiaweek.com/asiaweek/95/1013/feat1.html (accessed August 2004) and "Imelda Trial Called Off," *Manila Times* (27 February 2004), www.manilatimes.net/national/2004/feb/27/yehey/metro/20040227met8.html (accessed August 2004).

12. A semifictionalized account of these murders and the trial that followed can be found in Thomas Churchill (1995).

13. His wife, Imelda, was found innocent of the charges in 1991, two years after Marcos's death. She claimed her husband had been responsible for the transactions.

14. Luz, "Dictators Beware."

15. "Further Demand for Milosevic Wife," *BBC News Online* (18 April 2003), news.bbc.co.uk/2/hi/europe/2958781.stm (accessed 14 February 2004).

16. International Crisis Group, "Georgia: What Now?" (Tbilisi: International Crisis Group), Europe Report 151 (3 December 2003), p. 12, www.crisisgroup.org/home/index.cfm?id=2424&l=1 (accessed 14 February 2004).

17. Keti Borchorishvili, "New Georgian Leader Faces Up to Challenges" (London: International War and Peace Reporting), Caucasus Reporting Service 213 (8 January 2004), www.iwpr.net/index.pl?archive/cau/cau_200401_213_1_eng.txt (accessed 14 February 2004).

18. Taras Kuzio, "What Now for Leonid Kuchma?" (Jamestown Foundation), *Eurasian Daily Monitor* 1/131 (19 November 2004), jamestown.org/edm/article.php?article_id=2368885 (accessed 10 January 2005).

19. Jeremy Page, "Murdered Journalist Returns to Haunt Defeated Regime," *Times Online* (30 December 2004), www.timesonline.co.uk/article/0,,3-1419145,00.html (accessed 11 January 2005).

20. Krushelnycky, "Kiev Old Guard Try a Final Coup."

21. See the discussion in Thompson (1998: 218–220).

22. John Crewdson, "Marcos Graft Staggering," *Chicago Tribune* (23 March 1986), p. 20.

23. Once again, legal considerations constituted another important factor (see Campbell 1994: 190; Nwokedi 1994). The regional dimension of the power structure that needed to be preserved is stressed by Okoye (1999).

24. Michael Bitala, "Es herrscht die Familie: Der Streit um die Macht in Madagaskar ist einer um Pfründe," *Süddeutsche Zeitung* (6 June 2002).

25. See Krennerich (1996) and Carter Center and Council of Freely-Elected Heads of Government, *Observing Nicaragua's Elections, 1989–1990,* Special

Report 1 (May 1990), www.cartercenter.org/documents/1153.pdf.

26. This analysis draws on Linz and Stepan's distinction between totalitarian and authoritarian regimes (1996). A good, close-up view of the early Sandinista rule is provided by the journalist Shirley Christian (1986). The standard political science text is Booth (1985).

27. Carter Center, "Nicaragua," www.cartercenter.org/activities/country52.htm (accessed August 2004).

28. For a good discussion that includes a consideration of Poland's authoritarian regime type, see Linz and Stepan (1996: Chap. 16).

29. See Chehabi and Linz (1998b, 1998c), Linz and Stepan (1996: 51–54), and Linz (1975: 259–263). Statistical findings by Barbara Geddes (1999) lend additional evidence to this argument.

30. The sultanistic regime category has also been used to describe Milosevic's rule in Serbia. See, for example, Thomas (1999: 3–4, 424–426) and Antonić (2002: 435–468).

31. Linz and Stepan (1996: 52–53) and Chehabi and Linz (1998b).

32. The electoral dimension of the Marcos regime is stressed in the works of Hedman (1998) and Franco (2001). For Serbia, see Thomas (1999); for Madagascar, Marcus (2001); for Georgia, Fairbanks (2004); for Ukraine, Way (2004).

33. According to recent statements by Kenyan anticorruption officials, Moi has been granted immunity because of this decision not to resist the outcome of the election. Jeevan Vasagar, "Moi to Escape Corruption Charges," *Guardian* (22 December 2003), www.guardian.co.uk/international/story/0,3604,1111472,00.html (accessed 14 February 2004).

34. See Quandt (1998: 60–61). A different interpretation, emphasizing the selfish interests of the generals, is offered by Tahi (1995: 199–200).

35. For a psychological profile of Serbia's ruling couple, see Djukić (2001).

36. See Blair (2002) for a portrayal of Mugabe at that time.

37. See also Levitsky and Way (2002: 51–52) and Schedler (2002b: 36).

38. A similar argument has been made by Richard Snyder (in Chapter 13 of this book).

8

Armed Arbiters: When Does the Military Step into the Electoral Arena?

John F. Clark

In this chapter I look into the role of the military in the electoral authoritarian (EA) regimes of sub-Saharan Africa (SSA). EA regimes, like other kinds of authoritarian regimes, depend explicitly or implicitly on military support, or at least acquiescence, to remain in power. Yet military forces sometimes withdraw their support and intervene directly in the political process. The main question here is: Under what circumstances do they do so? This master question raises a series of others: What steps do the authoritarian regimes in power take to avoid military intervention in politics? How do administrative and economic factors affect the likelihood of military intervention in politics? And how do changes in the quality of subsequent elections affect the likelihood of military intervention?

One might usefully begin by asking how one can understand the variation in the incidence of military intervention, as some African EA regimes have avoided intervention by the military during recent years, whereas others have not. Some causes are best described as "permissive conditions," or social conditions that prevail throughout Africa (see Figure 8.1). For instance, no African state has as yet evolved a political culture that is entirely hostile to the possibility of military intervention, but that fact does little to explain the variation in military intervention. Similarly, the proximate cause of every case of military intervention is the presence of officers and troops who are ambitious—or disgruntled—enough to seek power for themselves. Since they are omnipresent, too, their motivations cannot explain variations in the incidence of military intervention either.

By contrast, there is considerable variation in the causal factors that we find in the middle columns of Figure 8.1. In particular, the levels of legitimacy of various regimes vary greatly. In turn, regime legitimacy is one major factor determining whether foreign actors are likely to intervene.

Figure 8.1 Explaining Military Intervention

Permissive Conditions		Contributing Conditions		Proximate Causes	
Culture tolerant of military intervention	+	Absent or declining legitimacy and/or Foreign support for intervention	+	Lack of military control mechanisms and Low likelihood of social protest	+	Ambitious officers and/or Disgruntled troops	→	Military intervention

There is less variation in the potential for protests against intervention, given the weakness of civil society throughout Africa. Whatever the restraining influence of civil society, the force of this restraint is also highly conditioned by legitimacy; that is, societal groups are far more likely to protest military intervention against relatively legitimate governments. Political legitimacy thus emerges as an important causal factor in understanding military intervention, and establishing tight controls over the military is clearly the only option for authoritarian rulers who cannot maintain even a pretense of legitimate authority.

The remainder of this chapter is divided into two parts. The first discusses the more specific conditions of military intervention in the EA regimes of sub-Saharan Africa, focusing on the relationship that one should expect to find between legitimacy and the incidence of military intervention. It concludes with several hypotheses about this relationship, based on the theoretical discussion. The second undertakes a systematic examination of the evidence of military intervention in sub-Saharan Africa's post-1990 EA regimes. It identifies the regimes that qualify as electoral authoritarian, examines the trajectories of their politics and their economic performance, and compares their records with the incidence of military intervention. This analysis, then, represents a first test of the hypotheses emerging from the section to follow.

Political Legitimacy and Military Intervention in Africa

African regimes prior to 1990 relied mostly on restraints external to the military itself to control intervention. The most typical instrument of such control has been an ultraloyal praetorian guard, such as Zairian president Mobutu Sese Seko's infamous Division Spéciale Présidentielle (Special Presidential Division). Herbert Howe (2001: 38–39) correctly notes that almost all African presidents have chosen to staff such units primarily with their ethnic kinsmen in order to ensure maximum loyalty. Samuel Decalo points out that in Gabon, President Omar Bongo continually augmented the size of his (all-Batéké) Presidential Guard until it reached a size of some 2,000 soldiers, about 80 percent of the size of the regular army (1998: 157–158). This guard protects the president from the unreliable, largely Fang regular army. Although extreme, this example is not entirely atypical of the African norm.

Aside from such specific mechanisms of control, Decalo (1998) identified two general modalities of direct civilian control over the interventionist predilections of African militaries: foreign guarantees for specific regimes and financial patronization of military elites. Gabon is his model for the first modality, in which an external guarantor (France) has assured the

Bongo regime of support and warned Gabonese soldiers against political interference. The model represented by Figure 8.1, however, suggests that foreign actors may encourage as well as deter military intervention. Indeed, in the quasi-states of sub-Saharan Africa, the signals of foreign supporters are often critical.

Decalo calls his second model of civilian control the "trade-off modality," but the relationship he describes has more commonly been referred to as neopatrimonialism. His argument is that civilian authorities essentially buy the loyalty of their armed forces by providing relatively high levels of pay, opportunities for rent seeking in society, and other paths to economic enrichment. Kenya serves as his prototypical case. Again, Decalo assumes that the military seeks a political role and views payoffs as a negative constraint on these natural instincts.

Each of these two modalities of civilian control remains relevant to Africa's EA regimes, but neither is easy to implement. Since EA regimes depend both on instruments of repression and on public support to remain in power, they cannot afford to appear entirely dependent on foreign powers. Hence, they must send a signal of warning to would-be coup makers that foreign supports will help quell military revolts while demonstrating their independence to the public. EA regimes will find the trade-off modality hard to employ because of the (at least minimal) public scrutiny that their financial dealings will draw. EA regimes cannot completely close down the political opposition or independent civil groups without losing the fig leaf of democratic legitimacy, and these independent groups will inevitably draw military patronage to the attention of the public.

Decalo's third model is the "legitimized modality," and one should note the fundamentally different quality of this form of civilian control. The other two models seek to control the (apparently inevitable) desire of soldiers for political power and illicit economic gain through external mechanisms. The legitimized modality seeks to condition or change the consciousness of soldiers so that the very idea of military intervention becomes anathema to them. This mode of civilian control is particularly relevant to the EA regimes of Africa because they depend more on legitimacy than the forthrightly authoritarian regimes of the pre-1990 era.

Unfortunately for the purposes of analysis, political legitimacy is a contingent and complicated phenomenon. Legitimacy cannot usefully be understood as an objectively present category, permanently sustained by any given political system or set of political outcomes. A clear election outcome may give a regime clear legitimacy for some period of time, but legitimacy may turn into a wasted asset in the hands of politicians who are inept or act in undemocratic ways, even if they were elected democratically. The question is rarely whether a regime has legitimacy, but rather how much legitimacy it has and whether its legitimacy is waxing or waning. Citizens' perceptions of the legitimacy of EA regimes are subjective and rather volatile.

Moreover, the non-Western observer must remember that political legitimacy is highly contextual and is not conferred only by free and fair elections. As Michael Schatzberg (2001) has brilliantly demonstrated, legitimacy in Africa depends on a regime's resonance with local cultures that emphasize the importance of "father, family, [and] food." This observation helps us understand how Decalo could present Malawi under Kamuzu Banda as a model of the legitimized modality of civilian control, despite the latter's failure ever to win a competitive election. Although the advent of widespread multiparty competition in Africa may slowly be eroding such patriarchal values, they have hardly evaporated overnight.

The capacity of some other nondemocratic political actions to confer legitimacy can be universally understood. In a setting of near-total political chaos in which no one's rights are assured, the simple process of restoring order can bestow a (temporary) legitimacy. This observation would be obvious to the citizens of Uganda, who welcomed Yoweri Museveni's rise to power by military means in 1986. Likewise, temporary legitimacy can be acquired by overthrowing hated alien or minority rule, as many revolutionary and anticolonial political figures in Africa have realized.

Yet Africa's EA regimes are different from the proudly nondemocratic regimes of pre-1990 Africa, whether they have a possible future as genuine democracies or not. Specifically, they seek at least some of their legitimacy from the evidence of popular support provided by regular, multiparty elections. Prior to 1990, only a very few African regimes staged regular multiparty elections. The large majority chose the one-party route of political control, a course that provided neither evidence of popular support nor military forbearance. Others were simply military dictatorships over long periods of time. Accordingly, the EA states share the desire to demonstrate popularity through multiparty elections with their more clearly democratic counterparts. For the study at hand, this desire begs the question, Do EA regimes face any unique challenges in seeking to establish and demonstrate their legitimacy?

In general, the most fundamental challenges for EA regimes apply to all African regimes, but these challenges are often more difficult for EA regimes to meet. First, like all developing world regimes, Africa's EA regimes must avoid the decline of state capacity at all cost. African states have enjoyed only a modest presence in the societies that they govern, and the state's "presence" is much less a matter of physical control than one of psychological acceptance of state legitimacy by local authorities and citizens. To the extent that the state is accepted, it is empowered vis-à-vis society. In the African context, legitimacy depends upon local authorities carrying out state policies, rather than using their official positions to extract rents. When local authorities fail to act in this manner, the reach of the state begins to contract, and local representatives begin usurping more and more power. This dynamic often leads to gradual state failure and eventually military intervention. Once public insecurity reaches an intolerable level, citizens may actually demand intervention by the military.

To meet this fundamental challenge, EA regimes must reliably and adequately compensate state agents, including military personnel. The failure to do so leads to a gradual but insidious erosion of state legitimacy, since unpaid state agents inevitably increase the rent-seeking activities that public office affords. Police and regular military forces typically attempt to extort money from defenseless populations, which in turn often leads to rebellion or at least accelerates the cycle of predation and erosion of legitimacy. When the unpaid agents include the military personnel themselves, the inducement to intervene is stronger still.

In turn, the appropriate compensation of state agents requires regimes to achieve two key tasks. The first is to raise a steady or growing level of income from whatever source. Although many African states get as much as half of their budget revenues from external aid, they also depend on internal economic growth to maintain robust state revenues. Of course, rising per capita incomes also accrue directly to the legitimacy of any given regime. If income increases are high enough and spread widely enough, populations are likely to tolerate nearly any sort of undemocratic behavior. The second task is to ensure that an adequate amount of this income is actually paid out to state agents. To achieve this, the EA regimes must keep corruption at a sufficiently low level that public funds are adequate to cover salaries, and they must also ensure that administrative mechanisms are in place to deliver them.

A second and more distinctive challenge for EA regimes is to demonstrate their democratic credentials. Although EA regimes are by definition authoritarian, they must avoid the appearance of being utterly repressive because such perceptions make it far more difficult to achieve electoral success, however manipulated. An EA regime that imprisons or otherwise openly molests its leading political opponents also provides coup makers with an obvious pretext for intervention. Therefore, in order to bolster their democratic credentials, EA regimes must disguise and limit the extent of their electoral manipulations. Blatantly stealing an election is one sure way for an EA regime to lose legitimacy rapidly. In any case, I hypothesize that the *trajectory* of a regime may be more important than the absolute *level* of its authoritarian misdeeds; a regime that exhibits gradual improvements in its democratic practices can avoid military intervention even if it starts from a low base.

A final challenge for EA regimes is to exhibit a modicum of respect for the rule of law, even if most regime loyalists feel little regard for the norm. Aside from the organization of elections, EA regimes must pay attention to the public perceptions of their legal probity in cases of institutional standoffs and in cases of individual persecution. Institutional standoffs most often occur when the representatives of different branches of government confront each other over constitutional interpretation. Where there is a lack of goodwill among political actors and/or when electoral outcomes are ambiguous, regime and opposition forces frequently disagree over the rules of the game. One form of confrontation occurs between presidents and legislative leaders, who struggle for control over the policy agenda. Likewise, EA regimes must appear to be respecting established law in their efforts to limit the political appeal of regime opponents.

These considerations allow us to make a number of related hypotheses about the circumstances for military intervention in the EA regimes of Africa. First, EA regimes will find it harder to employ the "external guarantor" modality of military control. In the post–Cold War environment, France is the only significant remaining external guarantor available. But the elected regimes that rule the former French colonies will often feel pressured to distance themselves from neocolonial French influence. When they do so, they will be more vulnerable to military intervention, unless they protect themselves otherwise.

Second, EA regimes that enjoy relatively strong economic growth will make themselves less vulnerable to military intervention for several reasons. For one, they can try to buy off their military establishments via the trade-off modality. As importantly, they will retain the possibility of compensating (nonmilitary) state agents, increasing the presence of the state throughout the territory and averting state decline. Yet, if an EA regime reaps a windfall of income (from rising commodity incomes, for instance) but fails to use it for the public good, rising revenues will not strengthen it. If the benefits of rising incomes are widely felt, however, popular support for the regime will rise, and military figures will be dissuaded from attempted intervention.

Third, EA regimes that launch themselves along a trajectory of increasingly liberal political practice will make themselves far less vulnerable to military intervention than they would otherwise be. Their legitimacy will gradually be enhanced by their respect for democratic norms and governance. Further, one would expect EA regimes experiencing both a trajectory toward greater liberalness and growing economic prosperity to be even less likely to experience military intervention. Inversely, regimes experiencing state failure, declining prosperity, and contracting liberties as well as those experiencing institutional crises are more vulnerable to coups.

Patterns of Military Intervention in
Africa's Electoral Autocracies

In this section, I examine military intervention in the EA regimes of Africa during the period from 1993 through 2003. The year 1993 is useful to begin the study because it represents the last year of the transitional period from the old, single-party regimes to the new, competitive, multiparty regimes. The last major group of formerly one-party or military-ruled African states all held their first multiparty elections in that year. We continue the study period through 2003, the last year for which data are readily available.

To make this part of our study as systematically comparative as possible, we need a definition of what states qualify as electoral autocracies for the period in question. The forty-eight states of SSA would have to meet two different criteria to fit into the category: first, they would have to hold competitive presidential and legislative elections on a regular basis; second, they would have to qualify as authoritarian states for some significant part of the selected eleven-year period. Twenty-nine of SSA's forty-eight states meet both criteria, as specified below.

With regard to the electoral part of the picture, the regularity of elections is important for a state to qualify as an electoral autocracy. Accordingly, only those states that held two or more competitive presidential elections between 1993 and 2003 are included in the population. Competitive is defined here in the narrow sense that opposition candidates and parties had the legal right to participate, whether or not they actually did so.[1] Nine states were eliminated by this stipulation: Angola, Burundi, the Democratic Republic of Congo (DRC), Eritrea, Lesotho, Liberia, Rwanda, Somalia, and Swaziland. All these states either held only one executive election, had only legislative elections, or had no elections at all. Uganda is included in the survey, though opposition parties were nominally banned under President Yoweri Museveni's no-party system, because opposition parties did function at a minimal level and Museveni faced serious opposition candidates in the presidential races of 1996 and 2001 (and later, in 2006). Opposition parties were legal—if often hamstrung in their activities—in all the other states included in the list of electoral autocracies.

Ten other states were eliminated from the pool because they were sufficiently liberal not to qualify as authoritarian. For our purposes here, authoritarian states were those that consistently impinged on either civil liberties or political rights to a significant degree according to Freedom House. Annual Freedom House surveys assess civil liberties and political rights by assigning scores of between 1 (most free) and 7 (most repressive) to individual countries. For purposes of assembling the population of electoral autocracies here, the two scores were simply added together and compiled for the eleven years in question. Only states that had scores of 7 or above for at least three of the eleven years in question were included in the population (see Table 8.1). The countries thus eliminated include Benin, Botswana, Cape Verde, Madagascar, Mali, Mauritius, Namibia, São Tomé, Seychelles, and South Africa, leaving the twenty-nine states in the table. This operation produces a surprisingly clear demarcation between authoritarian states (at least for some period of time) and their relatively liberal counterparts. Only Madagascar and Mali are mildly ambiguous cases under this scheme. Mali, though, scored 6 in only four out of eleven years and never once scored 7 or above. Madagascar is more controversial in that it scored a 7 in one year

Table 8.1 Combined Freedom House Scores of Electoral Authoritarian Regimes in Sub-Saharan Africa, 1993–2003

Country	1993	1994	1995	1996	1997	1998	1999	2000	2001	2002	2003
Burkina Faso	9	9	9	9	9	9	8	8	8	8	8
Cameroon	11	11	12	12	12	12	13	13	12	12	12
Central African Republic	7	7	7	8	8	7	7	7	10	10	12
Chad	11	11	11	11	11	10	11	11	11	11	11
Comoros	8	8	8	8	9	9	10	10	10	9	9
Congo-Brazzaville	8	8	8	8	12	12	11	10	9	10	9
Côte d'Ivoire	11	11	11	11	10	10	10	11	9	12	11
Djibouti	12	12	11	11	11	11	10	9	9	9	10
Equatorial Guinea	14	14	14	14	14	14	14	14	12	13	13
Ethiopia	11	11	9	9	9	8	10	10	10	10	10
Gabon	9	9	9	9	9	9	9	9	9	9	9
Gambia	4	13	13	13	13	12	12	12	10	8	8
Ghana	9	9	8	7	6	6	6	5	5	5	4
Guinea	11	11	11	11	11	11	11	11	11	11	11
Guinea-Bissau	11	7	7	7	7	8	8	9	9	9	10
Kenya	11	12	13	13	12	11	11	11	11	8	6
Malawi	11	5	5	5	5	5	6	6	7	8	7
Mauritania	13	14	12	12	12	11	11	11	10	10	11
Mozambique	11	8	7	7	7	7	7	7	7	7	7
Niger	7	8	8	12	12	12	10	8	8	8	8
Nigeria	12	13	14	13	13	10	7	8	9	9	8
Senegal	9	9	9	8	8	8	8	7	7	5	5
Sierra Leone	13	13	13	9	13	8	8	9	9	8	7
Sudan	14	14	14	14	14	14	14	14	14	14	14
Tanzania	11	12	10	10	10	9	8	8	8	7	7
Togo	12	11	11	11	11	11	10	10	10	11	11
Uganda	11	10	9	8	8	8	10	11	11	10	9
Zambia	7	7	7	9	9	9	9	9	9	8	8
Zimbabwe	10	10	10	10	10	10	11	11	12	12	12

Source: Freedom House (www.freedomhouse.org).
Note: Freedom House measures political rights and civil liberties on a 1-to-7 scale, with 1 representing the highest degree of freedom and 7 the lowest. Combined scores are the sum of both annual measures.

(2002) and 6 in the remaining ten years. There is, however, a relatively comfortable gap between Madagascar and the next most "illiberal" state, Mozambique. The latter state had a score of 7 for nine years and higher scores in the remaining two (1993 and 1994). Thus, this operational definition does an excellent job in distinguishing Africa's clearly authoritarian regimes from the more liberal ones.

Beyond merely serving to help identify sub-Saharan Africa's EA regimes, the presentation of the Freedom House data in Table 8.1 assists in evaluating our hypotheses, for two main reasons. First, during the 1990s, political rights (PR) and civil liberties (CL) became *the* major criteria for regime legitimacy in the African political context, unlike in earlier years. By the early 1990s, revolutionary and redistributional claims to legitimacy had largely been replaced by these democratic criteria. Accordingly, the PR-CL index serves as a useful proxy for political legitimacy based on democratic credentials. Second, the table shows the evolution of scores over time and thus helps to provide some sense of the political trajectory of the regimes, often an important element of their level of legitimacy.

As we also argued above, economic performance represents another important source of political legitimacy. Table 8.2 contains two important pieces of data for sub-Saharan Africa's EA regimes: the growth of their average annual gross domestic product (GDP) per capita and the year of their highest attainment of GDP per capita between 1975 and 2002. In general one would expect regimes that have reasonably high per capita economic growth and those attaining their wealthiest status in the 1990s or 2000s to be less vulnerable to military intervention.

A second phenomenon that needs specification for the purposes of our analysis is military intervention. Three different kinds of military intervention are included here: military coups d'état, attempted military coups d'état, and newly arising military rebellions aimed at overthrowing the regime. Successful coups d'état are rather easy to observe and are hence rather uncontroversial. Attempted coups d'état are often a matter of controversy because African states often use the fiction of attempted coups d'état or even alleged coup plots as a pretext for political crackdowns and persecution. Coup plots are so ubiquitous and so impossible to verify that they are formally left out of this study. Attempted coups, however, are included where there is sufficient evidence to show that they did in fact occur. For the period from 1993 to 2001, we rely on the data provided by Patrick J. McGowan (2003: 364); data for the subsequent two years have been added through a survey of the relevant media.

We also add cases of new armed rebellions aimed at overthrowing the state. These cases surely constitute "military intervention in politics," though they are not part of most studies of "military coups," like McGowan's. One notable case took place in Congo-Brazzaville in 1997. In that instance, an armed militia group attacked units of the Congolese military when the sit-

Table 8.2 Economic Performance of Electoral Authoritarian Regimes in Sub-Saharan Africa

Country	Average Annual Growth Rate of GDP per Capita, 1990–2002	Year of Highest GDP per Capita, 1975–2002
Burkina Faso	1.6	2002
Cameroon	−0.1	1986
Central African Republic	−0.2	1977
Chad	−0.5	1977
Comoros	−1.4	1985
Congo-Brazzaville	−1.6	1996
Côte d'Ivoire	−0.1	1978
Djibouti	−3.8	n/a
Equatorial Guinea	20.8	2001
Ethiopia	2.3	2002
Gabon	−0.2	1976
Gambia	0	1986
Ghana	1.8	2002
Guinea	1.7	2002
Guinea-Bissau	−2.2	1997
Kenya	−0.6	1990
Malawi	1.1	1979
Mauritania	1.6	2002
Mozambique	4.5	2002
Niger	−0.8	1979
Nigeria	−0.3	1977
Senegal	1.2	1976
Sierra Leone	−5.9	1982
Sudan	3.1	2002
Tanzania	0.7	2002
Togo	−0.7	1980
Uganda	3.9	2002
Zambia	−1.2	1976
Zimbabwe	−0.8	1998

Source: United Nations Development Programme, *Human Development Report 2004* (New York: UNDP), pp. 186–187.
Note: n/a = data not available.

ting president, Pascal Lissouba, attempted to arrest his rival in the forthcoming elections, Denis Sassou-Nguesso, starting a civil war (Clark 1998). Likewise, the successful "coup" in the Central African Republic in 2003 started as an army rebellion that led to a short civil war and eventually the overthrow of President Ange-Félix Patassé. The 2002 rebellion in Côte d'Ivoire is yet another example. As much as attempted and successful coups, these events are surely military interventions and are included in Table 8.3. The table does not include military mutinies not aimed at the overthrow of the regime but staged for other purposes such as forcing salary payments.

**Table 8.3   Military Coups, Attempted Coups, and
Armed Rebellions in Sub-Saharan Africa, 1993–2003**

Country	Successful Seizure of Power by Military	Failed Military Coups	New Armed Rebellions
Central African Republic	2003	1996, 1997, 2001	1996, 1997, 2002, 2003
Comoros	1999	1995, 2000, 2001	
Congo-Brazzaville	1997		1993, 1997, 1998, 2002
Côte d'Ivoire	1999	2000, 2001	2002
Equatorial Guinea		2003	
Gambia	1994	1994	
Guinea		1996	
Guinea-Bissau	1998, 2003	1993, 1998	1998
Mauritania		2003	
Niger	1996, 1999		
Nigeria	1993		
Sierra Leone	1996, 1997	1995, 1996, 2000	1991–
Zambia		1997	

Sources: Patrick J. McGowan, "African Military Coups d'État, 1956–2001: Frequency, Trends, and Distribution." *Journal of Modern African Studies* 41/3: 339–370; and author's database.

The sixteen EA regimes of our data set not listed in Table 8.3 did not experience any form of military intervention specified here. Senegal has experienced an ongoing rebellion in the Casamance region since the 1980s, but this rebellion does not appear to be aimed at the overthrow of the regime. Two other cases are of some interest. Djibouti experienced a brief rebellion of police officers in December 2000, quickly put down by the authorities, but this act was also not clearly aimed at the overthrow of the regime. Second, there was an alleged coup attempt in Chad in May 2002 (*Africa Confidential,* 22 October 2002), but this coup attempt could not be confirmed by other sources, and was not widely reported in the international media.

Explaining the Absence of Military Intervention

Among the states not listed in Table 8.3, several seem to confirm the "gradual liberalization" hypothesis, including Ghana, Senegal, Tanzania, and, most arguably, Kenya. These regimes exhibit a clear trajectory of greater freedom from 1993 through 2003. Kenya's repression score fell by 7 points, Ghana's and Tanzania's by 5, and Senegal's by 4, from their highs early in the 1990s to 2003. The successive elections held in each country over the period were of progressively better quality, leading to alternation in government in all cases but Tanzania. Three of the four countries (except Kenya) also experienced steady GDP per capita growth during the period. Hence, one may infer that the regimes in question experienced growing legitimacy from liberalization during the period, insulating them against military intervention.

The cases of Gambia (after 1994), Mozambique, and Nigeria (after 1993) also fit my theoretical expectations quite well. Mozambique did not improve its repression score as consistently as the cases just listed, but neither did it become any more repressive after the successful transitional elections of 1994. Although the 1999 elections were rather flawed and the opposition party rejected the results, the country's national elections commission and supreme court both reviewed the evidence and found that the reported results were accurate enough to be considered valid (Manning 2005). Meanwhile, the regime's impressive economic performance from 1994 to 2003 certainly shored up its popular legitimacy. Nigeria also fits our main hypothesis reasonably well. After the sudden death of the military dictator Sani Abacha in 1998, Nigeria returned to a civilian regime the following year in elections widely regarded as reasonably free and fair. Over the next five years, Nigeria enjoyed per capita GDP growth of 2.5 percent per year.[2] Thus it is not surprising that Nigeria did not experience military intervention aimed at overthrowing the regime.

Gambia would seem to be a contradictory case, since it had one of the most liberal regimes in Africa through the 1980s and early 1990s and since it did in fact suffer a coup d'état in 1994. Two things may be said, however, that mitigate the disconfirming power of the Gambian case. First, the old regime was in fact losing legitimacy leading up to the coup in 1994, even if it was comparably liberal by the standard of the times. Although the elections of 1987 and 1992 were regarded as generally free and fair, it was also the case that former president Sir Dawda Jawara had been in power continuously for twenty-nine years, leaving many Gambian and international observers to wonder how real Gambian democracy was. Also, as we see in Table 8.2, the year of Gambia highest GDP per capita attainment was 1986, and as of 1994, Gambia remained one of the poorest countries in the world. Lieutenant Yahya Jammeh and his men who overthrew Jawara cited the latter's increasing resort to repression, as well as his regime's corruption, as the reasons for their coup, even if their real motivations were otherwise (Howe 2001: 145). Second, one may note that since 1994, the trajectory of the new regime has been one of increasing liberalness. Since the coup, Jammeh has been successively elected and reelected president in the relatively fair elections of 1996 and 2001. In June 2002, Jawara returned from exile and took up an opposition role, and Gambia's Freedom House scores between 1997 and 2003 reflect the new regime's trend toward a return to political rights and civil liberties.

A rather large group of countries among sub-Saharan Africa's EA regimes witnessed neither military intervention nor significant movement in their repression scores for the 1993–2003 period. This list includes Burkina Faso, Cameroon, Chad, Djibouti, Ethiopia, Gabon, Sudan, Uganda, Togo, and Zimbabwe. In all ten cases, the same ruler was in power throughout the entire period. Among these same regimes, only Ethiopia and Sudan enjoyed significant per capita economic growth over the period in question, perhaps explaining their success in containing coups. These cases suggest that repressive regimes, even some that do not produce significant economic benefits from their citizens, can avoid military intervention in politics. As suggested by Decalo, these regimes tend to control their militaries through either the external guarantor modality or the trade-off modality, since they have only weak claims to legitimacy. All six of the former French colonies in the group appear to be relying on France to bolster the impression of their invulnerability to military intervention. Besides Gabon, that was certainly the case for Burkina Faso (Boudon 1997: 139) and Cameroon (Takougang 1997: 168).

The Sudanese regime relies somewhat on its Islamicist claim to legitimacy, though, of course, this claim resonates with the country's Muslim population only. Meanwhile, Zimbabwe's Robert Mugabe only has his waning status as an antiapartheid "hero" to bolster himself ideologically. Zimbabwe's recent economic record is even worse than indicated in Table 8.2. In fact, Mugabe's hands-on control of and collaboration with his military are the real secret of his anticoup success (*Africa Confidential,* 15 June 2001). Finally, South Africa's Thabo Mbeki has kept the international pressure off Mugabe, even if he has not exactly served as an external guarantor. In Uganda, the Museveni regime did not exhibit a clear trend toward either more liberality or more repressiveness. Nonetheless, it has enjoyed real legitimacy, based on two important grounds. First, Museveni rebuilt the country and restored order to Uganda after the debacles of the Idi Amin (1971–1979) and the second Milton Obote (1980–1985) regimes. Second, the Museveni regime has consistently and impressively produced economic results virtually unequaled in Africa. Museveni's successful effort to bring the military under civilian control (Brett 1995) is comprehensible in this context.

Explaining the Occurrence of Military Intervention

Now we come to the thirteen cases in which military intervention of some form did take place (in addition to the anomalous Gambian case, discussed above). In eight of these cases, the military intervention led to a change of power; in five others, it did not (see Table 8.3). Two of these cases, Equatorial Guinea and Comoros (1995), are rather aberrant and can reasonably be set aside without much controversy because both were generated from outside the country. The Equatorial Guinea case generated sensational media coverage because it apparently involved white mercenaries, some of whom were arrested in Zimbabwe (*Africa Confidential,* 19 March 2004, 17 August 2004). The regime of Teodoro Obiang Nguema Mbasogo enjoys very little real legitimacy because it is so transparently and ruthlessly repressive and corrupt, despite the country's spectacular, petroleum-fueled economic growth. The 1995 attempted coup in the Comoros was similar in that it was orchestrated by a collection of externally based mercenaries, led by the infamous mercenary Bob Denard.

Three cases of military intervention follow a similar pattern and can thus be usefully treated together: the Central African Republic, Congo-Brazzaville, and Niger. All three states underwent genuine transitions in the early 1990s, in each following "sovereign national conferences." Unlike some others, these sovereign conferences deserved the name, actually assuming sovereign powers and putting in place transitional regimes that organized elections leading to a change in the head of state. In each case, however, the political trajectory following the transitions was one of clearly decreasing legitimacy. This judgment is unassailable, even if it was far clearer to the country specialists studying each state than to the compilers of the Freedom House scores.[3] The newly elected rulers of each country, Ange-Félix Patassé (Central African Republic), Pascal Lissouba (Congo-Brazzaville), and Mahmane Ousmane (Niger), all acted in authoritarian ways that clearly violated the rule of law. All three also had absolutely dismal records of economic performance (though a gush of fresh petroleum revenues in 1996 obscures this fact for Congo-Brazzaville). Both the Lissouba and Ousmane regimes dissolved their respective parliaments when legislative elections produced national assemblies dominated by the opposition. Lissouba's illegal dissolution of parliament in late 1992 and the subsequent rerun of the legislative elections led to Congo-Brazzaville's first bout of civil war. After being forced out of power, Sassou returned to the presidency following another round of civil war in 1997. Likewise, in Niger, the legislative elections of both 1993 and 1995 produced assemblies dominated by the opposition and hostile to President Ousmane. The military coup of 1996 was a direct response to the standoff created by those elections (Villalón and Idrissa 2005: 38). Likewise, the successful 1999 military coup in Niger followed fraudulent, poorly organized elections in that year (p. 41). Finally, another outbreak of armed rebellion in Congo-Brazzaville coincided with President Sassou's staging of fraudulent and manipulated elections in 2002. Thus, the military interventions in these two countries are clearly associated with declining legitimacy and were triggered by fraudulent elections or institutional standoffs.

In the case of Patassé in the Central African Republic, the relationship between declining legitimacy and military intervention is not as readily confirmed by the timing, but a strong case for a linkage exists nonetheless. The 1996 army rebellions were related not only to Patassé's failure to make salary payments but also to his efforts to alter the country's constitution in order to increase his own power. Only the intervention of French troops saved him from being overthrown on this occasion. Having lost popularity and legitimacy, Patassé was able to stay in power only by heavily manipulating the 1999 presidential elections, which were of far lower quality than those of 1993 (Mehler 2005). Again it was Patassé's transparently unconstitutional attempts to manipulate the assembly that led to the armed rebellions of 2001. His perpetual attempts to circumvent the rule of law and the regime's awful economic performance had utterly undermined Patassé's legitimacy by this date. Accordingly, hardly anyone was surprised by the outbreak of yet another armed rebellion in 2003, this time leading to the feckless politician's demise. Here too, then, military intervention was linked to declining legitimacy.

Presidents Lissouba of Congo-Brazzaville and Patassé of the Central African Republic also share one other unfortunate distinction: both gave in to the political urge to defy French interests in their respective countries. Lissouba had the temerity to challenge the dominance of French petroleum companies, and Patassé squandered the military support that France had demonstrated in 1996 (Mehler 2005: 136–137) by criticizing the French, who subsequently closed their military base at Bouar in 1997. Both leaders thus sacrificed the protection—or at least the perception of protection—of their regimes by the French state, their potential external guarantor.

The story of Zambia's political trajectory differs from this set of cases only in that the attempted coup of 1997 failed, and the regime subsequently returned to a path of increasing, rather than declining, political legitimacy. Zambia's second election (in 1996) was far less free and fair than the founding election of 1991, and it took place in a far less open political environment. That election largely explains the increase in Zambia's political repression score in 1996. Meanwhile, the economic performance of the new regime of Frederick Chiluba proved to be as disappointing as his observance of democratic norms. The coup attempt of 1997, however, was a direct response to the political standoff created by the highly contested 1996 elections (Simon 2005). Once again, rapidly declining legitimacy marked by the need of a sitting president to manipulate elections led to military intervention. Interestingly, the 2001 elections, problematic though they were in some regards, seemed to put the regime in Zambia back on a path of increasing political legitimacy. After flirting with the idea of changing the constitution to stand for a third term in office, Chiluba backed down in the face of opposition. The new president elected in that year, Levy Mwanawasa, was of the same party as Chiluba but was far from a handpicked successor; indeed, Mwanawasa and Chiluba became bitter political rivals. The closeness of the 2001 elections also suggested that they were much less manipulated than in 1996 (Simon 2005). The competitiveness of these elections explains why Zambia's political freedom score improved from 5 to 4 in the subsequent two years after the elections.

The 1999 coup in Côte d'Ivoire was also linked to an (impending) election. As in Congo-Brazzaville, the military intervention took place before an election that was not expected to be free or fair by the most likely contestants. In hapless Côte d'Ivoire, Henri Konan Bedié had taken power after the death of Félix Houphouet-Boigny in December 1993. Bedié subsequently organized presidential elections in October 1995, but the two main opposition figures declined to participate on the grounds that Bedié had instituted an electoral code and prepared the elections in such a way as to ensure his own victory (Mundt 1997: 197). At the time of the 1995 elections and in the years afterward, Bedié kept the issue of "Ivoirité" on the front burner of Ivorian politics by insisting that only those of documented Ivoirian parentage could stand in subsequent elections (Akindès 2004: 20–21). This stance threatened to prevent the participation of the popular northerner, Alassane Ouattara, alleged to be of Burkinabè parentage. Indeed, that was only the most obvious way in which Bedié was then attempting to manipulate the coming electoral contest, scheduled for 2000, to ensure his own reelection. Accordingly, when General Robert Gueï seized power in December 1999, he cited Bedié's electoral manipulations as the main motive of the military intervention into politics (Akindès 2004: 31). Côte d'Ivoire's declining economic performance under Bedié was yet another source of his profound delegitimization in the eyes of the Ivoirian population (see Table 8.2).

The 1999 coup in Comoros was just as clearly linked to a decline in legitimacy, if not to a disputed election. In that case, President Mohamed Taki Abdulkarim, elected in 1996, died suddenly in November 1998, after which a military committee took power. Lacking any democratic credentials at all, the head of that committee, Tadjiddine Ben Said Massounde, was subsequently overthrown in a military coup in April 1999.

In Guinea-Bissau, João Bernardo Vieira, who had seized the presidency in 1980, confirmed his hold on power in noncompetitive elections in 1990 as well as in the reasonably free and fair elections of 1994. The military coup of 1998 interrupted the incipient electoral cycle and led to the downfall of President Vieira. By contrast, the 2003 coup against President Kumba Yala, winner of a dubious two-round presidential contest in 2000, reestablished minimally democratic elections and paved the way for Vieira's return to power in the 2003 presidential elections. With regard to both military changes of power, the analysis of a leading specialist seems more revealing than Freedom House scores. According to Joshua Forrest, the 1994 elections "did not help to restrain the autocratic character of the Vieira personalist regime, nor did it lead to a halt in the country's economic deterioration. These two factors contributed substantially to the subsequent rebellion of the country's armed forces in 1998" (2005: 255). In a similar fashion, Vieira's successor did not prove himself to be either democratically committed or economically competent. As Forrest states, "President Kumba Yala's strong-handed presidential style became increasingly manifested in a number of policy areas and issue disputes, calling into question his ability to resist reproducing the autocratic tendencies of his predecessors" (2005: 260). Like Lissouba and Patassé, Yala was not willing to lead his country on a path toward liberalization, and thus met the same fate as his counterparts in Congo-Brazzaville and the Central African Republic.

Finally, we turn to the two attempted coups in Guinea (1996) and Mauritania (2003), respectively. The coup in Mauritania represents perhaps the most anomalous case in our entire population of military intervention. According to Freedom House, Mauritania was gradually becoming more liberal in the course of the eleven-year period under review, descending from a combined score of 14 in 1994 to 10 in 2002; the country also experienced modest economic growth. Accordingly, one would not have expected an attempted coup against the regime. Although the coup attempt came only a few months before the presidential elections scheduled for November 2003, the would-be coup makers against President Maouiya Ould Sid'Ahmed Taya were not apparently reacting to presidential efforts to manipulate the polls. Rather, the military officers who attempted to oust President Taya did so because he was nurturing closer ties with the United States and Israel (*Africa Confidential*, 10 October 2003). It is easy to see that such policies would have diminished the legitimacy of the regime in the eyes of the (entirely Muslim) public and virtually invited a coup against its leader.

The attempted coup in Guinea in 1996 better supports our hypotheses. There is no evidence that the listless regime of President Lansana Conté in Guinea enjoys real popular support. President Conté came to power in a bloodless coup in 1984, and the elections that he has staged since 1993 have been exercises in attempted legitimization rather than genuinely competitive exercises. Conté has remained in power by keeping the opposition divided and by averting successful coups, rather than by forging a regime based on the real legitimacy that comes from success in fair elections. Conté was not protected by the possibility of French intervention because Franco-Guinean relations had never recovered from the rupture that occurred during Touré's rule in the 1960s.

Conclusion

I began this chapter with a claim that political legitimacy and control over the military, rather than more proximate or more fundamental factors, explain most of the variation in the military intervention that one observes in African states. Second, I inquired into the specific circumstances under which one would expect to observe military intervention in Africa's EA regimes. I argued that the trajectory of regime legitimacy would probably be the most important indicator of the likelihood of military intervention. One would expect that regimes that increase their legitimacy over time through increasingly free and fair elections would become increasingly invulnerable to military intervention. Regimes that grow increasingly repressive, however, or stage less free and fair second and third elections after the "founding" elections, would be more vulnerable to military intervention. As for all developing world regimes, increasing or stable levels of legitimacy also result partly from the economic performance achieved by those regimes. For regimes that never underwent any kind of genuine democratic transition and did not perform well economically, their ability to avoid military intervention depends largely on either international or monetary "control" mechanisms over the military.

In the main, the evidence bears out the major hypothesis produced in the first section. No regime that showed both a clear trajectory toward increasing liberality and positive economic performance experienced any form of military intervention. Ghana, Kenya, Senegal, and Tanzania fall into this category. A number of other states experienced democratic transitions in the early 1990s, but the regimes elected in the founding elections did not prove themselves to be genuinely democratic in their subsequent behavior, and all experienced military intervention. Another state that experienced a transition in this period, Benin, gradually developed a more legitimate regime, and it has avoided any attempted military coups. A number of other states made a nominal transition to multiparty rule without undergoing a genuine democratic transition, including most of the other states in our population of twenty-nine electoral autocracies. Whether these EA regimes avoided military intervention or not depended entirely on their ability to control their militaries through the "artificial" devices of financial payoffs or the threat of external intervention. The more competent and economically capable of them (e.g., Sudan and Uganda), as well as those protected by the threat of French intervention (e.g., Burkina Faso, Cameroon, Gabon, and Togo), avoided attempted coups. Meanwhile, the incompetent and unprotected regimes in Comoros, Congo-Brazzaville, the Central African Republic, Guinea-Bissau, and Sierra Leone all succumbed to military intervention.

Notes

1. In many cases, of course, opposition parties or candidates chose not to participate on the ground that the elections that were being prepared did not promise to be free and fair.

2. Calculated from the World Bank's annual *World Development Report* for the years 2000–2001 through 2005.

3. On the Central African Republic, see Mehler (2005); on Congo-Brazzaville, see Clark (2005); and on Niger, see Villalón and Idrissa (2005).

9

Tragic Protest:
Why Do Opposition Parties
Boycott Elections?

Staffan I. Lindberg

In this book several contributors refer to Larry Diamond's (2002) typology, ranging from closed authoritarianism to liberal democracy and situating types of electoral authoritarian regimes as intermediate categories along the continuum between these endpoints. Diamond's continuous conception of democracy is conversant with Robert A. Dahl's formulation of polyarchy (1971 and 1989), later refined by scholars such as Michael Coppedge and Wolfgang H. Reinicke (1990), and Kenneth Bollen and R. W. Jackman (1989: 612–618). The intermediate category of electoral authoritarianism is particularly important because these regimes carry the greatest potential to develop into democracies. In this chapter I take a closer look at the role of opposition parties in authoritarian elections. After operationalizing opposition behavior and identifying sub-Saharan Africa's electoral authoritarian regimes, I explore if (and if so which) opposition strategies help electoral authoritarian regimes transform into democracies. Concluding that boycotting strategies tend to derail rather than promote democratization, I then investigate the conditions under which opposition parties in electoral autocracies choose more beneficial strategies to enhance the freedom and fairness of electoral processes. As it seems, opposition parties sense when collaborative approaches are more likely to pay off in further reform and when hard-line autocratic rulers make boycott the most rational response. Finally, I discuss the lessons for Africa's political development in a comparative perspective.

Opposition Strategies

There are at least two interrelated reasons to study opposition strategies in authoritarian regimes. First, any form of political organization that makes binding decisions for all members requires some form of government. In a democracy, that entails representation of the people through competitive and participatory elections. The fundamental value of self-government therefore translates into both equal opportunity of political participation and political competition as the two core dimensions of democracy, or polyarchy, as Dahl (1971, 1989) labeled it. In order for the public to be able to exercise its sovereignty in elections, there must be choice. Without political opposition there is no choice, and when there is no choice, the public cannot exercise its discretion to indirectly rule via representation.

Second, however, electoral contestation alone is not sufficient to make a democracy, because the electoral process may be flawed, wholly orchestrated, or dominated by the incumbent party to the extent of making outcomes a foregone conclusion. Violence may mar the electoral campaign, and even if elections themselves appear more or less free and fair, the periods between them may be characterized by denial of political rights and civil liberties and autocratic behavior on the part of the incumbent regime. These are traits of electoral autocracies (Schedler 2002b). In response to authoritarian elections, opposition parties, first, must decide whether to participate in the electoral process and, second, after official results are announced, whether to accept those results.

1. *Opposition participation.* When do opposition parties choose to participate in or boycott elections in electoral autocracies? In order to respond to this question, I rely on an extensive database on elections in sub-Saharan Africa from 1989 to 2003 (Lindberg 2006). In the data set, I code opposition participation as a dichotomous variable. If some or all opposition parties boycott the poll, I count a "boycott." If all major political parties participate, I register full "participation." The variable records primarily the preelection period but extends over election day itself.

2. *Losers' acceptance.* When do opposition parties accept electoral results? In the database, I measure losers' acceptance on a three-point ordinal scale: none of the main losing parties accepts the outcome (no acceptance at all); some but not all losing parties do not accept the results, or some or all losing parties reject the results at first but within three months come to accept them (later/some acceptance); all losing parties concede defeat immediately after the results are pronounced (acceptance all at once).

Table 9.1 presents the rates of opposition boycott and acceptance for ninety-four presidential and 124 legislative elections in sub-Saharan Africa (from 1989 through mid-2003). As the table shows, all major opposition parties have contested the results in approximately two-thirds of all polls, presidential as well as parliamentary. In other words, boycotts of various kinds are not that common in Africa over the period. Losers' acceptance is much more

Table 9.1   Opposition Behavior in Sub-Saharan Africa, 1989–June 2003

		Presidential Elections		Legislative Elections	
		N	%	N	%
Opposition participation	Boycott	32	34	37	29
	Participation	63	66	88	70
	Total	95	100	125	99
Losers' acceptance	Not at all	42	45	36	29
	Later/Some	33	35	42	34
	All at once	19	20	46	37
	Total	94	100	124	100

Source: Author's database.

worrying, with only 20 percent of executive elections having been accepted immediately and less than 40 percent of legislative ones. Which of these opposition strategies furthers democratization? Do boycotts and protests increase pressures on authoritarian regimes, leading to further democratization, or is it rather collaboration and nonadversarial politics that pay off in the longer run?

Identifying Electoral Authoritarianism in Africa

In order to assess the effectiveness of opposition strategies, I classify African political regimes according to their trajectories. I distinguish electoral autocracies that have transformed into democracies from cases of self-reproducing electoral authoritarianism as well as cases of electoral authoritarian regimes that have broken down. Using a slightly modified version of Diamond's (2002) and Andreas Schedler's (2002b) proposals, I classify as liberal democracies all regimes scoring a maximum average of 2.0 in political rights and civil liberties according to the Freedom House scale. I will not be using the year of the election as a measurement point because elections typically start some time before polling day. Parties prepare for their campaigns, issues are debated and spread via media, potential voters start to ponder their decision, and voter registries and other organizational pillars of the electoral process are usually set up well before election day. Freedom House data are taken for the year preceding the election ($t-1$) to avoid taking stock too late in the process.

Electoral democracies are defined as those regimes that, at $t-1$, score an average of higher than 2.0 for political rights and civil liberties but no higher than 3.5. In addition, the election has to be judged free and fair by both local and international observers (or leave no doubt in case of missing reports). Free and fair elections create a fundamental distinction between democratically acceptable and unacceptable electoral processes. Although there is no such thing as an entirely clean election due to human and technical errors (see Mozaffar and Schedler 2002), flaws must not alter or predetermine the outcome.[1] All other cases of regimes holding de jure competitive and participatory elections are considered electoral authoritarian regimes. In this perspective, the organization of founding elections that are de jure competitive and inclusive marks the inauguration of an electoral authoritarian regime. Breakdown is defined as the abortion of electoral cycles as prescribed by the constitution. Regimes with no elections naturally do not constitute electoral regimes but are considered simply authoritarian. The empirical analysis in this chapter includes only regimes that were classified as electoral authoritarian at some point during the period from 1989 to June 2003.[2] Because I assess opposition behavior in electoral regimes, however, there is one important exception to this rule. Electoral regimes that were already present at the beginning of 1989 have been tracked backward to include their founding, second, and subsequent elections.

Based on these considerations, Table 9.2 offers a comprehensive classification of regimes in Africa. The classification builds on elections to the executive (i.e., to the office of president in presidential systems and to parliament in parliamentary systems). There are 210 elections in the data set, of which ninety-five are presidential and 125 are parliamentary.[3] In order to enhance the reading, Table 9.2 is organized such that within each category, regimes are grouped according to how many elections have been held as of June 2003. Within the category of electoral autocracies turned democracies, regimes are also ordered according to how many elections it took them to leave electoral authoritarianism behind.

Two regimes have been democratic from the start: Botswana and São Tomé and Principe (2) and are therefore excluded from the analysis. All the others have been EA regimes according to the criteria above at some point and must therefore be included, making a universe of fifty-three cases, out of which fourteen progressed to become electoral and liberal democracies, compared to thirty-nine unreformed electoral authoritarian regimes.[4] Out of the unreformed, nineteen have remained electoral autocracies over at least two consecutive electoral cycles, fifteen have broken down, and five regimes are pending a second election, which prevents further classification.[5] Despite its relative heterogeneity, this group of "unreformed" EA regimes is distinctive insofar as none of its members has ever transformed into a democracy. Yet, when do electoral autocracies become electoral or liberal democracies, as in the fourteen successful cases? Do different opposition strategies play a role in facilitating such a development?

Table 9.2 Trajectories of Electoral Regimes in Sub-Saharan Africa, 1990–2003

	Regime	Year Start	First Election	Second Election	Third Election	Fourth and Subsequent Elections	Breakdown
Democracies	São Tomé and Principe 2	1996	Liberal	Liberal	—	—	—
	Botswana	1969	Electoral	Liberal	Liberal	Liberal	—
Electoral autocracies turned democracies	Central African Republic 2	1993	EA	Electoral	—	—	2003
	Malawi	1994	EA	Electoral	—	—	—
	Mozambique	1994	EA	Electoral	—	—	—
	South Africa	1994	EA	Liberal	—	—	—
	Cape Verde	1991	EA	Liberal	Liberal	—	—
	Namibia	1989	EA	Electoral	Electoral	—	—
	Mali	1992	EA	Liberal	Electoral	—	—
	Seychelles	1993	EA	Electoral	Electoral	—	—
	Mauritius	1976	EA	Electoral	Electoral	Liberal	—
	Gambia 1	1982	EA	Liberal	Liberal	—	1994
	Ghana	1992	EA	EA	Electoral	—	—
	Madagascar	1982	EA	EA	EA	Electoral	—
	Senegal	1978	EA	EA	EA	Electoral	—
Oscillating	Benin	1991	EA	Liberal	EA	—	—
Electoral autocracies	Angola	1992	EA	—	—	—	1993
	Burundi	1993	EA	—	—	—	1996
	Central African Republic 1	1992	EA	—	—	—	1992
	Comoros 1	1990	EA	—	—	—	1995
	Comoros 2	1996	EA	—	—	—	1999
	Comoros 3	2002	EA	—	—	—	—
	Côte d'Ivoire 2	2002	EA	—	—	—	2002
	Guinea-Bissau 1	1994	EA	—	—	—	1998
	Guinea-Bissau 2	1999	EA	—	—	—	—
	Liberia	1997	EA	—	—	—	2003
	Niger 1	1993	EA	—	—	—	1996

(continues)

Table 9.2   continued

Regime	Year Start	First Election	Second Election	Third Election	Fourth and Subsequent Elections	Breakdown
Niger 2	1996	EA	—	—	—	1999
Niger 3	1999	EA	—	—	—	—
Nigeria 1	1993	EA	—	—	—	1993
Congo-Brazzaville 1	1992	EA	—	—	—	1997
Congo-Brazzaville 2	2002	EA	—	—	—	—
São Tomé and Principe 1	1991	EA	—	—	—	1995
Sierra Leone 1	1996	EA	—	—	—	1997
Sierra Leone 2	2002	EA	—	—	—	—
Burkina Faso	1991	EA	EA	—	—	—
Cameroon	1992	EA	EA	—	—	—
Chad	1996	EA	EA	—	—	—
Côte d'Ivoire 1	1990	EA	EA	—	—	1999
Djibouti	1993	EA	EA	—	—	—
Equatorial Guinea	1996	EA	EA	—	—	—
Ethiopia	1995	EA	EA	—	—	—
Gabon	1993	EA	EA	—	—	—
Gambia 2	1996	EA	EA	—	—	—
Guinea	1993	EA	EA	—	—	—
Mauritania	1992	EA	EA	—	—	—
Nigeria 2	1999	EA	EA	—	—	—
Sudan	1996	EA	EA	—	—	—
Swaziland	1993	EA	EA	—	—	—
Tanzania	1995	EA	EA	—	—	—
Uganda	1996	EA	EA	—	—	—
Kenya	1992	EA	EA	EA	—	—
Togo	1993	EA	EA	EA	—	—
Zambia	1991	EA	EA	EA	—	—
Zimbabwe	1980	Electoral	EA	EA	EA	—

Source: Author's database.

Notes: The cases reported here are regimes within the given countries. Within each category, regimes are ordered by the number of elections they conducted. Numbered country names denote successive regimes. "Electoral" and "liberal" refer to democracies. "EA" indicates an electoral authoritarian regime. "—" indicates that no elections were held.

The Consequences of Opposition Behavior

Table 9.3 couples our data on opposition behavior from Table 9.1 with our classification of regimes from Table 9.2. It is, in effect, a panel-group comparison of opposition participation and losers' acceptance. A total of fifty-three electoral authoritarian regimes have held elections over the period studied. Starting from the bottom of the table, as per June 2003, all major opposition parties participated and also accepted the results immediately in about half of all elections in unreformed EA regimes (54 percent and 45 percent, respectively).

A very different situation prevails for the other panel-group, consisting of the fourteen electoral regimes that have evolved into electoral or liberal democracies. In these regimes' transitional elections—elections held when they were still electoral autocracies—opposition participation hits 80 to 90 percent, and losers' acceptance reaches three-quarters of the elections. The same is true for elections held in these regimes once they have become electoral or liberal democracies, respectively. In short, opposition participation and acceptance of the outcome are clearly associated with the transformation of electoral autocracies into democracies over a sequence of multiparty elections. As of 2003, there are a number of electoral authoritarian regimes in which the opposition has participated so far in vain, although there are even fewer cases where opposition boycotts or postelectoral protests have led to democratic transitions. This empirical finding may reflect one of two causal relationships. Either the participation and rule abidance of opposition parties and candidates are facilitating conditions of democratization in electoral autocracies, or opposition players have a good sense of opportunity and agree to play in skewed games only when the likelihood of a fair game in the future seems reasonably high. Ghana is a case in point. When the Provisional National Defense Council (PNDC) regime under

Table 9.3   Trajectories of Africa's Fifty-three Electoral Authoritarian Regimes, June 2003

	N	Full Opposition Participation (percentage)	Loser Acceptance of Outcome (percentage)
Democratized EA regimes	14		
Transitional elections	21	81	75
Democratic elections	25	92	84
Unreformed EA regimes	39		
Authoritarian elections	65	54	45

Source: Author's database.

Jerry J. Rawlings finally agreed to hold multiparty elections in 1992, the main opposition party, the National Patriotic Party (NPP), protested fiercely at the conduct and results of the presidential elections and withdrew from the subsequent parliamentary contest. In the subsequent elections in 1996, the NPP and other opposition parties chose to participate fully and accepted the results, even if grudgingly. In 2000, the NPP swept to power in the most free and fair elections ever in this country. My own interviews with leading opposition figures over more than four years suggest that the strain and uncertainty of the boycott years (1992–1995) locked both opposition and the ruling party into uncooperative strategies. It also excluded the NPP from parliament, which later became a central arena for opposition parties to exert pressure for democratizing reforms. In conclusion, the comparison in Table 9.3 corroborates that opposition behavior constitutes a weighty causal factor for democratization in the foggy zone of electoral authoritarianism (Schedler 2002b).

The Contexts of Opposition Behavior

Having discussed the consequences of opposition participation, we may now turn to its structural conditions. When do opposition parties actually contest elections in electoral autocracies? In his review of the literature, Schedler (2002a, 2002b) suggests a range of factors that may influence opposition groups in deciding whether to play or exit the electoral game. Among these suggested factors, the following are singled out as particularly interesting to probe further.

Authoritarian Continuity

In Africa, the apparent transformation of previously highly authoritarian rulers into "democrats" is common. Schedler suggests that old authoritarian rulers are often inclined to use strategic interventions to prevent further democratic development, in particular to keep a threatening opposition from participating effectively (2002a: 42). In an important article, Bruce Baker noted that in twenty states, former authoritarian rulers were still in office as of 1997 (Baker 1998). Until proven otherwise, it seems reasonable to assume that those who fought to prevent political liberalization will not willingly further it. Hence, I hypothesize that the presence of old authoritarian rulers or their close associates will decrease the willingness and/or ability of opposition parties and candidates to contest elections. In my data set, I code the presence of former authoritarian rulers as an ordinal variable that admits three possibilities: (1) at least one of the presidential candidates or the leadership of one main party are former authoritarian rulers (old guard still active); (2) at least one candidate or leadership of one main party are former close associates (ministers or similar) of a former authoritarian regime (close allies still active); and (3) none of the main contenders are related to a former authoritarian regime (old guard gone). For the present analysis, I collapse the latter two categories, which yields a dichotomous variable: "yes" indicates the (either complete or partial) withdrawal of the old guard, and "no" its continuing presence.

Electoral Violence

The use of violence, during the campaign or on election day, is a core symptom of electoral authoritarianism. Assassination of political opponents, voter intimidation, attacks against the liberty and property of political adversaries, violence against elected officials or electoral administrators, politically motivated riots, and ethnic or other forms of "social" cleansing are examples of serious politically motivated violence (Schedler 2001: 70–71; Elster et al. 1998: 27). My hypothesis is that more violence will lead to less opposition participation in the election and less acceptance of the outcome. I code electoral violence as a three-point ordinal variable: (1) there is systematic and/or widespread politically related violence during the campaign, on election day and/or during the postelection period (significant violence); (2) there are nonsystematic and isolated incidents of violence, or geographically very limited outbreaks (isolated instances of violence); and (3) elections are entirely free of political violence (peaceful elections). Again, for the present purpose, I fuse the latter two categories, which yields a binary classification that contrasts violent elections ("no" peaceful process) with ("yes") relatively peaceful elections.

Electoral Systems

What is usually referred to as "electoral systems" encompasses both the rules concerning voting methods and the rules used in translation of votes into seats in the representative body (Sartori 2001: 99). The lawlike consequences of electoral systems first developed by Maurice Duverger (1954) and Anthony Downs (1957) have been confirmed by the work of scholars like Vernon Bogdanor and David Butler (1983), Arend Lijphart (1984), Lijphart and Carlos H. Waisman (1996), Peter Mair (1990), Bingham G. Powell (2000), Douglas Rae (1971), and Giovanni Sartori (1986). The imperative of the majoritarian vision—governing capacity—with a translation of votes-to-seats being (potentially) highly disproportional leads electoral competition to focus on the median voter. It also tends to exclude peripheral voting populations and to lower the incentives for participation. It is the essence of what is often referred to as adversarial, as opposed to consensual, politics. The imperative of consensual vision—representative justice—typically grants minorities better representation through PR systems, thereby reducing the incentives for antidemocratic behavior. Mixed electoral systems are those in which both the voting method and the allocation of seats are in part majoritarian and in part proportional. Such systems, it has been argued, offer the best solution to satisfy the two main, though contrary, imperatives of representative justice and governing capacity (Dunleavy and Margetts 1995). Students of democratization tend to agree that the consolidation of democracy requires, among other things, solid political institutions (e.g., Diamond 1999; Linz and Stepan 1996; O'Donnell 1996; Schedler 2001); yet few seem to consider whether the types of institutions that are put in place matter. I ask whether majoritarian, mixed, or proportional electoral systems are more conducive to opposition participation; and I hypothesize that majoritarian systems are less conducive to opposition participation. I distinguish between four types of systems for legislative elections: two-round majority systems, plurality systems, mixed systems, and PR systems.

The Key to Opposition Participation: Free, Fair, and Peaceful Elections

The empirical analysis of the context of opposition behavior in African electoral autocracies shows a mixed picture. When it comes to opposition behavior, there is a stark and statistically highly significant difference between flawed elections and free and fair ones. Table 9.4 shows that all opposition parties participated in only 40–45 percent of the flawed elections, whereas the equivalent rate hits around 90 percent in elections that were free and fair. That is indeed a healthy sign of opposition behavior. Apparently, opposition groups rarely use the weapon of boycotting to discredit democratic elections.[6] However, the results of democratic elections are rejected or contested far too often. Opposition parties do play along with the rules of the game but, to some extent, only when it suits their interests.

The data on losers' acceptance in Table 9.5 are worrying with regard to both presidential and parliamentary elections. Even among free and fair elections, the losing parties accepted the results immediately in only 40 percent of the cases of presidential elections and 65 percent in parliamentary elections. I should emphasize, though, that Table 9.5 does not report those cases in which opposition parties accepted election outcomes after some time of protest and hesitation. Eventually, losers acquiesced to electoral outcomes in almost all free and fair elections, even if they rejected them at first. Their strategic ambivalence seems to reflect ambivalent democratic convictions. Initially contesting the outcome, only grudgingly accepting it when it becomes clear one has more to lose from totally rejecting it than

Table 9.4   Political Contexts of Opposition Behavior in Electoral Autocracies, Sub-Saharan Africa, 1989–June 2003

Variables	Values	All Opposition Candidates/Parties Participate					
		Presidential Elections			Parliamentary Elections		
		%	N	p[a]	%	N	p[a]
Free and fair elections	Not at all	33	6	.752	29	7	.572
	Irregularities affected results	46	41	(.000)	43	49	(.000)
	Irregularities did not affect results	87	47		94	67	
	Free and fair	100	1		100	2	
Authoritarian guard gone	No	69	86	−.154	70	111	.013
	Yes	44	9	(.137)	71	14	(.833)
Peaceful process	No	42	19	.250	56	18	.130
	Yes	73	75	(.015)	74	106	(.151)
Electoral system	Majority	n/a			46	22	13.394
	Plurality				67	48	(.037)
	Mixed				71	14	
	PR				88	41	

Source: Author's database.

Notes: a. Spearman's correlation coefficients, except for electoral systems where Chi^2 value is reported.

n/a = not applicable.

from playing along, indicates instrumental rather than intrinsic support for democratic procedures.

The presence of old authoritarian rulers and/or their close associates, however, has no influence on opposition behavior, either in terms of the choice to contest elections or not, or in terms of accepting the outcome of the elections. It might be that particularly disgraceful old authoritarian rulers and their associates have a tendency to make use of the "menu of manipulation" (Schedler 2002b), but it does not seem to be a general trend. Although the analysis here does not suggest that authoritarian leopards can and do change their spots, their very presence in elections seems to have no negative effects on opposition behavior.

It is also often assumed in the literature that the use of violence and intimidation against opposition actors damages the legitimacy of electoral processes and dampens the prospects of opposition participation. The systematic use of violence definitely constitutes a denial of democratic values and rights, and it clearly influences opposition behavior to some extent, even if the differences we find are statistically significant (at the 0.05 level)

Table 9.5   Political Contexts of Losers' Acceptance in Electoral Autocracies, Sub-Saharan Africa, 1989–June 2003

| Variables | Values | All Parties Accepted Results Immediately | | | | | |
| | | Presidential Elections | | | Parliamentary Elections | | |
		%	N	p^a	%	N	p^a
Free and fair elections	Not at all	0	6	.634	0	7	.685
	Irregularities affected results	0	40	(.000)	2	48	(.000)
	Irregularities did not affect results	40	47		64	67	
	Free and fair	0	1		100	2	
Authoritarian guard gone	No	58	85	−.144	69	110	.116
	Yes	33	9	(.166)	86	14	(.200)
Peaceful process	No	32	19	.240	56	18	.140
	Yes/Only a few incidents	61	75	(.020)	74	106	(.121)
Electoral system	Majority	n/a			46	22	10.883
	Plurality				71	49	(.012)
	Mixed				93	14	
	PR				77	39	

Source: Author's database.
Notes: a. Spearman's correlation coefficient, except for electoral systems where Chi^2 value is reported.
n/a = not applicable.

only for presidential elections. The significance of violence in presidential elections hardly comes as a surprise. A vast majority of African regimes are presidential systems, and elections to the highest office are far more important than legislative contests. Opposition parties tend to stay out of presidential elections where politically motivated violence is systematic and/or widespread. In almost 60 percent of these cases, they recurred to either partial or total boycott. In only 42 percent, they participated fully. Among presidential elections where the use of political violence was only sporadic, boycotts were reduced to less than half, or 27 percent of cases (see Table 9.4). A similar pattern shows for losers' acceptance of the results. Once again, the differences are statistically significant only for presidential elections. Still, it seems that the hypothesized relationship between the incidence of electoral violence and the strategic behavior of opposition groups (e.g., Diamond 2002; Schedler 2002b) is corroborated by the empirical analysis of African regimes. The implication is clear: international assistance that helps to reduce the use of violence as a political means does have an effect on behavior of new opposition actors in these regimes. It is telling that it was shown to be important for electoral regimes to "graduate" into democracies (see Table 9.3). Without a field of opposition parties that not only participate but also accept the outcome of the contest, electoral autocracies are more unlikely to develop into democracies.

At first sight, the well-established hypothesis about the effects of electoral systems seems to be borne out by the analysis. Majoritarian systems are associated with lower levels of opposition participation and acceptance of the outcome. Yet, Tables 9.4 and 9.5 do not separate the effect of electoral systems from the effect of the democratic quality of elections. Simple cross-tabulation shows that 75 percent of all flawed elections occurred in majoritarian electoral systems. Although only 25 percent of elections in electoral autocracies operating PR systems were flawed, 60 percent of elections in majoritarian systems deserved this derogative epithet, and the relationship is strong and highly significant (Chi^2 13.758 p = .001). A two-level cross-tabulation shows that opposition participation and losers' acceptance are similar across the various electoral systems when controlling for freedom and fairness. In short, there seems to be no independent effect of electoral systems on opposition behavior among African electoral autocracies.[7] In sum, the context of elections is clearly important, as the literature suggests. However, only two factors have any generalizable effects on opposition behavior: the extent to which elections are free and fair and whether political violence is used during the campaign and on polling day.

Conclusion

Africa's electoral authoritarian regimes differ in many important and significant ways. Just as democracies are "bundled wholes" (Collier and Adcock 1999), so are electoral autocracies. Clearly, some African regimes are more repressive and closed than others. Furthermore, some have completed several electoral cycles, whereas others have broken down, giving way to new regimes. Africa's electoral regimes also differ with regard to how much political competition they allow. More than three decades ago, Dahl (1971) suggested that the extent of political competition in part determines how democratic a regime is. In a recent contribution, Nicolas van de Walle (2002) suggested that in Africa, the quality of competition and the power of the opposition could go a long way toward explaining the level of democracy that has developed in these countries. Thus, the behavior of opposition groups should be particularly important in electoral autocracies where the attainment of democracy is still an open question.

In this chapter I have shown that the participation of opposition parties plays an important role in transforming electoral autocracies into democracies. It seems that by choosing to contest elections and then accepting their outcome, opposition groups greatly enhance the likelihood that the regimes will become democratic. Yet, opposition participation in elections is far more likely to occur when at least minimal requirements of freedom, fairness, and peace are established. Hence, opposition parties display a good feel for which regimes are "softer" and more open to reform. In these cases it makes good sense to participate in the electoral arena, even if the conditions are not fully free and fair. It also makes sense to accept outcomes in order to gradually build strength both within legislatures and in society in general, in anticipation of winning subsequent elections. In tougher electoral autocracies, opposition parties face fewer incentives to adopt such cooperative strategies. Therefore, they tend to resort to confrontational strategies that may serve well to discredit the established regime, but they are of little practical use in furthering greater openness.

Here both domestic and international actors have a major role to play. There is no need to worry too much about the institutional context of elections or the presence or absence of old authoritarian "big men" and their associates. If democratizing forces inside or outside a given country wish to encourage the rise of opposition parties able to carry forward processes of "democratization by elections," they need to put in place the conditions for free, fair, and peaceful elections.

Notes

1. Even though it might seem contraintuitive that unfair elections can be competitive at all, they can. There are a couple of instances in Africa in which genuinely unfair elections have effected an opposition win against a long-term incumbent and previous authoritarian ruler. For example, the 22 October 2000 presidential elections in Côte d'Ivoire and parliamentary elections of 10 December the same year, Madagascar's presidential elections on 16 December 2001, the parliamentary elections in Malawi on 15 June 1999, and the constituent assembly–cum–parliamentary elections in Namibia on 11 November 1989 are good examples. Even though the "menu of manipulation" is long (Schedler 2002b), trying to cheat is one thing, and doing it with success is sometimes quite another. The normal pattern, of course, is that serious irregularities do not coincide with turnovers.

2. The reasons are simple. First, the object of study is electoral authoritarian regimes, hence the exclusion of continuously democratic or closed authoritarian regimes. Second, if we were to include only those regimes that were classified as electoral authoritarian at the entry point (that is, at the founding election for each regime), we would exclude cases that initially were democratic but regressed to be electoral authoritarian (even if it is only one case—Zimbabwe). In both cases, we would introduce selection biases in our sample.

3. The full data set, codebook, and background material are available from the author. Lindberg (2006) also contains a more detailed description. All processing was done in SPSS 11.0.2 for Macintosh. In the calculation of means, the geometric mean is used instead of the arithmetic mean because the geometric mean is not as sensitive to outliers and skewness as is its arithmetic cousin (Blume 1974; Datton, Greenies, and Stewart 1998). I have used the larger data set for studying the democratic qualities of

elections in Africa (Lindberg 2004a and 2006), women's legislative empowerment (Lindberg 2004b), and the political consequences of electoral systems (Lindberg 2005). None of these publications has addressed the logic of opposition participation under electoral authoritarianism.

4. One case—Benin—oscillated between electoral authoritarian and democratic, but given the benign political development in that country, it has been judged to be better classified as having "graduated," rather than stayed electoral authoritarian for the purposes of the present statistical analysis.

5. Notably, fourteen of them broke down after the founding election. Only in Côte d'Ivoire did an electoral autocracy ever break down after a second election had been held.

6. International observers also factor in opposition participation in assessing the freedom and fairness of elections, but only as one among many indicators, and in my sample they have not been a determining factor in their assessment. Hence, there is no significant conflation of the variables in question or possibility of reverse causality.

7. Yet, one could legitimately ask why two-round majority systems in particular hold so many unfair elections in Africa, but that is a very different issue than the one we are concerned with in this chapter, and it has been addressed elsewhere in part (see Lindberg 2005).

Part 4 _____

Shifting
Power Relations

10

Authoritarian Failure:
How Does State Weakness
Strengthen Electoral Competition?

Lucan A. Way

In this chapter I argue for a revision of our understanding of the relationship between state power and regime outcomes. Most authors have emphasized the importance of a strong state to the development of a democracy. Although these accounts capture important realities, they ignore alternative forms of state building oriented toward the preservation of nondemocratic rule. Many states that have been called weak due to an absence of the rule of law can be better conceptualized as different kinds of states oriented toward the monopolization of political control.[1] The authoritarian state is one in which state agencies are overwhelmingly subordinated to partisan political ends. Military and security organizations are used to intimidate political opposition, tax officials are used to bankrupt opposition donors, and local officials are used to coordinate vote fraud. Recognizing the existence of authoritarian state building is important not just for understanding the sources of autocratic rule—but for knowing why, in some cases, such rule fails to install itself. In key instances, the breakdown of authoritarian state control has created important room for electoral competition.

In this chapter, I provide a definition of authoritarian state power and describe efforts at authoritarian state building in three countries in the early 1990s. In Belarus, Moldova, and Ukraine in that period, executives sought to use state agencies to reduce electoral competition. Despite disproportionate access to state resources and weak civil societies, incumbents in all three countries lost presidential elections from 1994 to 1996. Such competitive outcomes can be partially explained by the fact that insubordination by local officials and coercive agencies undermined incumbent efforts to monopolize political control. The result was a kind of pluralism by default in which political competition resulted not from a strong civil society, robust democratic institutions, or democratically minded leaders but instead from failed efforts to impose nondemocratic rule. These cases illustrate the ways in which weak state control may undermine autocratic behavior and generate the hybrid democratic-authoritarian rule that has emerged since the end of the Cold War (Levitsky and Way 2002; Schedler 2002b).

Democracy and the State

Recent discussions of the relationship between state and regime have argued overwhelmingly that a strong state is essential for democracy. The argument is compelling. Guillermo O'Donnell, Stephen Holmes, and others have convincingly shown that a strong state is essential to prevent civil conflict and protect individual rights. As Holmes has noted, "the largest and most reliable human rights organization is the liberal state. Beyond the effective reach of such a state, rights will not be consistently protected or enforced" (Holmes 1997, 2002; O'Donnell 1999; Bunce 2003: 180–181). This type of strong state protects individuals from each other as well as from the arbitrary behavior of state leaders. The rule of law, which is basic to most of these discussions of democracy and the state, makes all citizens, including government leaders, equal before the law. Although history and scholarship provide numerous examples of other types of states, this "liberal" or "legal rational" state has in recent years become dominant in discussions of contemporary politics. Indeed, in contrast to virtually every other object of inquiry in comparative politics—regimes, party systems, and social welfare systems, among others—studies of the state in the contemporary era have been rooted in this single definition drawn from Western Europe and the United States (Darden, forthcoming).[2] As a result, states that do not provide a rule of law have often been called weak.

There are several important problems with this conflation of state strength and the rule of law. First, for many countries, the absence of a rule of law may have nothing to do with weakness but instead reflect the fact that the country's elites are not trying to create the rule of law (Allina-Pisano 2004; Darden, forthcoming). After all, not all political or economic leaders want to create a legal system that hampers their own discretion. In many countries, powerful governmental and nongovernmental actors benefit enormously from a weak court system. Second, it is odd to refer to certain violations of the rule of law as signs of weakness. For example, Russian president Vladimir Putin's grab of one of the world's largest oil companies, Yukos, using questionable legal means would seem to be a sign of state strength rather than weakness—just strength differently understood. Third, in the current international environment, it is very difficult and rare for most leaders to be both law abiding and autocratic. Because of the economic and political dominance of Western democratic powers, autocratic leaders today are forced to rely extensively on unwritten or informal laws to secure nondemocratic rule (Way 2005b; Darden, forthcoming). Most academic studies of the transition process have focused extensively on written laws and constitutions, but such a focus often draws our attention away from the autocratic elements of a country's regime. If we equate a strong state only with the rule of law, we are inevitably forced to call almost any autocracy weak.

Conceptualizing the Authoritarian State

Such problems suggest that we need to broaden our conceptualization of states to include those oriented toward nondemocratic rule. To understand the nature of the authoritarian state, it is useful to investigate the standard political science distinction between state and regime. Regime typically refers to the procedures that regulate access to state power. The state is most often understood as the apparatus used for the exercise of public power. The state is typically thought of as a much more permanent entity than the regime. Yet, although state and regime can always be conceptually distinguished, cases differ dramatically in terms of the extent to which the two are empirically distinct (Fishman 1990). In fact, regime type arguably hinges to an important degree on the extent of that separation. On the one hand, democracy necessarily involves a certain empirical separation between state and regime. In order for civil and political rights to be protected, state actors—police, tax authorities, local officials, and so on—must have a large degree of autonomy from political officials chosen by regime procedures.[3] Obviously, political freedoms are vulnerable if police are exposed to direct pressure from incumbent politicians regarding treatment of opposition figures. If those counting the votes are subject to partisan political interference, elections are unlikely to be free and fair.[4]

The authoritarian state is defined by the conflation of state and regime. Here, the actions of state officials are overwhelmingly oriented toward the manipulation of regime procedures in order to preserve incumbent power. In an authoritarian state, police and security officials are used to monitor, harass, and sometimes kill opposition activists. Tax officials may also be used to put pressure on businesses that fund the opposition. Directors of state schools, universities, hospitals, prisons, factories, farms, and military bases may be called on to mobilize support for the incumbent and steal votes during elections. State media may be pressured to provide biased coverage. State railways and bus lines may be used to carry incumbent supporters for rallies and multiple voting and prevented from carrying protesters to antigovernment demonstrations. State intelligence services may be used to collect embarrassing information on real or potential regime opponents. In such states, the law is not autonomous but is rather an instrument of power by the government. Thus, courts in authoritarian states are highly vulnerable to what in the Soviet era was known as "telephone law," or direct political interference into judicial decisionmaking.

In the post–Cold War era, few states have laws that permit such activity. Instead, authoritarian behavior is very frequently informal. As a result, authoritarian states today almost always lead dual lives. At one level, public institutions have a set of formally prescribed tasks. Schools educate; hospitals cure the sick; the tax administration collects revenue; the police prevent crime; intelligence services fight organized crime and foreign espionage. Simultaneously, though, these same institutions in autocratic states engage in a set of informal tasks associated with preservation of incumbent power, such as monitoring and harassment of the opposition and vote fraud.

Differences among authoritarian states can be understood according to the dimensions of control and scope (Way 2005a). Control refers to the extent to which subordinates obey orders of the executive. In strong authoritarian states, executives can rely on coercive agencies to follow orders to crack down on opposition, media to censor criticism of the government, and local governments to steal votes. Weak authoritarian states are ones in which those officials disobey orders to carry out these activities. Scope refers to the array of issue areas over which state leaders have discretionary control. For example, in strong authoritarian states, state actors have formal, or de facto, power over large sections of the economy. Such a high scope of control need not involve Soviet-style central planning but also includes cases in which state leaders or their friends own or control the main profit-making sectors in an economy—such as oil or other types of resource extraction. Strong authoritarian states also penetrate large numbers of civil society groups such as trade unions or churches. By contrast, a weak authoritarian state is one that confronts a large and autonomous business class and civil society.

The definition of authoritarian state strength is quite distinct from the definition of the liberal state. In fact, the same event could be considered as evidence of either strength or weakness, depending on the type of state under investigation. Thus, if US president George Bush ordered the army to arrest John Kerry and the army refused, most would see that as an example of state strength because state institutions had demonstrated autonomy from the executive. But if Robert Mugabe in Zimbabwe ordered the army to arrest an opposition figure and they refused, we could very well see that as a sign of weakness (i.e., a breakdown of central authoritarian control). Thus the same event (the failure of the army to arrest opposition) can be seen as a sign of either state weakness or strength. Even though both perspectives are in principle possible in any case, our choice of definition should probably hinge on the extent to which powerful actors in a particular country are oriented toward the construction of either a liberal or authoritarian state.

The rest of the chapter illustrates the utility of the authoritarian state-building perspective in the context of Belarus, Moldova, and Ukraine in the early 1990s. Although these countries were almost universally viewed as emerging democracies in the 1990s, key aspects of the transitions become much clearer when we focus on the construction of the authoritarian—not just the liberal—state. In particular, these cases provide useful illustrations of how—even in the absence of the rule of law—political competition can result from failed efforts by politicians to utilize state agencies for partisan political ends. In each case, the inability to maintain control over state subordinates created important openings for electoral competition. Partly as a result, incumbents in all three of these countries lost presidential elections in 1994–1996.

Building Authoritarian States in the Former Soviet Union

The vast majority of scholars have approached the study of regime development in post-Soviet (as well as other semiauthoritarian) countries in terms of the success or failure of democratic institution building. Thus, numerous studies have focused on the (failed) development of civil society, political party systems, parliamentary institutions, and pro-democratic forces in Russia and other parts of the former Soviet Union (see Fish 1995; Howard 2003; McFaul 2001; Remington 2001). These works have made invaluable contributions to our understanding of regime dynamics in this part of the world. At the same time, an approach that takes efforts to manipulate democratic institutions and monopolize political control as the main starting point also throws light on a whole set of processes that have hitherto mostly been ignored.[5] After all, leaders in the 1990s—almost all of whom had strong ties to the old regime—were not only writing constitutions and holding elections but also actively using extralegal measures to stay in power and undermine opposition. Viacheslav Kebich in Belarus shut down an opposition radio station and attempted to manipulate the vote in his favor in 1994. Mircea Snegur in Moldova successfully manipulated electoral laws in 1991 to disqualify other serious contenders for the presidency and passed a law that outlawed criticism of the president. Finally, Leonid Kravchuk in Ukraine closed an opposition TV station and ordered parliament to be shut in 1994 (Way 2005a). These and other actions provide strong evidence that authoritarian state building needs to be taken seriously.

The Soviet era provided elites with ample resources and opportunities to create a powerful authoritarian state. Above all, the Soviet experience left states with a wide scope of control over the economy and society. First, the Soviet inheritance supplied post-Soviet states with large apparatuses of societal control—all-embracing bureaucracies of state officials in every population center, large security forces, and extensive infrastructures of surveillance such as listening devices. In addition, the extremely large state economic sector meant that well into the mid-1990s, state actors—in principle at least—had an extremely wide range of tools of influence at their disposal. Leaders sat at the top of a hierarchy that included a vast array of enterprises, local governments, and state-run TV and radio that had almost no competition from private sources. Jessica Allina-Pisano (2005) compellingly argues that the "overlapping character of social, political, and economic spheres" in the Soviet system generated powerful mechanisms of social control available for use in the post-Soviet era. Further, the extremely recent experience with Soviet rule meant that state actors were accustomed to promoting incumbent interests. The authoritarian state model was not something foreign. Finally, Marc Howard (2003) has convincingly shown that the communist system very successfully undermined independent societal organizations—leaving postcommunist countries with especially weak civil societies. Thus, post-Soviet governments faced relatively unorganized societies.

With such resources at their disposal, post-Soviet leaders thus would seem to have been in a good position to manipulate and win elections. Yet, as noted above, incumbents in all three countries lost presidential elections: Kebich in Belarus lost to Alyaksandr Lukashenka in 1994, Snegur in Moldova lost to Petru Lucinschi in 1996, and Kravchuk in Ukraine was defeated by Leonid Kuchma in 1994. Several factors help to explain why leaders lost elections and the systems remained competitive in the early 1990s. First, the collapse of the Communist Party, the introduction of elections, and the emergence of the international liberal hegemony in the 1990s created radically new challenges for autocratic leaders for which Soviet rule had done nothing to prepare them. The Soviet state had successfully destroyed virtually all vestiges of an opposition. Simultaneously, Soviet leaders had been socialized in a system that rewarded conformity and strict subordination above all else. In the Soviet era, the Communist Party had functioned as a powerful mechanism of elite control. However, Mikhail Gorbachev's promotion of open discussion, his failure to seriously punish dissenters, and the introduction of competitive elections fundamentally undermined this tradition and made it increasingly difficult for party leaders to rein in those members seeking to destroy the system (Hill 1991). The failed coup of August 1991 discredited the party completely and led to its dissolution throughout most of the former Soviet Union, including Belarus, Moldova, and Ukraine. Experience with Soviet-era façade elections and dependence on central authorities in Moscow gave incumbents little understanding of how to survive in the face of even rudimentary forms of political opposition. In contrast to Malaysian, Tanzanian, and some other authoritarian leaders, who had to cope with active oppositions and semicompetitive elections over the 1960s, 1970s, and 1980s, post-Soviet leaders were thus particularly unprepared for the collapse of authoritarianism.

Second, leaders confronted problems of controlling the vast bureaucracy that they had inherited. Many key agencies had been embedded in a Moscow-centered hierarchy and often resisted efforts by republican leaders to dictate their actions in the post-Soviet era. In addition, the economic collapse that attended the fall of the Soviet Union meant that leaders in the early post-Soviet years were often unable to pay salaries or economic subsidies or to send funds to localities. All this made it much harder for leaders to maintain control. Further, executives coming to power in the early 1990s often lacked extensive personal networks encompassing leadership over key bureaucracies. Heads of different bureaucracies were often independent political actors with few direct ties to the executive. Authoritarian state control was also undermined by elite fragmentation. High-level defections by former incumbent allies weakened authoritarian state hierarchy. Subordinates in the military, regional governments, and state-run media have generally been less likely to follow orders to favor the incumbent if they thought that he or she faces serious challenges (Way 2005a). In such a context, it has often been perceived as much safer for subordinates to ignore autocratic demands in an effort to avoid doing anything that might offend an opponent who might subsequently gain power. Orders to the media to provide biased coverage, to the military to fire on opponents, or to local governments to steal votes have been more likely to be ignored.

The sections below review how leaders in post-Soviet Belarus, Moldova, and Ukraine attempted and partially failed to construct autocratic states in the face of the obstacles described above. Focusing on control over coercive agencies and local governments, I demonstrate the mechanisms by which weak control has promoted greater electoral competition.

Belarus

In the early 1990s, Belarus witnessed dynamic political competition prior to the rise of the highly autocratic Alyaksandr Lukashenka in the country's first presidential election in 1994. In the early 1990s Belarus lacked a presidency, and power was centered in the hands of Prime Minister Viacheslav Kebich, who had been chosen by parliament in 1990. Kebich's efforts at authoritarian state building mainly involved drawing on the support of intelligence services to collect compromising materials on his political enemies and the use of local state officials to support his campaign for president in 1994 by distributing campaign material and engaging in moderate vote stealing. Yet, the discretionary power of the prime minister over bureaucratic agencies was relatively weak in the early 1990s. Although the governing elite remained much more intact in Belarus than in the neighboring republics, low-level fragmentation created a kind of de facto pluralism because no single leader was able to gain unquestioned dominance.

First, Kebich's weak control over the police and intelligence services strengthened his opponents. In the early 1990s, the prime minister faced a relatively autonomous police and KGB apparatus. Heads of these two agencies frequently took positions independent of the government (Kharitonov 2003; *Narodnaia hazeta,* 18 May 1991, p. 1). The Belarusian KGB, the only such agency in the former Soviet Union to retain its name, barely changed staff after independence and maintained extremely close ties to Moscow. It was generally felt that—even though Belarus was an independent state— the head of the KGB could not be fired without Moscow's agreement. It was often referred to as "a state within a state" (Lukashuk 1992: 18; Mihalisko 1997: 252). The relatively autonomous nature of this agency directly contributed to the rise of Lukashenka, then a relatively unknown parliamentary deputy from a rural region. Lukashenka obtained key assistance from the KGB after he was chosen in 1993 to head a legislative commission to fight corruption. According to several KGB sources who spoke with the author, the head of the agency at the time fed Lukashenka with material aimed at undermining Kebich's reputation.[6] Partly as a result, Lukashenka gained wide renown as a fighter against corruption in the run-up to the 1994 presidential elections.

Unable to fire the heads of the KGB or police without the backing of the Council of Ministers, Prime Minister Kebich sought to undermine the heads of police and KGB by increasing the intelligence and police functions of the border guards that were controlled by a Kebich ally. Kebich also appointed a long-time associate, Gennadi Danilov, to audit their work and provide regular reports to the Council of Ministers (Kharitonov 2003: 33–34)—a move that was widely interpreted as an effort to undermine the autonomy of the police and KGB by collecting compromising material on them.[7] Eventually Kebich used a scandal in January 1994 surrounding the illegal arrest of Lithuanian communists to replace the heads of police and KGB with Kebich loyalists. As a result, Kebich had his own people in key positions just ahead of Belarus's presidential elections. Nevertheless, officials who worked in the KGB at that time report that many officers in the service continued to cooperate with Lukashenka during his campaign and that overall KGB support for Kebich was quite weak.[8]

In addition, Kebich also faced problems controlling district governments and local enterprises. Although formally, heads of regional governments until 1994 were chosen by popularly elected regional committees and could not be fired by the prime minister, there was a widespread informal practice of vetting potential heads with the prime minister before appointment. Given the financial dependence of regional governments on government allocations, it was broadly assumed that Kebich's opposition could kill an appointment.[9] Yet, this informal system of control appears to have been relatively weak and dependent on the voluntary cooperation of lower-level officials. For example, an anti-Kebich mayor of one large city was able to resist efforts by Kebich to fire her in early 1994 by simply refusing to resign in the face of pressure from the Council of Ministers.[10]

Such relatively weak central control had a direct impact on Kebich's capacity to use administrative resources during the 1994 presidential campaign against Lukashenka. Although a great many local officials officially signed up as representatives of the Kebich campaign, they often failed to support Kebich in practice.[11] Thus, the deputy mayor of Gomel city recalled that pro-Kebich leaflets dropped off at the city council were never distributed because of widespread support for another candidate, Stanislau Shushkevich.[12] Another former local official from Mogilev reported that many from his region would "go to [the capital] and report to Kebich 'we support you 100 percent'—but then fail to do the most basic activities to support his candidacy."[13] Finally, a regional official from Gomel province explained that although open rebellion was not an option, "it was always possible to smile but at the same time do nothing."[14] Such weak de facto control by Kebich over regional governments meant that—despite the prime minister's apparently overwhelming resource advantage going into the 1994 election—little was done to support his candidacy.

Ultimately, such administrative obstacles to electoral control were hardly insurmountable. Thus when Lukashenka came to power in 1994, he secured autocratic rule by installing loyalists in the KGB and establishing formal—rather than simply informal—control over local and regional governments.

Moldova

Leaders in Moldova in the 1990s faced even more serious problems of authoritarian state construction. Throughout the 1990s, political competition was promoted by an inability of incumbents to secure control over either security agencies or local governments. First, incumbents in the 1990s had uncertain control over seriously weakened security forces. Ethnonational conflict in eastern Moldova in 1990–1992 led to the large-scale flight of high-level ethnic Russian police and especially KGB officials, who had dominated these agencies in the Soviet era. Thus to a greater extent than in Belarus or Ukraine, security agencies had to be built from scratch. Between 1991 and 1996, control over existing security agencies was highly divided between the head of parliament, Petru Lucinschi, Prime Minister Andrei Sangheli, and President Mircea Snegur, who were considered to each have "their" people in these services. For example, when Snegur attempted unsuccessfully to fire the minister of defense ahead of the 1996 presidential elections, he sent in "his" people to evict the minister. The prime minister, however, successfully fought this firing, and as a result Snegur never gained secure control over coercive agencies (Way 2003).

Efforts at authoritarian state construction in this context became more extensive under the second president, Petru Lucinschi, who was elected in 1996. After his election, he proposed the creation of a Department for Organized Crime and Corruption Prevention, a move that was broadly interpreted as an effort to create an agency to collect compromising material on Lucinschi's enemies. Although the department was formally subordinated to the Ministry of the Interior, Lucinschi appears to have informally controlled it directly through his close associate Nicolae Alexei (Way 2003). Alexei became very active in publicly accusing and sometimes harassing a number of politicians who had disagreements with the president. Among other tasks, Alexei appears to have been involved in setting blackmail traps for politicians who might oppose him.[15] In one case, Lucinschi set up a politician, Valeriu Matei, with a questionable funder and then had Alexei expose Matei for this connection after Matei opposed Lucinschi in parliament (Way 2003). In this way, Lucinschi used nominally nonpartisan government agencies to attack his political enemies. Nevertheless, Lucinschi was never able to gain support from the police or military as a whole—a fact that significantly undermined efforts at political control.

Second, Moldovan leaders also faced severe problems in their efforts to control local governments. Regions such as Transnistr and Gagauzia broke on the basis of ethnonational issues. This led to a civil war in 1990–1992 and the creation of an independent Transnistran state that survives today. In Gagauzia, violence was mostly averted, but the region retains a great deal of autonomy. Open rebellion, by contrast, was not a problem in other parts of Moldova. As in Belarus in the early 1990s, many felt that the central financing gave the central government strong influence over local governments despite the inability to fire local officials. Yet the severe decline in central resources relative to the Soviet era translated into a significant loss of control. As one deputy head of a rural district reported to the author,

> During the Soviet era the key to discipline of enterprises [and local governments] was the fact that the government and party provided the main funds. But by the early 1990s, those funds had completely dried up. Now when they tried to dictate things, we could just ignore them. Under the new conditions they could do little to help us or hurt us.[16]

This loss of control, combined with fragmentation at the top, had a direct impact on authoritarian state control during the 1996 presidential election. Many predicted that Prime Minister Sangheli would use his power over local governments to employ "administrative" measures that seem to have been successful in 1994. He was accused of purging the government administration of anyone opposed to his Agrarian Party (*Basapress,* 6 December 1995; *Infotag,* 12 September 1996). Many worried that his administrative resources would give Sangheli's supporters greater opportunity to steal votes (*Basapress,* 18 November 1996; *Infotag,* 8 November 1996; *Infotag,* 26 June 1996; *Infotag,* 1 December 1996). Yet, this proved difficult in practice. Given the fact that each of the presidential contenders held a high position—president, prime minister, and head of parliament—it was relatively easy for each of them to gain support from competing local officials and heads of farm enterprises that at the time functioned as important centers of electoral mobilization. Further, local officials often could not be relied on to follow through on providing support. For example, one Sangheli official complained that although local leaders often promised full support, "it was very difficult to follow up on such promises and to know if they would keep their word."[17] As a result, the elections in 1996 were extremely competitive, and both heads of executive power—Prime Minister Sangheli and President Snegur—lost to the head of parliament, Petru Lucinschi.

Because of greater division among elites, pluralism survived much longer than in Belarus. However, the victory of a highly organized and disciplined Communist Party in 2001 led to increasing regime closure—despite the fact that Moldova became a parliamentary republic in that year (Way 2003; 2005a).

Ukraine

In Ukraine, problems of authoritarian state construction were especially serious in the early 1990s under President Leonid Kravchuk. The authoritarian state became more robust in the late 1990s and early 2000s under Leonid Kuchma. However, division at the top in the early 2000s and the release of damaging audiotapes led to regime breakdown in 2004.

As Ukraine's first president, Leonid Kravchuk faced particularly serious difficulties in imposing autocratic rule. First, Kravchuk had only weak control over coercive agencies. In the early 1990s, there was tremendous uncertainty concerning the loyalty of troops and especially officers, who were overwhelmingly Russian (Foye 1993: 62–63). Simultaneously, Ukrainian nationalist officers were extremely dissatisfied with Kravchuk in late 1993, and coup rumors abounded (Kuzio 1993). Further, as in Belarus and Moldova, heads of security and police acted as independent forces and had few if any ties of loyalty to Kravchuk.

Such weak control significantly reduced Kravchuk's options during the 1993 crisis with parliament. Almost certainly inspired by Boris Yeltsin, who had just dissolved the Russian Supreme Soviet, Kravchuk prepared plans to break up parliament (Kravchuk 2002: 227; FBIS-SOV, 1 October 1993, p. 25). However, according to his own account, Kravchuk changed his mind and decided not to take action against parliament when the heads of the

Intelligence Agency and the Ministry of Internal Affairs rejected the idea. "Taking such a step without the support of the Ministry of Internal Affairs would have been risky" (Kravchuk 2002: 228). Simultaneously, parliament had forced Kravchuk to appoint a new defense minister opposed to any kind of action against the legislature (FBIS-SOV, 12 October 1993, p. 88; FBIS-SOV, 15 October 1993, p. 39).

Kravchuk also faced significant problems controlling regional governments. In contrast to leaders in Belarus and Moldova, he had formal authority to appoint regional representatives. Nevertheless, de facto central control was undermined by strong regional differences between east and west. Kravchuk had become president in December 1991 while supporting independence from the Soviet Union and by 1993 was strongly supported by forces in western Ukraine. As the economy declined precipitously in the early 1990s due to the collapse of trade with other Soviet republics,[18] eastern industrial elites grew increasingly hostile toward Kravchuk and began calling for greater autonomy and stronger links to Russia (UPI, 16 December 1993; Kuzio 2000: 207–209).[19]

Such regional problems directly affected competition in the 1994 presidential elections. Despite an apparent belief among Kravchuk's staff that they would be able to manipulate election results and win (Kuzio 1996: 132), the president faced trouble in part because of his inability to control his own subordinates. Local officials and even his own appointees often directly undermined the president during the election. Election commission workers in eastern and southern regions openly supported Kuchma and influenced the voting process in his favor. For example, local officials in a number of cases prevented Kravchuk supporters from monitoring the vote (Kuzio 1996: 132–133). An observer reported that Kravchuk-appointed government officials frequently campaigned actively against the incumbent (FBIS-SOV, 3 August 1994, p. 38). Another election observation report noted that pro-Kravchuk fliers sent to Kravchuk-appointed representatives in eastern Ukraine went unused, while "anti-Kravchuk materials were distributed widely by local officials" (Democratic Elections in Ukraine 1994: 14). Weak control over local governments also undermined Kravchuk's capacity to monopolize the media. Thus, although central state TV was heavily biased in favor of Kravchuk, local media controlled by governments in the south and east were often biased in favor of Kuchma. In addition, Kravchuk complained that during the elections he was unable to find out from the Intelligence Agency whether or not election violations were being made against him (Kravchuk 2002: 229). Kravchuk's inability to control his own officials contributed to the relative weakness of pro-incumbent "administrative resources" in 1994.

The use of administrative resources became increasingly systematic in the mid- and late 1990s as Kuchma gained increasingly effective control over the state. Despite being elected on a platform calling for greater regional autonomy, Kuchma successfully resolved regional problems and reestablished vertical political control. However, the president's reliance on oligarchic support, combined with the release of damaging audiotapes in 2000, led to a gradual hemorrhaging of his support base (Way 2005b). In 2004, following an attempt by Kuchma's chosen successor to steal an election and enormous protests in the capital, the regime fell to Victor Yushchenko.

Conclusion

This chapter has argued for a rethinking of the relationship between state power and regime outcomes. Many nondemocratic states that are referred to as weak because they lack a strong rule of law are better understood as different kinds of states, rather than as lesser versions of a liberal or legal rational state. An authoritarian state is one in which state officials are widely used to manipulate regime procedures to preserve incumbent power. The ability or inability of state leaders to control subordinates in such states has a direct impact on the success or failure of authoritarian consolidation. Focusing on three post-Soviet cases of authoritarian state building, I have demonstrated the mechanisms by which weak authoritarian state control contributes to the persistence of competitive politics in otherwise autocratic regimes. In this way, weak states have contributed to the emergence and persistence of hybrid rule in the post–Cold War era.

Notes

1. Jessica Allina-Pisano (2004) and Keith Darden (2001 and forthcoming) make similar arguments about the diversity of state power in the context of economic reform and corruption, respectively.

2. Exceptions to this dominance of a single-state conception come from the political economy literature, which focuses on different state strategies for economic development. However, such state typologies have mostly been absent from discussions of regimes.

3. At the same time, many dimensions of state power have little apparent relation to regime type. Thus, the monopoly of violence by public authorities over a bounded territory and the capacity of state actors to extract resources are equally important in a democratic as an authoritarian regime. The provision of public goods such as roads, universal education, and certain types of regulation would also seem to be unrelated to regime type.

4. At the same time, it is important to note that the rule of law and nondemocratic regimes are not always incompatible. For example, Bismark, Germany, and South Africa under apartheid were two countries with well-developed legal systems that worked to restrict individual and democratic rights. Yet in the post–Cold War era, such rule of law autocracies have become extraordinarily rare.

5. For recent work on competitive regimes that takes such an approach, see the chapters in this book as well as, especially, Darden (2001 and forthcoming); Fish (2005); Howard and Roessler (2006); Ledeneva (2001); McFaul (2002); Roeder (1994); Schedler (2002b); Wilson (2005).

6. Author interview with Vladimir Alekseevich Reznikov, KGB official, 13 July 2004, Minsk, Belarus; author interview with Sergei Anis'ko, former counter-intelligence official, 14 July 2004, Minsk, Belarus.

7. Author interview with Aleksandr Dabravolski, vice chairman, United Civil Party, 21 June 2004, Minsk, Belarus.

8. Author interview with Vladimir Alekseevich Reznikov, KGB official, 13 July 2004, Minsk, Belarus; author interview with Sergei Anis'ko, former KGB official, 14 July 2004, Minsk, Belarus.

9. Author interview with Aleksandr Sosnov, former leader in the Belarusian parliament, 21 June 2004, Minsk, Belarus.

10. Author interview with Svetlana Gol'dade, former mayor of Gomel, 9 July 2004, Gomel, Belarus.

11. Author interview with Valerii Fadeev, former Council of Ministers official in charge of local government relations, 28 June 2004, Minsk, Belarus.

12. Author interview with Aleksandr Kornienko, 30 June 2004, Minsk, Belarus.

13. Author interview with Vladimir Novosiad, 8 July 2004, Minsk, Belarus.

14. Author interview with Nikolai Voitenkov, head of Gomel province from 1989 to 1994, 9 July 2004, Gomel, Belarus.

15. For a detailed discussion of the use of blackmail in state building, see Darden (2001 and forthcoming).

16. Author interview with Vasile Galadi, former deputy head of Nesporene rayon, 3 August 2004, Chisinau, Moldova.

17. Author interview with former Sangheli official, February 2002, Chisinau, Moldova.

18. By the end of 1993, the Ukrainian gross domestic product had dropped by almost 40 percent relative to its level in 1989.

19. Backed by regional leaders, coal miners in the eastern region of Donetsk struck for higher wages as well as greater regional autonomy in 1993 (Wilson 1993; Solchanyk 1994: 59).

11

Creative Constitutions: How Do Parliamentary Powers Shape the Electoral Arena?

M. Steven Fish

This chapter addresses how constitutional choices about the strength of the national legislature influence political regime change. It focuses specifically on the postcommunist region. I show that the power invested in the national legislatures by the new, postcommunist constitutions, adopted in the early years of regime change, subsequently influenced the resulting political regimes of the mid-2000s. Countries that opted for strong legislatures underwent substantial democratization. By the mid-2000s, these countries enjoyed regimes that were liberal democracies or electoral democracies. Countries whose constitutions provided for weak legislatures developed electoral authoritarian or closed autocratic regimes. This generalization holds with remarkable consistency, even controlling for other factors that might have also affected trajectories of regime change, such as starting points in terms of levels of democratization and socioeconomic development. A strong legislature promotes a successful transition to democracy, but a weak one sets the stage for nondemocratization or for democratization followed by backsliding to electoral authoritarianism or closed autocracy.

The first section reviews the debate on the effect of constitutional choices on democratization. The second introduces a new way to measure the powers of parliaments and assesses the strength of parliaments in postcommunist countries. The third presents empirical evidence showing that the choice of a strong parliament was an unmixed blessing for democratization. It also shows that the extent of democratization at the time of the constitution's adoption did not affect the strength of the legislature to nearly as great an extent as the strength of the legislature subsequently affected democratization. The fourth section of the chapter considers why a strong parliament is so beneficial for democratization. For empirical illustration, it draws on the experiences of two countries that exemplify divergent trajectories of regime change. Russia started its post-Soviet incarnation as an electoral democracy and subsequently regressed to electoral authoritarianism. Bulgaria also began its postcommunist existence as an electoral democracy but then advanced to liberal democracy. These cases show how a strong parliament restrains executive power and promotes political parties, thereby shielding the polity from the rise of, or reversion to, electoral authoritarianism or closed autocracy.

Many studies have considered the implications of constitutional forms for the survivability of democracy. Some authors have argued that parliamentarism provides a superior institutional basis for avoiding the breakdown of democracy, but others have held that presidentialism might be better for this purpose. This chapter differs in several respects from such studies. First, it departs from the usual nominal classification of constitutional types (e.g., parliamentary, presidential, semipresidential, premier-presidential, president-parliamentary) and offers instead a continuous measure of the powers of legislatures. Second, rather than focusing on the stability of democracy, meaning the lifespan of democratic regimes or the consolidation/breakdown of democratic regimes within an extensive block of historical time, this chapter investigates the effect of the legislature's power on trajectories of regime change, meaning progress toward democracy or erosion of democratic gains over a relatively brief interval (here, the early 1990s until the mid-2000s). In sum, here the independent variable (the power of the national legislature) is measured differently, and the dependent variable (democratization) is specified differently than in most other writings.

The Debate over Constitutions

The relative merits of constitutional types for democratization are the source of a lively debate. Some scholars advocate parliamentarism. Under such a constitution, the government is formed by elements of the legislature, the prime minister exercises considerable executive power and is answerable primarily or exclusively to parliament, and the president either does not exist, is elected by the legislature, or is elected by direct suffrage but holds only modest power. Advocates of parliamentarism are generally suspicious of unconstrained executive power and laud the permanent dependence of the most powerful executive (the prime minister) and his or her government on the legislature. They note that no matter how powerful the prime minister might appear to be, in a parliamentary system he or she serves at the pleasure of the assembly and can be dismissed by that assembly if he or she loses his or her majority. They contrast the rigidity of the fixed terms that presidents serve—which may force electorates to live with an incompetent or malign executive for years—with the flexibility of parliamentarism, where legislatures may depose undesirable prime ministers and their governments in short order (Linz and Valenzuela 1994; Stepan and Skach 1993).

Presidentialism also has its advocates. In that system, the president is directly elected, the government is appointed by and answerable to the president alone, and the president enjoys considerable prerogatives. Presidentialism's defenders sometimes tout the advantages of the separation of power. The presence of two entities (the presidency and the legislature), each with its own source of electoral legitimacy and an ability to check the other, may reduce the danger of radical missteps that may exist if legislative and executive power spring from a single source. A president elected by the whole people may better embody the national will than a legislature can. In times of crisis, a president, as a unitary actor, may be more capable of rapid, decisive action than a legislature (Mainwaring and Shugart 1997; Horowitz 1996).

Semipresidentialism, sometimes called a "dual" or "mixed" system, combines features of presidentialism and parliamentarism. Maurice Duverger (1980) formulated the classical definition. According to Duverger, a system is semipresidential if the constitution that established it combines three elements: (1) the president of the republic is elected by universal suffrage; (2) the president possesses quite considerable powers; (3) the president has opposite him or her, however, a prime minister and ministers who possess executive and governmental power and can stay in office only if the parliament does not show its opposition to them. The first two points require some minimum of presidential authority. The third sets some minimum of parliamentary influence. It specifies the distinctive feature of semipresidentialism: the mutual and often contested control of the prime minister and the government as a whole by the president and the legislature.

Semipresidentialism may be defended on the same grounds as parliamentarism and presidentialism. Since it provides for some separation of powers, it may, like presidentialism, temper the blunders of either the parliament or the president. Since it involves direct election of the president, the people as a whole have a decisive voice in the selection of the chief executive. Yet since it affords the legislature some say over the government, it may reduce the risks of overweening presidential power.

A New Means of Assessment: The Parliamentary Powers Index

As useful as the usual system of classifying constitutional types may be, it is a blunt instrument. It establishes some basis for discerning the contours of the constitutional system but does not necessarily get us very far in understanding where power really lies. For example, both the United States and Mexico have presidential systems. Yet it is intuitively obvious to most observers that the US Congress has more say over policy and more clout in its relations with the president than does its Mexican counterpart. In the postcommunist region, nine countries have semipresidential constitutions. They are Croatia, Kazakhstan, Lithuania, Moldova (until 2001), Mongolia, Poland, Romania, Russia, and Ukraine. Each of these countries fulfills (in Moldova's case, fulfilled) Duverger's criteria for semipresidentialism. In each the president is directly elected and possesses considerable powers, but the government is in some way dependent on parliamentary approval. Each country has a prime minister who must be confirmed by parliament in order to have the right to assume office.

Yet it is obvious even to the casual observer that there are stark differences among these countries in the powers vested in the main agencies of government. The presidents of Russia and Kazakhstan hold enormous power. Certainly, each is less constrained by the legislature than is the US president. In contrast, in Lithuania and Mongolia, parliaments occupy center stage in national politics.

If we wish to assess more precisely how constitutions really allot power and where power actually resides, we need an instrument designed to measure the capacity of a specific agency. In an effort to measure the powers of national legislatures, Matthew Kroenig and I have created a Parliamentary Powers Index (PPI; see Fish and Kroenig 2006; also Fish 2005). Several other efforts to quantify the powers of parliaments have been made (Shugart and Carey 1992; Krouwel 2000). Yet they are dated, cover a small number of countries, or are based on only a handful of criteria. The PPI overcomes these limitations. It is based on thirty-two items that cover the parliament's ability to monitor the president and the bureaucracy, its freedom from presidential control, its authority in specific areas, and the resources that it brings to its work. Some answers are readily available in constitutions. Addressing other items requires country expertise. In order to enhance the accuracy of assessments, we surveyed experts and obtained a minimum of five expert responses per country. The survey commenced in 2002 and is still in progress, but as of early 2006 we have complete data for the postcommunist countries (except for Bosnia, Turkmenistan, and Yugoslavia/ Serbia and Montenegro, which are excluded from the survey). The items in the survey are posed in such a way that affirmation of the statement indicates greater rather than lesser power for the legislature. More affirmative answers indicate a more powerful legislature. The Legislative Powers Survey (LPS), on which the PPI is based, is presented in Table 11.1.

The PPI is calculated for each country by dividing the number of affirmative answers by thirty-two (that is, by the total number of questions). This technique, which assigns equal weight to each item, obviously involves difficult and arbitrary distinctions. So, too, would weighting the questions involve difficult and arbitrary distinctions. Despite the limitations inherent

Table 11.1   The Fish-Kroenig Legislative Powers Survey

1. The legislature alone, without the involvement of any other agencies, can impeach the president or replace the prime minister.
2. Ministers may serve simultaneously as members of the legislature.
3. The legislature has powers of summons over executive branch officials, and hearings with executive branch officials testifying before the legislature or its committees are regularly held.
4. The legislature can conduct independent investigation of the chief executive and the agencies of the executive.
5. The legislature has effective powers of oversight over the agencies of coercion (the military, organs of law enforcement, intelligence services, and the secret police).
6. The legislature appoints the prime minister.
7. The legislature's approval is required to confirm the appointment of individual ministers; or the legislature itself appoints ministers.
8. The country lacks a presidency entirely, or there is a presidency but the president is elected by the legislature.
9. The legislature can vote no confidence in the government without jeopardizing its own term (that is, without, the threat of dissolution).
10. The legislature is immune from dissolution by the executive.
11. Any executive initiative on legislation requires ratification or approval by the legislature before it takes effect; that is, the executive lacks decree power.
12. Laws passed by the legislature are veto-proof or essentially veto-proof; that is, the executive lacks veto power, or has veto power but the veto can be overridden by a simple majority in the legislature.
13. The legislature's laws are supreme and not subject to judicial review.
14. The legislature has the right to initiate bills in all policy jurisdictions; the executive lacks gate-keeping authority.
15. Expenditure of funds appropriated by the legislature is mandatory; the executive lacks the power to impound funds appropriated by the legislature.
16. The legislature controls the resources that finance its own internal operation and provide for the perquisites of its own members.
17. Members of the legislature are immune from arrest and/or criminal prosecution.
18. All members of the legislature are elected; the executive lacks the power to appoint any members of the legislature.
19. The legislature alone, without the involvement of any other agencies, can change the constitution.
20. The legislature's approval is necessary for the declaration of war.
21. The legislature's approval is necessary to ratify treaties with foreign countries.
22. The legislature has the power to grant amnesty.
23. The legislature has the power of pardon.
24. The legislature reviews and has the right to reject appointments to the judiciary, or the legislature itself appoints members of the judiciary.
25. The chairman of the central bank is appointed by the legislature.
26. The legislature has a substantial voice in the operation of the state-owned media.
27. The legislature is regularly in session.
28. Each legislator has a personal secretary.
29. Each legislator has at least one nonsecretarial staff member with policy expertise.
30. Legislators are eligible for reelection without any restriction.
31. A seat in the legislature is an attractive enough position that legislators are generally interested in and seek reelection.
32. The reelection of incumbent legislators is common enough that at any given time the legislature contains a significant number of highly experienced members.

in this or any other index, the PPI may provide a useful tool for assessing the power of national legislatures.

Table 11.2 presents the PPI for each postcommunist country. The powers of legislatures have not been fixed in all countries since the adoption of the original postcommunist constitutional arrangements. Albania, Belarus, Kazakhstan, Kyrgyzstan, Moldova, Poland, Slovakia, and Ukraine all made changes between the time of the adoption of their first post-Soviet constitutions and the present day that may be of relevance to the powers of their legislatures. Albania adopted its first postcommunist constitution in May 1991 but revised it in October 1998. The basic powers of the legislature, which are of concern here, are essentially the same in the two constitutions, though they are spelled out with greater clarity in the later document. Since 1998, officials have observed the constitution more faithfully than during 1991–1998, when then-president Sali Berisha made a habit of trying to break out of the constitution's constraints. Belarus adopted changes in November 1996 that strengthened the president's powers. Kazakhstan and Kyrgyzstan enacted changes that strengthened presidencies in August 1995 and February 1996, respectively. Moldova changed its constitution to put the parliament in charge of electing the president in 2001. Poland did not have a constitution until May 1997, but between 1992 and 1997 it operated under a "little constitution" that was the blueprint for the constitution that it finally enacted formally in 1997. Slovakia switched from election of the president by parliament to direct election of the president in 1999. Ukraine undertook changes in 2005 that promised to boost the power of the legislature. The scores shown in Table 11.2 and used here reflect the powers of legislatures in the countries' original constitutions, before the changes just enumerated were made.

The Strength of Parliaments and Patterns of Democratization

The data help us assess the relationship between the powers of parliaments, on the one hand, and democratization, on the other. To assess the extent of democratization, I use the average Freedom House freedom scores (hereafter, "FH scores") from the 2005 survey (Freedom House 2005). In Freedom House's assessment, 1 stands for "most free" and 7 for "least free."

The relationship between the strength of parliaments and the extent of democratization is intimate. The correlation is very high ($r = -.91$; $p < .001$). Before concluding that stronger parliaments necessarily make for more open politics, however, we must consider whether stronger parliaments are a mere effect of more open politics.

Table 11.2 **Parliamentary Powers and Levels of Democracy in Postcommunist Countries at the Time of Constitutional Choice**

Country	Parliamentary Powers Index[a]	Freedom House Score[b]	Date of Enactment of New Constitution
Albania	.75	6.5	May 1991
Armenia	.53	3.5	July 1995
Azerbaijan	.44	6.0	November 1995
Belarus	.28	4.5	March 1994
Bulgaria	.78	3.5	July 1991
Croatia	.72	n/a	December 1990
Czech Republic	.78	2.0	December 1992
Estonia	.75	2.5	June 1992
Georgia	.59	5.0	October 1995
Hungary	.69	4.5	October 1989
Kazakhstan	.31	5.0	January 1993
Kyrgyzstan	.41	3.0	May 1993
Latvia	.84	n/a	1991 (1922)
Lithuania	.72	2.5	October 1992
Macedonia	.78	n/a	November 1991
Moldova	.72	5.0	July 1994
Mongolia	.81	2.5	February 1992
Poland	.66	2.0	November 1992
Romania	.72	5.5	December 1991
Russia	.44	3.5	December 1993
Slovakia	.72	2.0	January 1993
Slovenia	.78	n/a	December 1991
Tajikistan	.41	7.0	December 1994
Ukraine	.50	3.5	June 1996
Uzbekistan	.28	5.5	December 1992

Notes: a. Figures indicate measurements following enactment of the new constitution.
b. Average of Freedom House civil liberties and political rights scores, for the year preceding enactment of the new constitution.
n/a = not available.

Definitively establishing the direction of causation is difficult. The data do not lend themselves to statistical techniques that tease out the direction of causation, such as two-stage least squares regression or Granger causality analysis. The causal arrow probably goes both ways. The extent of political openness at the time of the constitution's inauguration may well have influenced the powers granted to parliament. Certainly, one would expect that constitutions made in closed polities would provide for weak legislatures while lodging the bulk of power in the president (or the general secretary of the hegemonic party or the head of the military).

To measure the openness of the polity at the time that the constitution was adopted, I use FH scores for the last year before the enactment of the constitution. They capture the state of political openness at the constitutional moment. Table 11.2 shows the time that each country originally adopted its fundamental law and the FH score that reflects conditions at that time.

Freedom House data for some countries cannot be included. Those of the former Yugoslavia enacted constitutions before FH freedom scores were published for them. Latvia is excluded for the same reason. In May 1990, before the demise of the Soviet Union and before FH freedom scores were available for Latvia, the republican legislature reverted to the 1922 constitution of the Republic of Latvia. The document has subsequently been amended but has remained in force to the present day. Alone in the region, Latvia did not adopt a new postcommunist constitution.

There is a link between political openness at the constitutional moment and the powers of the parliament. We may treat the PPI as the dependent variable, under the assumption that the openness of the polity affected the powers that parliament received. In general, countries that had more open polities at the time that they chose their constitutions did create stronger national legislatures. There is a correlation between countries' FH scores at the time that they adopted their original constitutions on the one hand and the strength of the legislature on the other.

Yet the link is not tight ($r = -.41$; $p = .07$). In many countries the powers of parliament are not what one would expect them to be if political openness translated into an expansive role for parliament. Hungary was just beginning democratization at the time that it adopted its fundamental law, and its FH freedom score was still quite low, yet it embraced a constitution that provided for a powerful legislature. Romania's FH freedom score was even lower at the time it adopted its constitution. Nicolae Ceausescu had been deposed, but Ion Iliescu, a holdover from the old regime, grabbed the presidency. Iliescu and most other power holders at the time were in no hurry to democratize. Yet the Romanian constitution provided for a strong legislature. In contrast, Kyrgyzstan was a relatively open polity when it embraced a constitution that vested more modest powers in the legislature. Russia was more open in 1993, when it adopted its constitution, than Romania was in 1991. Yet Russia's constitution created a comparatively weak legislature. The evidence does not support the notion that the powers of legislatures were mere effects of the extent of democratization at the time that the powers of legislatures were defined.

In fact, myriad explanatory factors can be understood only in the context of each country's political experience and of the struggles that shaped the decisions defining the powers of legislatures. Constitutions were drawn up in the heat of regime change. Some analysts treat constitution making as a bargaining game among elite actors pursuing their own interests. Yet under the chaotic conditions that obtained in most postcommunist countries, most elite actors could not gauge which institutional arrangements would best serve them. What is more, mass opinion molded constitutional choice in some countries.

While the origins of choices about the powers vested in legislatures varied across cases, the consequences of those choices did not. Stronger legislatures facilitated subsequent democratization. As mentioned, determining the direction of the causal arrow in the relationship between political openness and the power of legislatures is difficult, and in practice the relationship probably runs both ways. But the correlation between FH scores in 2005 and the PPI is much higher than between the PPI and FH scores at the constitutional moment. Thus, the power of parliaments, as established in constitutions adopted between the late 1980s and mid-1990s, predicts political openness in the middle of the current decade more accurately than political openness at the time of the adoption of constitutions predicts the power of parliaments.

For more evidence, one may calculate the change in FH scores between the time of the constitution's adoption and 2005 and examine the correlation between this change and the PPI. The correlation is fairly strong ($r = -.70$; $p < .001$). All seven of the countries whose FH score deteriorated over the years between the constitution's adoption and 2005 had a PPI score of less than 0.6. Eleven of the fourteen countries whose FH score improved had a PPI score higher than 0.6.

Furthermore, the effect of the PPI on change in FH scores is robust to controls. In the regression presented in Table 11.3, the change in the FH score between the time that constitutions were adopted and 2005 is the dependent variable. In the regression, the level of economic development in 1990, measured as gross domestic product (GDP), and the FH scores at the time of the constitution's adoption are added as controls. Along with the PPI, they are the independent variables in the analysis. Even controlling for "starting points" in economic development and political openness, the PPI is a good predictor of how countries fared in democratization after they adopted their constitutions.

How the Strength of Parliament Shapes Democratization

How does a weak legislature inhibit democratization? It reduces the possibilities for effective "horizontal accountability," which Guillermo O'Donnell (1999: 185) defines as "the controls that state agencies are supposed to exercise over other state agencies." In polities where authoritarian regimes have

Table 11.3   Multiple Regression of Changes in Freedom House Scores on Hypothesized Determinants

Variable	
Constant	13.43**
	(2.51)
Economic development (log GDP p/c 1990)	–1.55*
	(0.63)
FH score at time of constitution's adoption	–0.86***
	(0.12)
Parliamentary Powers Index	–9.33***
	(0.90)
Adj. R^2	.85

Notes: OLS regression. N = 21 countries. Entries are unstandardized regression coefficients, with standard errors in parentheses.

$*p < 0.05$; $**p < 0.01$; $***p < 0.001$.

broken down and new regimes are taking their place, the temptation to concentrate power in the executive is great. People often confuse concentrated power with effective power, and the president is usually the beneficiary. Although one might expect the judiciary to provide some protection against abuse of power, habits of judicial quiescence commonly inherited from the authoritarian period often ensure that the courts will not counterbalance executive power, at least not in the early years of transition (Holston and Caldeira 1998). Under such circumstances, the legislature is the only agency at the national level that is potentially capable of controlling the chief executive. Where the legislature lacks muscle, presidential abuse of power—including interference in the media, societal organizations, and the conduct of elections—frequently ensues, even under presidents who came to office with reputations as democrats.

Legislative weakness also inhibits democratization by undermining the development of political parties. In polities with weak legislatures, political parties drift and stagnate rather than develop and mature. Parties are the main vehicles for structuring political competition and for linking the people and their elected officials. The underdevelopment of parties therefore saps political competition of its substance and vigor and checks the growth of "vertical accountability," meaning the ability of the people to control their representatives.

Precise information on party development in the postcommunist region is scarce, but what is available suggests that weaker parliaments furnish fainter incentives for participation in parties. The 2000 World Values Surveys (WVS) have data on the percentage of respondents who are members of political parties for seventeen postcommunist countries for which I also have PPI data. Adding data from the 1995 WVS for the three countries of the Caucasus, for which data are missing in the 2000 survey, yields a sample of twenty countries (Inglehart et al. 2004; Inglehart 2002). Among these countries, controlling for economic development (measured, as above, as GDP per capita in 1990), the partial correlation between the PPI and the percentage of the population that belongs to a political party is substantial ($r = .56$; $p < .01$). What is more, the level of participation in parties and the extent of democratization are also linked. In a partial correlation controlling for economic development, the relationship between party membership and FH scores for 2005 is noteworthy ($r = -.44$; $p < .05$). The numbers are consistent with the possibility that the power of the legislature affects party development and that party development, in turn, influences democratization.

Some qualitative evidence drawn from cases may help flesh out the argument. A telling comparison is found in the trajectories of regime change in Russia and Bulgaria. Both countries experienced substantial but incomplete political openings as their communist party regimes collapsed. Neither country opened up as dramatically and suddenly as did, for example, Poland and Lithuania. At the time that Poland adopted its "little constitution" in November 1992 and Lithuania its new constitution in October 1992, each was already a liberal democracy. Poland's FH score for 1992 was 2.0 and Lithuania's 2.5. On the other end of the spectrum, Uzbekistan's FH score was 5.5 at the time that it adopted its post-Soviet constitution in December 1992. Uzbekistan never really underwent a substantial political opening. It merely slid from one form of authoritarianism to another. Bulgaria and Russia were, in the context of the postcommunist region, intermediate cases. Each had an FH score of 3.5 at the time it adopted its constitution (Bulgaria in July 1991, Russia in December 1993). Each was therefore an electoral democracy at the time of its constitutional moment.

Yet the two subsequently went separate ways. Bulgaria's FH score improved to 2.5 during the 1990s and climbed to 1.5 in the current decade. By 2005 Bulgaria had reached a mark that placed it on par with Japan and South Korea. Russia moved in the opposite direction. Its FH score deteriorated steadily during the 1990s and early 2000s. In 2005 it stood at 5.5, placing it at the same level as Pakistan and Rwanda. While Bulgaria advanced decisively from electoral democracy to liberal democracy, Russia moved just as definitely from electoral democracy to electoral autocracy.

How to explain this dramatic divergence? Many factors may affect regime change. In terms of their starting points, Russia and Bulgaria differed in some traits and matched one another in others. In general, it would be difficult to say that one country had a structural or cultural profile that made it decidedly more likely to democratize than the other. The style of Sovietism practiced in the two countries during the 1960s–1980s was similar. Todor Zhivkov, the party first secretary of Bulgaria, self-consciously imitated Leonid Brezhnev's style of rule. Brezhnev's Russia and Zhivkov's Bulgaria were both thoroughly closed polities with fully closed economies. At the onset of regime change, Russia was the richer country. Its GDP per capita in 1990 was about $3,700, compared to about $1,700 in Bulgaria. In both countries, 14 percent of the workforce was engaged in agriculture as of 1990 (UNDP 2000; World Bank 1997). Bulgaria had what may be regarded as the advantage of continuity in its statehood, whereas Russia grappled during the early postcommunist years with redefining its territorial boundaries. Russia was not part of Europe, but Bulgaria was. Bulgarians also experienced the enticements of possible membership in the European Union, whereas Russians did not. Bulgaria, however, is tucked away in the corner of a tumultuous region (southeastern Europe) and does not share a border with any Western European country, whereas Russia is the preeminent entity in the Slavic world and the site of world-class cities that are home to a large and vigorous intelligentsia. Both are predominantly Orthodox Christian societies with large Muslim minorities. In the early 1990s, both countries appeared to hold some hope for democratization; yet neither appeared as promising as the predominantly Catholic countries of East-Central Europe that bordered Germany and Austria.

The key determinant of the divergence in paths of regime change may have been constitutional choice. Bulgaria opted for a strong parliament. It chose a system in which the parliament forms the government. Bulgaria's PPI score is 0.78, which means that twenty-five of the thirty-two questions in the LPS are affirmative for Bulgaria. Russia opted for a strong president. Russia's PPI score is 0.44; only fourteen of the thirty-two questions in the LPS are affirmative for Russia. Unlike in Bulgaria, the parliament in Russia has little influence over the government. It has little say in the formation of the government, scant oversight authority, and meager resources—particularly in comparison with the colossal resources available to the executive branch.

The relative clout of legislatures has deeply affected trajectories of democratization. Presidential abuse of power, committed in the presence of a legislature that cannot prevent it even when it has been inclined to do so, has been a hallmark of postcommunist Russian politics. The weakness of the legislature has thereby undermined vertical accountability. It has left the president free to pursue his aims by virtually any means he chooses. Both of Russia's postcommunist presidents, Boris Yeltsin and Vladimir Putin, used their freedom from constraint to undermine rights and freedoms and distort elections. Putin has gone much further than his predecessor, seizing all electronic media with national reach and ensuring that only his own version of the news reaches the masses. In doing so, he explicitly violates Article 29 of the constitution, which guarantees freedom of speech and information. But there is no one to stop him. In contrast, Bulgarian presidents have been hemmed in by a strong legislature. Of course, they have not been happy with this state of affairs. In an interview with the author, Zhelyu Zhelev, who served as Bulgaria's first postcommunist president (1990–1996), stated that he had coveted Yeltsin's powers and thought that a Russian-style constitution would have been wonderful for Bulgaria.[1] Zhelev and his successors, after all, were and continue to be boxed in by a strong legislature. Bulgarian democratization has profited immensely as a result.

The strength of parliaments has also affected the development of political parties in the two countries. The impetus to build parties depends largely on the power of the national legislature, and in Bulgaria, where the legislature occupies center stage, politicians must invest in parties in order to advance their careers. The Bulgarian Socialist Party (BSP) was born out of the remnants of the formerly hegemonic communist party; it established a strong presence on the left. The Union of Democratic Forces (UDF) brought together Bulgaria's liberals, and the Movement for Rights and Freedoms (MRF) represented much of the country's large Turkish minority. Throughout the entire 1990s, these three parties structured political competition in Bulgaria. The BSP and the UDF each served stints in government, and they offered voters distinct choice. Each party developed a fairly coherent social basis, with the BSP faring better in the countryside and small towns and among less educated voters and the UDF enjoying strong support in the major urban centers and among upwardly mobile strata. The MRF did a remarkable job of integrating Turks into the mainstream of Bulgarian political life and checked the scourge of ethnic demagoguery (both Turkish and ethnic Bulgarian) in a country that had a history that made it as vulnerable to intercommunal violence as any of the countries of the former Yugoslavia (Fish and Brooks 2000; Ganev 2004).

The two largest parties faltered in 2001, when a new party arose to challenge the then-governing UDF. The National Movement of Simeon the Second (NMSS), led by the former tsar, drew support from the traditional bases of both the UDF and the BSP and won a large plurality in June 2001. The BSP and the UDF nevertheless weathered the crisis and maintained coherent organizations. For its own part, the NMSS created a broad coalition government, giving two cabinet posts to the MRF and two to BSP-affiliated technocrats. In appointing regional governors, the NMSS leadership nodded to the liberal partisan complexion of the capital and appointed a UDF politician governor of the Sofia region. It gave the governorship of Kardzhali to an MRF representative, although some feared granting the Turks too much power in a region that borders Turkey. In the legislative elections of 2005, the BSP won about a third of the vote and leadership of the government. The NMSS picked up a fifth of the vote, followed by the MRF and the UDF.

Although some small parties come and go in Bulgaria, as they do in almost every polity, several major parties represent constituents, provide meaningful sources of identification for politicians, compete vigorously with one another, and impose order on political life. They fulfill the functions that Richard Katz (1980: 1–2) says parties must in order for elections to be meaningful expressions of popular preferences: namely, the parties "structure campaigns, provide continuity from one election to the next, and provide links among candidates in different locales for different offices." They promote what O'Donnell calls vertical accountability.

None of this may be said of Russia's political parties, which have failed to establish a coherent arena for political competition (Fish 2003; McFaul 2001). Electoral volatility is much higher in Russia than in Bulgaria. In each election voters face a different lineup of parties. Half of all deputies are elected on party lists, and committee chairmanships are distributed on the basis of party affiliation in the Duma, which provides a stimulus to party building. But the countervailing effects of the legislature's diminutive role erase the potentially favorable effects of these rules. For the political operative, the attractive positions are in the executive branch, and party work is not a prerequisite for a position there. The system of strong-president-weak-legislature animates the growth not of political parties, but rather of small, well-endowed interest groups that specialize in targeting officials in executive branch agencies. Consequently, well-heeled cliques representing narrow business interests, rather than political parties, have constituted the growth sector in sociopolitical organization in post-Soviet Russia (Zudin 1999).

Russia shows that the ultimate consequence of a weak legislature may be the reduction of political parties to supplicants for presidential favor. In the party-lists portion of balloting in the most recent elections for the Duma, held in December 2003, United Russia, whose sole raison d'être is supporting President Putin, won a large plurality. Vladimir Zhirinovskii's misnamed Liberal Democratic Party of Russia, which does little but collect bribes from the presidential administration in exchange for unstinting support, and a nondescript, mainly pro-Putin organization that emerged only months before the election, the Motherland Party, each received about one-tenth of the vote. The Communist Party of the Russian Federation (CPRF), the rump of the former single party and the only party in Russia with anything resembling a mass membership, received about one-eighth of the vote. The two main liberal parties and the only parties besides the CPRF that were inclined to oppose the president, Iabloko and the Union of Right Forces, both failed to cross the 5 percent threshold for representation in the legislature.

In Bulgaria, the strength of the legislature stimulated the formation of parties that structured political competition. It also encouraged public participation in parties. As of 2000, 4 percent of Bulgarian adults declared themselves members of a party, and 3 percent said that they engaged in voluntary, unpaid work on behalf of a party. The numbers may seem modest, but in Russia the analogous figures were 1 and 0 percent, respectively (Inglehart et al. 2004). Party membership, like membership in other societal organizations, is much lower in the postcommunist region than in other regions of the world (Howard 2003). The figures for participation in parties in Bulgaria are actually higher than the mean for postcommunist countries.

Bulgaria, with its relatively low level of economic development and other conditions that did not presage robust democratization, did not top anyone's list of likely future democratic success stories in 1990. Yet, a decade and a half later, it stands out as a case of remarkable achievement. Among the eighty-eight countries of the world with at least 1 million inhabitants that had incomes per capita of $2,000 or less in 1990, Bulgaria is the only one that received an FH score as favorable as 1.5 in 2005.

Bulgaria is not the only pleasant surprise in the postcommunist region. Four countries in the region had incomes per capita of less than $1,000 in 1990. They (and their level of per capita income in 1990) are Albania ($800), Macedonia ($800), Mongolia ($500), and Tajikistan ($700). Among these disadvantaged countries, one (Mongolia) became a liberal democracy, and two (Albania and Macedonia) received FH scores of 3 in 2005, marking them as electoral democracies. Within this impoverished quartet, only Tajikistan, with a score of 5.5 in 2005, failed to undergo substantial democratization. Strikingly, all three of the poor-but-open polities opted for strong legislatures early in their postcommunist existence. The PPI scores for Albania, Macedonia, and Mongolia are 0.75, 0.78, and 0.81, respectively. These scores place the three at or near the top of postcommunist countries in terms of the powers vested in legislatures. In addition, these polities have strong party systems. The WVS lack data for Mongolia, but available sources suggest that participation in political parties is exceptionally high in regional terms. As much as one-fifth of the adult population belongs to a political party. The country has a robust party system that has been consistently structured by a party of the left, the Mongolian People's Revolutionary Party, and a right-center liberal party, the Mongolian Democratic Party (Fish 1998). Among postcommunist countries for which the WVS do have data for 2000, Albania and Macedonia rank first and second in terms of public involvement in political parties. In Albania, 15 percent report membership in a party, and 11 percent perform voluntary work for a party. The analogous figures for Macedonia are 12 and 8 percent. These numbers are by far the highest in the postcommunist region; the next highest figures are for Slovakia, where 7 percent belong and 5 percent engage in voluntary work (Inglehart et al. 2004). The evidence suggests that vesting power in the legislature spurs party development, which in turn bolsters democratization. It shows that even impoverished countries emerging from long spells of totalitarian domination can democratize.

Conclusion

Stronger parliaments are better for democratization than are weaker parliaments. In the postcommunist region, all countries that opted for constitutional arrangements that produced legislatures that scored over 0.6 on the PPI—a group that included countries that were deeply disadvantaged by initial structural conditions—were liberal democracies or electoral democracies as of 2005. All countries that adopted constitutions that provided for legislatures that scored below 0.5 on the PPI—a group that included countries in which other initial conditions were relatively auspicious—ended up with electoral authoritarian or closed autocratic regimes. Opting for weak legislatures early in the course of regime change was a sufficient condition for failing to advance to or maintain status as a liberal or electoral democracy.

Stronger legislatures served as a weightier check on presidents and thus a more reliable guarantor of horizontal accountability than did weaker legislatures. They also provided a stronger stimulus to party building. Where legislatures were more powerful, people invested more in political parties, and parties consequently grew stronger. The strength of parties varies positively with the strength of the legislature. What is more, the extent of democratization varies positively with popular participation in political parties. Parties that had a major role in the legislature and some roots in society were better at linking the people and elected officials—that is, at promoting vertical accountability—than were parties whose role in the legislature was modest and whose roots in society were shallow.

The practical implications of the findings for political actors are clear: to enhance the chances of democracy's success, focus on creating a powerful legislature. Federalism, interethnic relations, national identity, economic reform, and myriad other matters may occupy the minds of would-be democratizers during the heated and disorderly days of political regime change. But if democracy's well-wishers fail to establish a national legislature with far-reaching powers, they will in any event soon find themselves living under an electoral authoritarian or closed autocratic regime.

How will we know whether we may have confidence in the causal scheme offered here? If, as of the year 2015, countries with weak legislatures (e.g., Russia, Belarus, Kazakhstan, and Azerbaijan) have become liberal or electoral democracies even in the absence of prior changes that enhance the powers of national legislatures, my argument will be undermined. Furthermore, if political parties in any of these polities become serious forces in the absence of major changes in the powers of national legislatures, or if lasting democratization occurs even without the prior growth of political parties, the causal argument presented here will be shown to be faulty or at best incomplete. Given that nearly two-thirds of the people in the postcommunist region live in polities with legislatures that score 0.5 or lower in the PPI, one can only hope that the argument put forward in this chapter shall indeed be swiftly consigned to the dustbin of discredited social-scientific scribbling.

Note

1. Author interview with Zhelyu Zhelev, 14 January 1998.

12

Linkage and Leverage: How Do International Factors Change Domestic Balances of Power?

Steven Levitsky and Lucan A. Way

The end of the Cold War posed an unprecedented challenge to authoritarian regimes. The collapse of the Soviet Union (and consequent drying up of external assistance to Soviet and US client states), the military and economic ascendance of Western democracies, and the virtual disappearance of legitimate regime alternatives created powerful incentives for developing world elites to adopt formal democratic institutions. As a result, overtly authoritarian regimes disappeared from many parts of the globe, giving way, in most cases, to regimes based on multiparty elections. Yet as this book makes clear, many of these electoral regimes did not democratize. In countries as diverse as Belarus, Cambodia, Croatia, Kenya, Mexico, Malaysia, Peru, Serbia, Russia, and Zimbabwe, competitive elections coexisted with widespread abuse of democratic procedure.[1] We call these regimes competitive authoritarian: civilian regimes in which democratic institutions exist and are taken seriously as a means of obtaining power, but in which incumbent abuse tilts the electoral playing field so heavily against the opposition that the regime cannot be labeled democratic (see Levitsky and Way 2002).

Competitive authoritarian regimes followed diverging paths during the post–Cold War period. Although some democratized (Croatia, Mexico, Peru, Slovakia, Taiwan), many others remained stable or hardened (Cambodia, Cameroon, Malaysia, Russia, Zimbabwe). In still other cases (Zambia in 1991, Malawi and Ukraine in 1994, Georgia in 2003), autocratic governments were removed from power, but regimes failed to democratize.

In this chapter we argue that post–Cold War competitive authoritarian regime trajectories were powerfully shaped by the international environment and, specifically, by the nature and extent of countries' ties to the West. We treat the post–Cold War international environment as operating along two dimensions: Western leverage, or governments' vulnerability to international democratizing pressure; and linkage to the West, or the density of economic, political, social, organizational, and communication ties to the United States, the European Union (EU), and Western-led multilateral institutions. We argue that the use of leverage—via diplomatic pressure, conditionality, or military intervention—was rarely sufficient to democratize post–Cold War competitive authoritarian regimes. Rather, the diffuse and decentralized effects of linkage contributed more consistently to democratization. Linkage raised the cost of authoritarianism by heightening the international salience of repression, fraud, and other abuses; increasing the likelihood that Western governments would respond to those abuses; and creating domestic constituencies with a political, economic, or professional stake in adhering to democratic norms. Thus, in regions with extensive linkage to the West, such as Central Europe and the Americas, international pressure was intense after 1989, contributing to democratization even under unfavorable domestic conditions. Low-linkage regions were characterized by a more permissive international environment. Where both linkage and leverage were low, as in parts of the former Soviet Union and East Asia, external democratizing pressure was limited and domestic forces predominated, which frequently resulted in authoritarian persistence. Where linkage was low but leverage high (as in much of Africa) external pressure was only intermittent and partially effective, at times weakening autocracies but—in the absence of a strong domestic push—rarely achieving democratization.

Two Dimensions of International Pressure: Leverage and Linkage

It is by now clear that the international environment had a powerful impact on post–Cold War regime outcomes (see Whitehead 1996). However, it did not affect all countries evenly. International democratizing pressures—in the form of diffusion, diplomatic or military pressure, multilateral conditionality, governmental and nongovernmental democracy assistance programs, or the activities of transnational human rights and democracy networks—were more intense and sustained in some regions (Central Europe, the Americas) than in others (sub-Saharan Africa, East Asia, the former Soviet Union) (see Kopstein and Reilly 2000). This variation can best be understood by conceptualizing the post–Cold War international environment along two dimensions: Western leverage and linkage to the West. Both leverage and linkage raised the cost of authoritarianism during the post–Cold War period, but they did so in different ways and with different implications for democratization.

Western Leverage

Western leverage may be defined as governments' vulnerability to external democratizing pressure. International actors may exert leverage in a variety of ways, including conditionality and punitive sanctions, diplomatic pressure, and military intervention. Where leverage is high, the probability that Western states or multilateral institutions will effectively employ such punitive measures is greatest.

Western leverage varies considerably across states. Leverage is primarily a function of countries' raw size and (military and economic) strength. Weak, aid-dependent states with underdeveloped economies (e.g., much of sub-Saharan Africa) are more vulnerable to external pressure than those countries with substantial military and/or economic power. In larger, more powerful countries such as China, India, and Russia, instruments of external pressure, including diplomatic isolation, trade sanctions, and the threat of military force, are less likely to be employed and, when employed, less likely to be effective. Two additional factors shape the degree of leverage. First, leverage is reduced where there exist important competing issues or goals on Western foreign policy agendas. For example, where Western governments have important economic or security interests at stake, as in much of the Middle East and East Asia, regimes are less vulnerable to external democratizing pressure. In these regions, Western demands for political reform are rare, and when they occur, such demands are less likely to achieve an international consensus or be sustained over time (Crawford 2001: 211–217). Second, a state's vulnerability to Western democratizing pressure may be reduced if it has access to political, economic, and/or military support from an alternative regional power. Russia, for example, has provided critical support to autocrats in Armenia, Belarus, and Ukraine, and China has played a similar role in East Asia. France has at times served as a regional counterhegemon in Africa, lending vital assistance to autocrats in Cameroon, Côte d'Ivoire, Gabon, and other former colonies.[2] In Central Europe and the Americas, by contrast, no alternative regional power exists, leaving the United States and the EU as the players setting "the only game in town."

Leverage raises the cost of repression, electoral fraud, and other government abuses. Where Western powers exert substantial leverage, as in much of sub-Saharan Africa, Central Europe, and Latin America and the Caribbean, international pressure has often played an important role in deterring or ending full-scale authoritarian rule. During the 1990s, for example, pressure by Western governments and multilateral institutions helped thwart or roll back coups in Ecuador, Haiti, Guatemala, and Paraguay, and it was critical in forcing autocrats to hold competitive elections in countries like Cambodia, Kenya, Malawi, Nicaragua, and Zambia.

Although leverage is an important source of antiauthoritarian pressure, it is rarely sufficient to achieve democratization. Even during its heyday in the 1990s, Western democracy promotion was often inconsistent and ineffective (Nelson and Eglinton 1992; Crawford 2001). With the exception of the EU enlargement process, political conditionality was generally too blunt an instrument to achieve full-scale democratization. International actors focused almost exclusively on elections, often neglecting other essential components of democracy such as civil liberties and a level political playing field (see Ottaway 2003). Countries frequently slipped out of the international spotlight once elections had been held—even when they did not bring democracy (e.g., Zambia in 1991, Kenya in 1992, Peru in 1995). Indeed, outside the EU, the consistent monitoring and enforcement necessary to ensure civil liberties and a level playing field was largely absent (Nelson and Eglinton 1992; Stokke 1995). Hence, although military coups, canceled elections, and other blatantly authoritarian acts often triggered strong (and in many cases, effective) international reactions during the post–Cold War period, external pressure routinely failed to deter more subtle abuses, including government manipulation and control of the media, harassment of the opposition, and substantial electoral fraud.

Linkage to the West

Leverage is most effective when combined with linkage to the West. By linkage, we mean the concentration of ties between a country and the EU, the United States, and Western-dominated multilateral organizations. We focus on five dimensions of linkage: (1) economic linkage, which includes flows of trade, investment, credit, and assistance; (2) geopolitical linkage, which includes ties to Western governments and participation in Western-led international organizations; (3) social linkage, which includes migration, refugee and diaspora communities, tourism, and elite education in the West; (4) communication linkage, which includes cross-border telecommunications, Internet connections, and Western media penetration; and (5) transnational civil society linkage, which includes local ties to Western-based nongovernmental organizations (NGOs), religious groups, and party organizations.

Although linkage is rooted in a variety of factors, including histories of colonization and military occupation, geostrategic alliances, and economic development and openness, its primary source remains geography (Kopstein and Reilly 2000). Countries located near the United States or the EU are generally characterized by greater economic interaction; a larger number of intergovernmental connections; and higher cross-border flows of people, information, and organizations than are more geographically distant ones. Thus, with a few notable exceptions (Israel, Taiwan), Central Europe and the Americas are characterized by greater linkage to the West than are Africa, the Middle East, and most of East Asia and the former Soviet Union.

The Effects of Linkage

Linkage raises the cost of authoritarianism in at least four ways: it (1) heightens the salience of government abuse in the West, (2) increases the probability of an international response, (3) creates domestic constituencies with a stake in adhering to democratic norms, and (4) strengthens democratic forces vis-à-vis autocrats.

The International Salience of Government Abuse

First, linkage intensifies the salience of government abuse in Western countries. Where there is extensive penetration by Western media and NGOs, dense communication flows, and widespread elite contact, it is more likely that government abuses will reverberate in Western capitals. Transnational human rights networks, exile and refugee groups, and international party organizations have an amplifying effect, such that even relatively minor violations of democratic procedure (such as harassment of the opposition and media) become "news" in Western capitals. For example, when the Peruvian government stripped Baruch Ivcher of his television station in 1997, Ivcher used his ties in Washington to mount an effective lobbying campaign that resulted in public denunciations by Secretary of State Madeleine Albright, the US House and Senate, and the *Washington Post*. Similarly, due in part to the Slovak opposition's close ties to Western politicians and party networks, the government of Vladimir Meciar was once cited by the EU for violating informal parliamentary norms of committee assignment (Deegan-Krause 2004). By contrast, the international attention given to lower linkage countries such as Belarus, Cambodia, Georgia, Kenya, and Zimbabwe is sporadic and tends to focus only on the most extreme abuses.

The Probability of International Response

Linkage also increases the likelihood that Western governments will take action in response to autocratic abuses. Greater media coverage and lobbying by NGOs, exile and refugee groups, and their Western allies increases the pressure on Western governments to act (Keck and Sikkink 1998). For example, intense lobbying by Haitian refugee organizations, human rights groups, and the Congressional Black Caucus played an important role in convincing the Clinton administration to take action against Haiti's military regime in 1994 (Kumar 2000). In Central Europe, extensive Hungarian lobbying forced the EU to pressure the Romanian and Slovakian governments to eliminate discriminatory policies against Hungarian minorities. By contrast, because US- and European-based constituencies for African human rights and democracy are relatively weak, Western governments felt little domestic pressure to take action against human rights abuses in that region (Moss 1995: 198–199). Western governments also tend to perceive that they have concrete interests at stake in high-linkage cases. Political instability in the Caribbean Basin and Central Europe is far more likely to have consequences—such as refugee flows—that are directly felt in the United States and Europe than is instability in other regions.

Reshaping Domestic Preferences

Linkage also has an important effect on the preferences of domestic actors. It increases the number of individuals, firms, and organizations that, due to financial, professional, or other ties to the West, have a stake in adhering to international norms. Because government abuses could threaten their country's standing within the Western democratic communities, thereby putting valued markets, investment flows, grants, future job prospects, and reputations at risk, these "intermestic" actors have an incentive to oppose— or at least distance themselves from—such abuses. For example, economic integration increases the number of business firms that depend on transnational economic activity and for whom sudden shifts in trade or investment flows caused by regional or international isolation would be costly (Pridham 1991: 220–225). Linkage also increases the number of foreign-educated elites with ties to Western universities, NGOs, and international organizations such as the World Bank and the International Monetary Fund (IMF). These technocrats often enjoy—or aspire to—access to resources and employment opportunities offered by Western institutions, which creates an incentive to avoid reputations as authoritarians or rights violators. Close ties to the West may thus induce key elites either to reform autocratic parties or governments from within, as in Croatia, Mexico, and Taiwan, or to defect to the opposition altogether—as occurred in Slovakia and (to a lesser extent) Romania during the mid-1990s (Vachudova 2004: 162–172). Linkage may even shape voter preferences. Mexican, Croatian, or Slovak citizens who expect integration with the United States or Europe to bring prosperity may be expected to oppose governments whose behavior appears to put that integration at risk.

By heightening domestic actors' sensitivity to shifts in a regime's image abroad, linkage thus blurs international and domestic politics, transforming international norms into domestic demands. This blurring makes it difficult to build and sustain authoritarian coalitions. In countries that can credibly aspire to join Western democratic "clubs," the reluctance of political, economic, and technocratic actors to endorse government actions that could lead to international isolation undermines autocrats' efforts to maintain a stable governing coalition. As one European official put it,

> You can never prevent an adventurer trying to overthrow the government if he is backed by the real economic powers, the banks and the businesses. But once in the [European] community, you create a network of interests for those banks and businesses. . . . As a result, those powers would refuse to back the adventurer for fear of losing all those links.[3]

The difficulty of maintaining authoritarian coalitions in a context of high linkage was clearly seen in Latin America during the 1990s. For example, when Alberto Fujimori's 1992 presidential "self-coup" threatened Peru's reintegration into the international financial system, technocratic and business elites lobbied him to abandon plans for a Pinochet-style dictatorship and call early elections, and when Guatemalan president Jorge Serrano led a similar coup in 1993, the specter of international sanctions triggered such widespread business and military opposition that Serrano was forced to resign.

Reshaping the Domestic Balance of Power

Finally, linkage to the West reshapes the distribution of domestic power in ways that favor democracy. First, ties to influential foreign actors can help to protect opposition groups from repression by enhancing their international prestige (Keck and Sikkink 1998). In Mexico, for example, international media coverage and pressure by a vast array of transnational human rights and indigenous rights groups helped protect the Zapatista movement from military repression during the mid-1990s (Dresser 1996). Second, ties to Western governments, parties, and transnational organizations may be an important source of financial and organizational support for opposition movements (Pridham 1999). In 2000, for example, the Serbian opposition benefited from massive US and European assistance, which was used to finance opposition party activity, independent media, election monitoring, and an enormous get-out-the-vote campaign—all of which helped to level the playing field vis-à-vis Slobodan Milosevic (Carothers 2001). Similarly, in Slovakia, support from EU and European party networks helped a weak and fragmented opposition defeat Vladimir Meciar in 1998 (Pridham 1999: 1229–1230), and in Nicaragua, US funding of opposition parties and civic and media organizations sufficiently narrowed the power asymmetries between the governing Sandinistas and the National Opposition Union (UNO) to permit the latter's victory.

Third, ties to the West may enhance public support for democratic actors. Powerful friends in the West may enhance opposition leaders' public support by linking them with valued Western ideals or, more concretely, convincing voters and economic elites that they are best able to secure a position for their country within Western democratic "clubs." For example, in Nicaragua, where the Sandinista government suffered a costly US-sponsored war and trade embargo, UNO's credible promise of better relations with the United States was a major source of electoral support. Opposition forces in Croatia and Slovakia benefited in a similar way from ties to the West. At the same time, autocrats' pariah status vis-à-vis Western governments often has a significant cost in terms of domestic public support.

Unlike most mechanisms of leverage, the effects of linkage are diffuse and often difficult to detect. Yet they are frequently more pervasive, and more persistent than those generated via leverage alone. Where linkage is extensive, it creates multiple pressure points—from investors to technocrats to voters—that even powerful autocrats cannot afford to ignore.

Leverage, Linkage, and the Fate of Competitive Authoritarian Regimes

Cross-national variation in leverage and linkage is critical to explaining the diverging fates of post–Cold War competitive authoritarian regimes. Competitive authoritarian regimes are characterized by the coexistence of meaningful democratic institutions and autocratic governments. This combination is a potential source of instability. Due to the existence of formally empowered legislatures and courts, independent media outlets, and meaningful (if flawed) elections, opposition forces may periodically pose serious challenges to autocratic incumbents. These challenges present incumbents with a difficult dilemma. On the one hand, overt repression—canceling elections, jailing opponents, ignoring Supreme Court rulings, or closing the legislature—is costly, because the challenges are formally legal and internationally legitimate. On the other hand, if opposition challenges are allowed to run their course, incumbents risk losing power. Hence, incumbents in competitive authoritarian regimes must periodically choose between allowing serious opposition challenges to proceed, at the cost of possible defeat, and egregiously violating democratic rules, at the cost of international condemnation and even isolation.

Government responses to these crises—and consequently, regime outcomes—during the post–Cold War period were heavily influenced by countries' relationship to the West. Where linkage was extensive, the cost of repression, large-scale fraud, and other serious violations of democratic procedure was often prohibitive, which limited governments' capacity to sustain or consolidate competitive authoritarian rule. That was the case even in countries—such as Mexico and Taiwan—where Western leverage was limited. Where linkage and leverage were low, the international environment was more permissive, and domestic political dynamics predominated. Autocratic governments could crack down on opposition challenges—via repression and/or fraud—without paying a heavy international cost, which enhanced the prospects for regime survival. Where linkage was low and leverage was high, the cost of large-scale abuse was often high, but external incentives to play by fully democratic rules were weaker. Hence, in the absence of strong domestic pressure, stable democratization was unlikely.

High Linkage and Democratization: Central Europe and the Americas

In countries with extensive linkage to the West, competitive authoritarian regimes were exposed to intense international democratizing pressure during the post–Cold War period. Where linkage was combined with high Western leverage, intensive scrutiny from the media, NGOs, and international organizations drew widespread attention to even relatively minor government abuses, which triggered—or threatened to trigger—costly punitive action by Western powers. The international "boomerang effect" (Keck and Sikkink 1998) caused by these abuses was frequently magnified by pressure from intermestic actors with an interest in preserving their country's standing in the international community. Although autocrats who enjoyed strong public support and/or faced weak oppositions could temporarily maintain themselves in power without resorting to large-scale abuse (e.g., Fujimori in Peru, Meciar in Slovakia), opposition ties to the West quickly narrowed those power asymmetries, and the cost of cracking down on serious opposition challenges eventually induced these governments to cede power. Because opposition forces almost always maintained close ties to the West, successor governments consistently adhered to democratic norms.

Central Europe and much of the Americas fall into the high-linkage/high-leverage category. Countries in both regions confront significant military and economic power asymmetries vis-à-vis EU members and the United States. In most countries, leverage is enhanced by the absence of either an alternative regional power or competing foreign policy issues that trump democracy promotion. At the same time, both Central Europe and the Americas are closely linked to the West via economic integration; extensive cross-border communication; large-scale flows of tourists, students, and immigrants; and substantial Western media and NGO penetration.

Central Europe is marked by the distinctive role of the EU. The EU enlargement process enhanced both linkage and leverage. EU membership entails a high level of integration and policy coordination, including regulations encompassing virtually every aspect of domestic governance. EU political conditionality differs from that of other multilateral organizations in several ways (see Kelley 2004: 459). First, it is not limited to elections but includes respect for human rights, free expression, and the rule of law. Second, European demands are reinforced by extensive monitoring, as the EU and related organizations rigorously observe electoral processes; scrutinize constitutions; and meet regularly with party leaders, parliamentarians, and bureaucrats. Simultaneously, the "big prize" associated with EU membership creates a strong incentive for compliance. Indeed, governments or parties that are viewed as an obstacle to integration often suffer political isolation and an erosion of public support.

Central Europe's competitive authoritarian regimes exhibited a clear democratizing pattern after 1990—despite the fact that the region had little previous experience with democracy. By 2000, Bulgaria, Croatia, Serbia, Slovakia, and—more ambiguously—Romania had undergone democratic transitions. In Croatia, public frustration with the country's isolation from Europe contributed to the 2000 victory of the democratic opposition following the death of Franjo Tudjman. Although Tudjman's party regained power in 2003, democratic reformers—with an eye on EU accession—had by then seized control of the party. In Serbia, massive Western assistance to opposition and media organizations prior to the 2000 election helped democratic forces defeat autocrat Slobodan Milosevic at the ballot box and thwart his efforts to steal the election. In Slovakia, Vladimir Meciar's autocratic behavior triggered the EU's rejection of the country's application to begin accession negotiations, which hurt his public image and isolated the governing party from potential coalition partners. Buttressed by EU and European party support, opposition forces united to defeat Meciar and remove him from power in 1998. Finally, Romania is "perhaps the most spectacular case of the EU's active leverage in helping to create a more competitive . . . political system" (Vachudova 2004: 165). Intensive EU engagement heavily constrained the less-than-democratic Iliescu government during the early 1990s and made possible Iliescu's defeat in a relatively clean election in 1996.[4] Until recently, Albania was an exception to the regional democratizing pattern. It remained unstably competitive authoritarian through 2004. Yet even in Albania, a country whose low level of development and weak state would pose serious obstacles to democratization in any context, abusive governments consistently failed to consolidate power, and in July 2005 the country finally experienced minimally acceptable democratic elections.

Mechanisms of leverage and linkage in the Americas are less institutionalized. Multilateral institutions such as the Organization of American States (OAS) and the emerging Free Trade Agreement of the Americas lack the EU's encompassing ties and monitoring and sanctioning capacity. Nevertheless, economic, social, communication, and technocratic linkage are extensive, particularly in Central America and the Caribbean. Both linkage and leverage were enhanced by the 1980s debt crisis and the economic reforms of the 1990s. US-educated technocrats—most of whom maintain close ties to North American academic and policy circles—now hold top government positions throughout Latin America. Technocratic ties are reinforced by a dense web of transnational civil society networks, particularly in the areas of human rights and democracy promotion.

Competitive authoritarian regimes in Latin America and the Caribbean also democratized during the post–Cold War period. In Guyana and Nicaragua, autocratic governments lost internationally scrutinized elections and peacefully yielded power. In the Dominican Republic, longtime autocrat

Joaquín Balaguer attempted to steal heavily monitored elections in 1994, but in the face of intense international criticism and diplomatic threats from the United States, Balaguer agreed to OAS-mediated negotiations that produced his early resignation and new democratic elections in 1996. In Peru, although Alberto Fujimori's popularity and a weak opposition allowed competitive authoritarianism to endure for nearly a decade, the country's increasing isolation in the aftermath of Fujimori's flawed 2000 reelection (denounced as unfair by OAS observers) eroded elite support for the regime and helped trigger its collapse in late 2000. The only competitive authoritarian regime in the region that did not democratize was Haiti, a country that, like Albania, possesses highly unfavorable conditions for democracy. Even there, however, autocrats failed to consolidate power after 1990. The competitive authoritarian government of Jean-Bertrand Aristide, largely cut off from US assistance after 2000, collapsed in 2004.

Finally, Mexico's democratization merits special attention because it occurred without substantial Western leverage. US-Mexican relations are characterized by extensive linkage, which broadened and deepened with the North American Free Trade Agreement (NAFTA). However, US leverage was limited by the existence of numerous competing foreign policy priorities (including economic relations, drugs, immigration, and security). Even during NAFTA negotiations, US governments refused to impose political conditionality. Nevertheless, NAFTA exposed the Mexican government to intense international scrutiny and vastly increased the number of domestic actors with a stake in their country's international standing. In this context, the governing Institutional Revolutionary Party (PRI)—which was led by US-educated technocrats who were highly sensitive to international opinion—undertook a series of electoral reforms and abstained from many of the authoritarian practices upon which its hegemonic rule had been based. Although this self-restraint may have enhanced the PRI's image internationally, it left the party increasingly vulnerable to electoral challenges. In 2000, opposition candidate Vicente Fox won the presidency in a heavily scrutinized election, and the PRI leadership—unwilling to pay the cost of a crackdown—ceded power peacefully. Although Mexico's democratization was in many respects a product of domestic factors, the incentives and constraints created by extensive linkage—even in the absence of direct external pressure for democratization—were critical to keeping PRI elites on the path of reform.

Low Linkage and International Permissiveness

Countries in regions with less extensive ties to the West faced weaker international democratizing pressures during the post–Cold War period. As a result, domestic factors played a more pronounced role in shaping regime outcomes. Where low linkage was combined with high Western leverage, international pressure often worked to undermine full-scale autocracy, but in the absence of a strong domestic push, it was usually insufficient to induce full democratization. Where both linkage and leverage were low, the international environment was far more permissive, which enhanced the prospects for authoritarian stability.

Leverage without linkage: Intermittent and limited international pressure. Where Western leverage was high but linkage was low, the post–Cold War international environment weakened authoritarianism but contributed less decisively to democratization. On the one hand, political conditionality made full-scale autocracy far more difficult to sustain than in earlier periods. In weak, aid-dependent states, governments that failed to meet minimal international standards with respect to elections and human rights often suffered debilitating losses of external assistance. Yet the international community's near-exclusive focus on elections and inability to monitor and enforce civil liberties and a level playing field permitted many autocrats to remain in power via competitive authoritarianism. Even when autocrats fell, turnover frequently did not lead to democracy. Lacking close ties to the West or powerful external incentives to play by fully democratic rules, successor governments often ruled in an autocratic manner. Hence, the combination of high leverage and low linkage facilitated the emergence and persistence of competitive authoritarian regimes.

Much of sub-Saharan Africa falls into the high-leverage/low-linkage category. Africa is easily the poorest and most aid-dependent region in the world, and most of the region's governments are highly vulnerable to external pressure.[5] At the same time, linkage to the West is very low. Low literacy and the paucity of televisions, telephones, fax machines, and Internet hookups means that flows of ideas and information from the West reach only a narrow elite (Ott and Rosser 2000: 143–144). In addition, geographic distance, weak economic integration, low media penetration, and a relative dearth of international NGOs means that political developments in the region have little salience in Western capitals. US academic and media coverage of the region is minimal, and NGOs and other groups devoted to African issues are "small and non-influential" and "rarely have the power to significantly alter U.S. Africa policy" (Schraeder 1994: 4–5, 44–45).

The end of the Cold War triggered far-reaching regime transformations in sub-Saharan Africa, as a steep decline in external support and the unprecedented use of political conditionality triggered the widespread collapse of established autocracies. Throughout the region, autocrats either allowed multiparty electoral competition or fell from power—or both (Bratton and van de Walle 1997). Yet multiparty elections rarely led to full democracy. In the absence of rigorous international monitoring and enforcement, many autocrats "learned that they did not have to democratize" to maintain their international standing (Joseph 1999: 61). Thus, in Cameroon, Ethiopia, Gabon, Mozambique, Tanzania, Togo, Zimbabwe, and—until 2002—Kenya, autocrats remained in power via competitive authoritarianism. In other countries, such as Madagascar, Malawi, and Zambia, autocratic incumbents fell, but successor governments were less than democratic. Zambia's 1991 election, in which autocrat Kenneth Kaunda was defeated by Frederick Chiluba, gained widespread international attention and led analysts to describe the country as a "model for democratic change" (Joseph 1992). Yet Zambia never democratized. The Chiluba government declared a state of emergency, assaulted the independent media, and banned Kaunda—Chiluba's leading opponent—from the 1996 election. The international community failed to respond vigorously or consistently to these abuses, and competitive authoritarianism persisted through early 2006.

Parts of the former Soviet Union—most notably Georgia and Moldova—can also be categorized as low linkage and high leverage. Like their African counterparts, both these countries are poor and aid-dependent, leaving governments vulnerable to external pressure.[6] At the same time, both countries are weakly integrated into the global economy and have only limited ties to the EU. Since 1990, Georgia and Moldova have been governed by unstable competitive authoritarian regimes. In each country, autocratic governments fell from power twice between 1990 and 2004, but neither country democratized. In Georgia, where international intervention was forceful but sporadic, Western pressure helped convince President Eduard Shevardnadze to resign amid mass protest following flawed parliamentary elections in 2003. In the aftermath of these events, however, reduced international attention allowed new president Mikheil Saakashvili to harass antigovernmental media and manipulate the March 2004 parliamentary elections (in which no opposition parties won seats) (see OSCE/ODIHR 2004; Peuch 2004). Thus, the regime remains competitive authoritarian.

Low linkage and leverage: Weak international pressure and the predominance of domestic factors. Where both linkage and leverage were low, autocratic governments were exposed to relatively little external democratizing pressure. In the absence of extensive linkage, even serious abuses frequently often did not reverberate in the West, and in the absence of leverage, these abuses often failed to trigger punitive responses from Western governments. When international sanctions were imposed, governments were less vulnerable to them. At the same time, because major political, economic, and technocratic actors held a weaker stake in maintaining ties to the West, they had less to lose from association with an autocratic government. In this more permissive international environment, autocrats enjoyed greater room for maneuver in cracking down on opposition challenges. Governments could manipulate electoral results, arrest major opposition leaders, and virtually eliminate the independent media without paying a heavy international cost. As a result, democratization was less likely.

Low-leverage/low-linkage countries are found in much of the Middle East and parts of the former Soviet Union and East Asia. Stable nondemocracies are most likely to be found in these countries. During the 1990s, competitive authoritarian regimes existed in low-leverage/low-linkage countries such as Malaysia, Belarus, Russia, and—albeit with somewhat higher levels of Western leverage—Armenia, Cambodia, and Ukraine. Neither Armenia nor Cambodia had democratized by early 2006. Ukraine, since the "orange revolution" of 2004, remains a fluid, ambiguous case. In Malaysia, Prime Minister Mahathir Mohamad was able to jail his leading challenger, Anwar Ibrahim, in 1998 and crack down on the reform movement. Anwar's arrest transpired without incurring large-scale external costs. Notwithstanding US and IMF support for Anwar and the *reformasi* movement, the international community never seriously threatened Mahathir's grip on power (Singh 2000). Russia's size, geostrategic importance, and large oil and gas reserves, as well as its limited economic integration and elite exposure to the West, left Presidents Boris Yeltsin and Vladimir Putin largely unfettered as they cracked down on opposition challenges. Serious abuses, including the bombing of the legislature in 1993, the flawed 1996 presidential election, massive human rights violations in Chechnya, and more recently, Putin's systematic destruction of the independent media and virtual elimination of viable opposition forces, elicited few serious responses from the West. Finally, although Belarus lacks Russia's military and economic strength, its close ties to Russia helped insulate the autocratic government of Alyaksandr Lukashenka from Western democratizing pressure. Russia provided key political backing to Lukashenka when he shut down parliament in 1996, and although the regime's increasingly closed nature resulted in increasing estrangement from the Western democratic community, Russian energy subsidies and other assistance—valued at about 20 percent of Belarus's gross domestic product (GDP) (Aslund 2002: 182)—cushioned the impact of this isolation.

A similar pattern can be observed in sub-Saharan African cases in which support from an alternative regional power (usually France) limited Western leverage. In Cameroon, Gabon, Zimbabwe, and Côte d'Ivoire until autocrat Félix Houphouet-Boigny's death in 1993, diplomatic, financial, and other assistance from France (or in the Zimbabwean case, South Africa) helped autocratic governments survive opposition challenges after 1990. Although Western leverage remained relatively high in these countries, this alternative assistance blunted the impact of external pressure and thus enhanced the stability of nondemocratic regimes.

Comparing Regions

A comparison of post–Cold War competitive authoritarian regime trajectories thus reveals a striking pattern of regional variation. We classified thirty-eight regimes as having been or become competitive authoritarian between 1990 and 1995: thirteen in the high-linkage regions of Central Europe (seven) and the Americas (six) and twenty-five in the lower linkage regions of East Asia (three), sub-Saharan Africa (sixteen), and the former Soviet Union (six). Table 12.1 shows how these regimes evolved through mid-2005, classifying them as cases of democratization (free elections, broad protection of civil liberties, and a reasonably level political playing field); turnover without democratization (autocrats lose power, but successor governments remain nondemocratic); and authoritarian stability (autocratic governments or their chosen successors remain in power through 2005).[7]

In the high-linkage regions, Latin America, the Caribbean, and Central Europe, democratization was widespread. Ten of thirteen competitive authoritarian regimes had unambiguously democratized by 2005, and two others—Albania and Macedonia—were nearly democratic. The only clear

Table 12.1   Competitive Authoritarian Regime Outcomes in Five Regions, 1990–2005

	Number of Cases	Democratic Transition	Turnover Without Democracy	Stable Nondemocratic Regime	Ambiguous
High-linkage regions	*13*	*10*	*3*	*0*	*0*
Latin America and Caribbean[a]	6	5	1	0	0
Central Europe[b]	7	5	2	0	0
Medium/Low-linkage regions	*25*	*5*	*9*	*10*	*1*
East Asia[c]	3	1	0	2	0
Africa[d]	16	4	5	7	0
Former Soviet Union[e]	6	0	4	1	1
Total	*38*	*15*	*12*	*10*	*1*

Notes: a. Dominican Republic, Guyana, Haiti, Mexico, Nicaragua, Peru.
   b. Albania, Bulgaria, Croatia, Macedonia, Romania, Serbia, Slovakia.
   c. Cambodia, Malaysia, Taiwan.
   d. Benin, Cameroon, Côte d'Ivoire, Ethiopia, Gabon, Ghana, Kenya, Madagascar, Malawi, Mali, Mozambique, Senegal, Tanzania, Togo, Zambia, Zimbabwe.
   e. Armenia, Belarus, Georgia, Moldova, Russia, Ukraine.

case of nondemocratization, Haiti, lacked even minimal conditions favorable to democracy. Equally impressive is the failure of authoritarianism in the two regions. In not a single country did a competitive authoritarian government or chosen successor survive through 2005. Thus, even in countries that failed to democratize, nondemocratic governments were unable to sustain themselves in power.

In regions characterized by medium to low levels of linkage, the pattern is strikingly different. Of the twenty-five competitive authoritarian regimes that existed in East Asia, sub-Saharan Africa, and the former Soviet Union between 1990 and 1995, only five democratized (Benin, Ghana, Mali, Senegal, and Taiwan)—and Taiwan is a case of exceptionally high linkage to the United States. At the same time, the prospects for competitive authoritarian stability were somewhat greater in lower linkage regions. Although competitive authoritarian governments or their chosen successors failed to survive in a single Central European, Latin American, or Caribbean case, ten of twenty-five survived in East Asia, Africa, and the former Soviet Union.

Conclusion

Since 1989, Western powers have played a distinctly positive role in promoting democracy throughout much of the world. Nevertheless, the precise mechanisms of Western influence remain poorly understood. Although analysts and policymakers tend to focus on mechanisms of leverage such as conditionality and diplomatic pressure, we argued in this chapter that leverage has rarely been sufficient to induce democratic change. Instead, the democratization of post–Cold War competitive authoritarian regimes has been most frequent in countries with extensive economic, social, political, communication, and civil society linkages to the West. Linkage involves the use of soft power. Its effects are diffuse and often operate below the radar screens of international observers. Yet linkage can be crucial to democratization. Where extensive, linkage raises the cost of autocratic behavior by heightening the salience of government abuses, increasing the odds of an international response, and creating powerful intermestic constituencies for democratic change. By blurring the distinction between the international and the domestic and converting international norms into domestic demands, linkage generates democratizing pressure that is often more systematic—and effective—than the punitive measures taken by Western powers.

Linkage is critical to understanding cross-national variation in the intensity and effectiveness of international democratizing pressure. That suggests that debates over the relative importance of domestic versus international variables in explaining regime change have been somewhat miscast. The weight of the international environment varies considerably across cases and regions. Where linkage is extensive, international influences may be decisive, contributing to democratization even in countries with highly unfavorable domestic conditions (Albania, Nicaragua, Romania). Where linkage is lower, international influences are weaker, and regime outcomes are more likely to be a product of domestic factors.

A few policy implications are worth noting. First, although the use of leverage may be effective in deterring the worst authoritarian abuses, it is more likely to contribute to sustainable democracy in high-linkage cases (Dominican Republic, Panama, Slovakia) than in low-linkage cases (Cambodia, Georgia, Malawi). Second, linkage is primarily a structural variable. Mostly a product of geography, historical factors such as colonialism and geostrategic alliances, and long-term processes of social and economic integration, it is far less malleable—and hence, less amenable to short-term foreign policy goals—than are individual leaders or constitutional frameworks. Yet as the experience of EU enlargement in southern and Central Europe (and to a lesser extent, NAFTA) demonstrate, sustained policies of integration can broaden and deepen linkage over time—with impressive results in terms of stable democratization. An implication is that over the medium-to-long haul, Western policies of broad-based engagement are more likely to have a democratizing impact than those of isolation and sanctions (e.g., US policy toward Cuba and Iran).

Finally, it is worth reiterating that the dynamics discussed in this chapter are a product of a particular world historical moment: the Western liberal hegemony that followed the end of the Cold War. During the 1930s and during the Cold War period, powerful military and ideological rivals both provided support to autocratic governments and induced Western democracies to prioritize security issues over democratization in much of the world. During the 1990s, like the interwar period in Europe, the absence of a serious threat to the liberal West created an international environment that was highly favorable to democratization. Whether the resurgence of security issues triggered by the 2001 terrorist attacks in the United States will eventually alter this environment remains to be seen.

Notes

1. See the articles on "Elections Without Democracy" in the April 2002 issue of the *Journal of Democracy*.

2. Another example is South Africa, which provided critical assistance to the Mugabe government in Zimbabwe.

3. Quoted in Pridham (1991: 220).

4. Although there were some government abuses (particularly against the media) after Iliescu's return to the presidency in 2000, the extent of democratization in

Romania—a country that had never experienced the democratic removal of a head of state before 1996—is remarkable.

5. African countries' average per capita GDP is barely one-sixth that of Latin America. And whereas foreign aid constitutes less than 1 percent of GDP in Latin America, in much of Africa it is greater than 10 percent.

6. According to the World Bank's World Development Indicators, foreign aid accounted for 33 percent of central government expenditures in Moldova and 75 percent in Georgia in 2002.

7. We classify one case, Ukraine in 2005, as ambiguous, because its transition was too recent to determine the character of the regime.

Part 5

Conclusion

13

Beyond Electoral Authoritarianism: The Spectrum of Nondemocratic Regimes

Richard Snyder

It is increasingly evident that the Third Wave of democracy had a strong undemocratic undertow. Despite the fact that an unprecedented number of countries experienced transitions to democracy since the mid-1970s, a wide range of nondemocratic regimes persisted across the globe. For example, entrenched totalitarian or post-totalitarian regimes kept a firm grip on power in North Korea, Cuba, China, Laos, and Vietnam. Long-standing monarchies endured in Saudi Arabia, Morocco, and Jordan.[1] Personalistic dictators survived in Libya, Zimbabwe, and Togo. And theocracies, ethnocracies, and military regimes remained in power in Iran, Syria, and Burma. Moreover, many countries experienced processes of political regime change that did not result in democracy. Regime change led to state collapse and protracted civil wars in Liberia, Cambodia, Somalia, Afghanistan, and Zaire. In other instances, including many of the countries analyzed by the contributors to this volume, regime change resulted in the emergence of new nondemocratic regimes. The growing realization that the "victory of democracy" celebrated during the euphoria at the end of the Cold War was far from complete has led scholars increasingly to switch their focus from democratic transitions to the nondemocratic regimes of the contemporary era.

This switch requires that we tackle a key conceptual challenge: how to get beyond studying politics through the prism of democracy. The contributors to this book take a significant step in this direction because they break with what Thomas Carothers (2002) calls the "transition paradigm."[2] From this perspective, which dominated the comparative study of regimes during the 1980s and 1990s, the many countries across the world in the "gray zone" between liberal democracy and full-blown authoritarianism were seen as qualified democracies in the process of moving toward full democracy. By contrast, the contributors regard these gray-zone countries as neither democratic nor in transition toward democracy. Instead of seeing such regimes as democracies "with adjectives" and calling them, for example, "illiberal democracies" (Zakaria 1997) or "semi-democracies" (Case 1996), the contributors to the present volume understand them as authoritarianisms with adjectives, calling them electoral authoritarian regimes.[3] This change in labels marks an important gestalt shift away from the transition paradigm.

Despite this gestalt shift, students of world politics still face a series of key unresolved challenges in their quest to understand the variety of nondemocratic regimes. In this chapter, I argue that the burgeoning literature on contemporary nondemocratic regimes, much like the literature on democratic regimes, places an overwhelming emphasis on the electoral process and thus overlooks other fundamental dimensions that are critical for analyzing regimes. This focus on elections results in two important shortcomings. First, it leads to a neglect of how the political consequences of elections depend on their interaction with key extra-electoral factors. To get beyond this limitation, I highlight four extra-electoral dimensions deployed in a long tradition of comparative research on political regimes: (1) Who rules? Party elites, a personal leader, the military, or the clergy? (2) How do rulers rule? By means of patron-client networks, ethnic ties, or a mass-based party?[4] (3) Why do rulers rule? Out of greed, ethnic hatred, or a commitment to a religion or ideology? and (4) How much do rulers rule? That is, does anybody really rule and, if so, to what degree?[5] Second, the heavy emphasis on electoral competition in research on nondemocratic regimes leads to a severe underappreciation of the wide range of regimes in the world today that lack even the trappings of democracy. Understanding the full spectrum of nondemocratic regimes requires a broader conceptual framework, one that gets beyond the limited focus on electoral politics and competition seen in much recent work.

Setting Elections in Context:
Who Rules, How, and Why?

The fortunes of nondemocratic regimes that hold elections are shaped in crucial ways by variation in the type of rulers (e.g., military, personal leader, or a political party); whether the rulers govern mainly through patronage networks, ethnic ties, or mass parties; and the motives that drive rulers in their quest for power (e.g., greed, religion, ideology). Understanding how such regimes work and evolve thus requires that we explore the interactions among electoral processes and other dimensions of nondemocratic rule. A brief comparison of electoral processes in military and personalistic regimes illustrates this point.

A fundamental fact distinguishes elections in most military regimes from elections in other types of nondemocratic regimes: the incumbents have guns, whereas the opposition does not.[6] Because they directly control the means of coercion, rulers in military regimes may have a stronger capacity than rulers in other types of regimes to reverse processes of change set in motion by elections.[7] Indeed, military rulers can even lose competitive elections yet still keep office, as occurred in Burma in 1990 and Algeria in 1992.[8] In these cases, competitive elections and incumbent defeat at the polls resulted not in democratization but in the reequilibration of the nondemocratic regime.[9] Understanding this outcome requires that we focus on who rules: because a cohesive military organization governed in both Burma and Algeria, incumbents were able to survive defeat at the polls and keep their grip on power.

In contrast to military regimes, the ruler in personalistic regimes does not always directly control the means of coercion: depending on how far the ruler's patronage network penetrates the armed forces, the military apparatus may be able to act autonomously from the ruler (see Snyder 1992 and 1998). In cases such as Haiti and the Philippines in 1986, the military played a central role in toppling personalistic dictators in the context of a wider societal crisis. The case of the Philippines is especially interesting, because the crisis that led factions of the military to turn against Ferdinand Marcos was precipitated by the dictator's decision to hold "snap elections."[10]

Yet a focus on elections by itself is insufficient to explain why autonomous groups turn against a ruler: electoral competition may galvanize defections by disgruntled elites, but it does not explain why a pool of disaffected actors emerges in the first place. Addressing this question requires a focus on the prior issue of how personalistic regimes rule—that is, via patron-client networks. As a result, personalistic rulers usually fill the top leadership posts in the armed forces and other government agencies with their cronies, relatives, and clients. This practice can form a "crony glass ceiling" that alienates career officers, cadres, and bureaucrats, thus potentially generating a large pool of disgruntled elites prone to turn against the regime in a crisis. For example, in the Philippines, approximately 10 percent of military officers were members of the Reform the Armed Forces Now Movement (RAM), which had been organized by officers disturbed by the influx of Marcos's patronage appointees (Buss 1987; Bonner 1988: 372). In the context of widespread public outrage over Marcos's use of violence and fraud during the "snap elections" of February 1986, a group of some 300 officers from the RAM launched a military coup against the dictator. Although the coup failed, it emboldened tens of thousands of civilians, mobilized by the Catholic Church, who formed a human buffer to protect the mutinous officers. This outpouring of "people power" led to a wave of military defections and to Marcos's departure from the country three days later (Bonner 1988).

As seen in the overthrow of Marcos in the Philippines, electoral competition may galvanize disgruntled members of the regime who defect from the ruler, but it does not explain why a group of disgruntled elites forms in the first place. Understanding the prior question of why splits emerge in some personalistic regimes in the face of elections thus requires that we look beyond elections, which may merely be the proximate trigger for such splits, by considering whether the infrastructure of political power, that is, patron-client networks, generates a pool of frustrated actors, like the RAM in the Philippines, ready to turn against the ruler in a crisis.

Moreover, a focus on why rulers rule (that is, on the purpose of power) can also help explain the contrasting consequences of crises in nondemocratic regimes, whether or not these crises are linked to elections.[11] Personalistic rulers rarely rule in the name of religion or ideology. Instead, they are more often motivated by greed (Chehabi and Linz 1998a). Hence, their willingness to relinquish power in the face of a crisis may be greater than that of theocratic or totalitarian rulers, who rule in the name of a "cause" for which they may even be willing to die. By contrast, if their Swiss bank accounts are large enough, personalistic rulers may be willing to relinquish power if guaranteed a safe haven abroad. Jean-Claude Duvalier, who left Haiti for a peaceful life in France; Alfredo Stroessner, who fled Paraguay for Brazil; Mobutu Sese Seko, who left Zaire for Morocco; and, more recently, Charles Taylor, who fled Liberia for Nigeria, illustrate this possibility. Still, new international norms of holding former dictators accountable through the International Criminal Court may make variation in why rulers rule less relevant for predicting which rulers cede control peacefully. As the possibility of a comfortable life in exile as a "retired dictator" diminishes, even rulers motivated by greed, instead of a utopian vision of societal transformation, may refuse to leave office except by force.

Elections and Stateness: How Much Do Rulers Rule?

In addition to setting elections in the context of the means of nondemocratic rule and the motives of nondemocratic rulers, students of contemporary nondemocratic regimes should focus more attention on how elections interact with a further extra-electoral dimension: the degree of rule, or stateness. Elections in nondemocratic contexts can have sharply contrasting effects on stateness, subverting state capacity in some instances and strengthening it in others. In turn, electoral processes themselves are influenced in crucial ways by how much the rulers rule.

State-Subverting Elections

Although elections in some nondemocratic regimes may be mere window dressing, in other instances they have important consequences for the stability of the incumbent regime. Hence, as Andreas Schedler (2002b: 49) puts it, elections may be "regime-sustaining," or "regime-subverting."[12] Yet the power of elections in nondemocratic regimes may be even greater than students of electoral authoritarianism have generally acknowledged: in addition to affecting the stability of regimes, elections can also influence the stability of states. For example, in the Soviet Union, Yugoslavia, and Haiti, elections contributed to state collapse and hence can be considered state-subverting. By contrast, in Spain, elections played an important role in holding together the state.[13] Such cases further highlight why it is important not to analyze elections and other democratic trappings of nondemocratic regimes in isolation from the broader political and societal context. In particular, we need to explore how the degree of rule affects elections and, in turn, how elections affect the degree of rule.

Events in Haiti highlight how electoral competition can contribute to state collapse. In Haiti, an impasse stemming from fraudulent legislative and boycotted presidential elections was a major cause of state breakdown. After his fraudulent victory in legislative elections in 2000 and his subsequent reelection to a five-year term as president, Jean-Bertrand Aristide focused his efforts on repressing the only internationally legitimate opposition group: the "electoral opposition" comprised of moderate elites who were willing to play by the rules of the electoral game but had boycotted Aristide's reelection. Aristide's strategy of repressing moderate elites ironically helped strengthen the hand of armed rebels who would eventually take control of much of the country. Moreover, Aristide's dismantling of the army in 1995 and his "patrimonialization" of the police (for example, by installing cronies as police chiefs to make the police force loyal to his person) helped further strengthen the hand of the armed opposition, which was led by former members of the disbanded Haitian Army and by paramilitary forces, such as the "Cannibal Army" of Gonaives, that had previously been loyal to Aristide. These armed groups took advantage of (1) the Haitian state's weak coercive apparatus (i.e., no army and a small, poorly equipped police force); (2) its inability to control the 200-mile-long border with the Dominican Republic, where many of the rebels took refuge and organized; and (3) the weakness of the moderate opposition, which resulted in part from Aristide's repressive measures against them. Combined with state weakness, the stalemate between the regime and moderate, nonarmed opposition groups resulting from the electoral boycott of 2000 helped trigger Haiti's collapse into civil war and chaos in 2004. Elections held by a nondemocratic regime thus proved state-subverting.

Elections Without States?

When elections are held in the context of collapsed states and civil war, as occurred in Liberia in 1997 and Sierra Leone in 1996, they do not confer power because there is no usable state apparatus that becomes available to the winners of elections.[14] Rather, elections serve at best to ratify the balance of power over territory, people, and resources created by war. Hence, the winners of "elections without states" must supply their own infrastructure of power—soldiers, administrative personnel, and so forth—in order to govern.

In collapsed states, phenomena routinely associated with elections, such as parties, pluralism, and competition, acquire bizarre meanings. The parties who compete in elections are armed groups led by warlords; pluralism refers to the number and variety of armed groups in the territory; and competition is waged by bullets, not ballots. A focus on elections in such cases ignores the far more fundamental matter of competition among armed groups for control over territory and resources. Yet the holding of elections has curiously led some observers to classify cases of civil war and collapsed states, like Liberia and Angola, as "hegemonic electoral authoritarian" regimes (see, for example, Diamond 2002: 30–31). Moreover, because international observers may certify elections in collapsed states as relatively clean and fair, such cases may even earn a semirespectable, "partly free" rating from Freedom House, as seen in Sierra Leone's score in 2001 of 4 on the political rights index and 5 on the civil liberties index.[15] Yet classifying such cases as electoral authoritarian regimes makes little sense: in the absence of a state, there is no regime, and that holds true whether or not there are competitive, internationally certified elections. Instead of classifying such cases based on their democratic trappings, we should focus instead on their low degree of rule, that is, on the prior, more fundamental issue of state(less)ness.

Inside the Black Box of "Closed Regimes"

A focus on extra-electoral factors is necessary not only to understand the dynamics of regimes that hold elections but also to describe and hence classify the full spectrum of contemporary nondemocratic regimes. Recent efforts to conceptualize regimes that occupy what Schedler (2002b: 37) calls the "foggy zone" between liberal democracy and closed authoritarianism take a useful step toward understanding the variety of regimes in the post–Cold War world. Yet the emphasis on hybrid regimes that hold elections has led to an unfortunate neglect of the wide range of cases that lack democratic features or trappings. Although the agenda of research on the foggy zone is valuable, we should not overlook the dark zone inhabited by so-called closed regimes with no democratic aspects.

The neglect of the dark zone has resulted in the shoehorning of cases as distinct as China, Somalia, and Saudi Arabia into the catch-all category "closed regimes."[16] This category suffers from serious limitations. First, the category of closed authoritarianism lumps together a wide variety of quite distinct cases, including totalitarian and post-totalitarian systems like China, Vietnam, Cuba, North Korea, and Laos; theocracies like Iran and Afghanistan under the Taliban; sultanates like Brunei; nontraditional personalistic regimes like Turkmenistan and Libya; traditional monarchies like Swaziland, Qatar, and Saudi Arabia; military regimes like Burma; and ethnocracies like Syria and Burundi.

The category closed authoritarianism also collapses the important distinction between totalitarian and authoritarian regimes, thereby creating an unnecessary and counterproductive disjuncture with prior research on nondemocratic systems.[17] The category closed authoritarianism lumps regimes that are mass-mobilizing and ideologically based, such as North Korea, Vietnam, Cuba, China, and perhaps Iraq until the US invasion of 2003, with regimes that are not. Likewise, closed authoritarianism glosses over important distinctions drawn in earlier typologies between military and personalistic regimes. In sum, using the category of closed authoritarianism to classify nondemocratic regimes that lack democratic trappings creates a disconnect with previous regime typologies, thereby making it harder to achieve cumulative knowledge about world politics.

A final limitation of the category closed authoritarianism concerns its lumping together of countries where, to use Samuel P. Huntington's language, the "government governs" (e.g., China, Vietnam) with countries where the government does not govern, if there even is a government (e.g., Somalia, Democratic Republic of Congo, Liberia, Sierra Leone, and Rwanda). As Huntington (1968: 1) famously put it, "the most important distinction among countries concerns not their form of government but their degree of government." The category of closed authoritarianism fails to differentiate collapsed states that lack political order from totalitarian regimes that suffer the opposite problem—too much order. In countries with a high degree of government, life is predictable and stable for most citizens, whereas predictability is utterly lacking in cases where warlords, bandits, and chaos are the dominant force.[18] Indeed, in cases of state collapse it makes little sense to speak of any regime, much less a closed one, because the metaphor "closed" falsely implies that access to power is restricted by incumbent rulers. In the context of state collapse, a more appropriate metaphor is a false door, as on a movie set, that has no real edifice behind it: a doorway to nowhere. If the putatively "closed" regime were to "open" by holding free and fair elections, the victors who pass through the "opening" would not gain access to power, because there is no state apparatus to confer power.[19] Likewise, where state institutions are collapsed, those "inside" a so-called closed regime do not have power by virtue of their location, because there is no state apparatus. Instead, they must supply or create their own power resources and infrastructure. Thus a victorious rebel army in a country without a state cannot govern by taking over the state's coercive and administrative apparatus, because there is no such apparatus to take over. It makes little sense to classify such cases as closed regimes.

Two sharply contrasting pathways into the dark zone can readily be identified: too much political order (e.g., North Korea) and too little political order (e.g., Democratic Republic of Congo). In fact, the lack of a robust state apparatus capable of intensive, widespread repression may partly explain Larry Diamond's (2002: 26) observation that the "steady overall rise of freedom in the world" is "partly seen in the shrinking number and proportion of states with the two most repressive average freedom scores of 6.5 and 7.0." Hence, in 2001, a collapsed state like Sierra Leone received an average freedom score of 4.5, whereas North Korea, which had the state capacity to fully extinguish political and civil liberties, earned a score of 7.[20] Yet is it fruitful to call Sierra Leone in 2001, where chaos and anarchy prevailed and life approximated the Hobbesian state of nature, more "free" than North Korea?

Classifying regimes on the basis of closedness proves unsatisfactory because it (1) creates a disconnect with earlier frameworks for conceptualizing nondemocratic regimes, thus making it harder to generate cumulative knowledge about the political world; and (2) ignores other, more important dimensions, especially stateness, that are crucial for successfully mapping the wide range of polities in the world today.

Conclusion: Steps Ahead

Although electoral competition is a notable feature of many contemporary nondemocratic regimes, we should not overstate the importance of elections. First, many nondemocratic regimes lack elections or other democratic features. Second, even in nondemocratic regimes that do hold elections, the effect of electoral competition on the fortunes of these regimes depends on extra-electoral factors. Third, as students of democratic regimes increasingly emphasize, democracy itself involves far more than just elections (see, for example, O'Donnell 2001). Understanding the spectrum of political regimes in the post–Cold War era thus requires a conceptual framework that goes beyond the electoral process. In this chapter, I took two steps toward building such a framework. First, I specified four critical dimensions that interact with electoral contestation and thus determine how it affects the fortunes of nondemocratic regimes: Who rules? How do rulers rule? Why do rulers rule? And how much do rulers rule? Second, I opened the black box of closed regimes and showed how a focus on the degree of rule, or stateness, provides a stronger basis for understanding these cases than does a focus on closedness.

What further steps should be taken to strengthen our understanding of the spectrum of nondemocratic regimes? First, we need to do a far better job taking stock of existing conceptual frameworks before we propose new ones. Because they put the democratic trappings of nondemocracies, that is, elections and political contestation, at the center of analysis, recent efforts to classify nondemocratic regimes often fail to connect with prior categories and typologies of nondemocratic regimes, which focused centrally on variations in who rules, how rulers rule, and why rulers rule. This delinking from the stock of knowledge is often a deliberate move justified with the argument that the nondemocratic regimes of the post–Cold War era are sui generis and hence do not fit the old categories. New concepts are thus required to describe and understand these regimes. Yet the costs of delinking from earlier efforts to conceptualize nondemocratic regimes are high: conceptual fragmentation poses a serious barrier to theory building and the accumulation of knowledge. Because of these potentially high costs of conceptual innovation, prudence is warranted.

Maximizing the prospects for achieving cumulative knowledge requires a conservative bias with regard to concept formation. We should resist the naturalist's temptation to proclaim the discovery, naming, and classification of new political animals. Instead of rushing willy-nilly to coin neologisms in the hope of reaping a handsome profit in the marketplace of ideas, we should first carefully evaluate the "null hypothesis" that the political phenomena of interest, in this case, contemporary nondemocratic regimes, are actually *not* sufficiently novel to warrant any new categories and labels. If this null hypothesis proves false, then we should try to salvage and retain as much as possible from earlier conceptual schemes. In either case, an earnest and careful effort to take stock of earlier conceptualizations is required before a legitimate claim can be made for a new type or subtype. Otherwise, we run a grave risk of conceptual amnesia and chaos that can block the accumulation of knowledge in regime studies, and, even worse, cause the loss, or decumulation, of knowledge.

In the spirit of avoiding conceptual amnesia, a fruitful starting point for achieving a stronger understanding of the spectrum of contemporary nondemocratic regimes is Juan Linz's (1975) influential typology of regimes, arguably the most comprehensive effort in modern social science to map the variety of regimes. Linz's typology is organized around three core dimensions: (1) the degree of pluralism; (2) the degree of mobilization; and (3) the degree of ideology.[21] How relevant are Linz's three dimensions for understanding nondemocratic regimes thirty years later? Does the task of developing an updated typology require new dimensions? If so, what might these dimensions be?

A focus on the degree of pluralism clearly remains relevant for analyzing variation among nondemocratic regimes today. Indeed, the pluralism dimension has absorbed virtually all the attention of scholars whose work highlights the democratic trappings (e.g., electoral contestation and competitiveness) of modern nondemocratic regimes. By contrast, Linz's other two dimensions—mobilization and ideology—have been strikingly neglected. At first glance, the tendency to fixate on pluralism to the exclusion of mobilization and ideology seems justified by the paucity of patently mobilizational regimes in the world today. The mobilizational forms that characterized the fascist and communist regimes of the twentieth century—mass rallies animated by songs and pageantry, endless parades of goose-stepping troops, mass parties, and so on—seem extinct with the exception of a few vestigial cases like North Korea and Cuba. The apparent demise or, at least, hiatus, of mobilizational regimes goes hand in hand with the crisis of ideology that accompanied the end of the Cold War—after all, mass political mobilization probably requires ideology. Still, as Linz (2000) himself cautions, it may be premature to declare the end of mobilization and ideology. The most likely candidates today for a new wave of mobilizing regimes are religious fundamentalism, especially Islamic fundamentalism, and nationalism. Indeed, a variety of "anti-Western" ideologies can be seen among opposition groups across countries with democratic and nondemocratic regimes, ranging from Islamic fundamentalists in the Middle East and Asia to factions of indigenous movements across Latin America (most notably in Bolivia, Ecuador, and Mexico), which seek political and cultural autonomy in response to exclusion from national democratic politics and the extraction of natural resources by foreign companies. It remains to be seen whether and how these opposition groups will win power and the kind of regimes they will establish if they do. In addition to these strongly anti-Western ideologies, a softer strand of anti-Western thought can be seen in the "Asian values" invoked to legitimate developmental authoritarian regimes in Singapore and Malaysia. Another example of soft anti-Westernism can be found in the nationalist populism of the Hugo Chavez regime in Venezuela, which has demonstrated a strong capacity to mobilize poor, urban dwellers. As these examples suggest, it would be a mistake to treat the post–Cold War era as postideological, and hence, postmobilizational.

If the three core dimensions of Linz's 1975 typology—pluralism, mobilization, and ideology—still have great relevance, are any new dimensions warranted to understand the spectrum of contemporary nondemocratic regimes? The proliferation of failed and collapsed states after the end of the Cold War, especially in Africa, points clearly to one such dimension: the degree of rule, or stateness. This dimension highlights the territorially uneven nature of political power and authority, which in turn brings into focus subnational nondemocratic regimes, ranging from petty despots (e.g., subnational sultanism) to more institutionalized, subnational authoritarian enclaves, such as the state- and local-level party machines in some regions of India and Mexico. A territorially disaggregated, geographically nuanced perspective on political regimes, one that captures variation in the reach of the central state as well as in the forms of rule at the subnational level, would strengthen our understanding of contemporary nondemocratic politics.[22]

A final dimension that merits consideration concerns how advances in information technology affect the capacity of nondemocrats to capture and keep political power. Information is a key aspect of control and hence political power, both in democratic and nondemocratic systems. Although a few political scientists and sociologists have turned to the study of "e-democracy," focusing, for example, on electronic voting and how citizens interact with government agencies and state officials through Internet websites and e-mail,[23] little, if any, work has been done on "e-authoritarianism." It could prove fruitful to explore the implications of recent advances in the technology of surveillance for the maintenance of modern nondemocratic regimes (that is, for how rulers rule). The case of Singapore, where hidden sensors and cameras are reportedly installed in public elevators and bathrooms, probably approximates most closely the Orwellian Big Brother nightmare. Still, the increasing miniaturization and rapidly falling cost of surveillance technology presumably makes Singaporean-style voyeurism more feasible for a wide range of nondemocratic rulers.[24] New information technologies—especially e-mail and websites—may also make it easier for rulers to disseminate their propaganda and hence cultivate support, both domestically and internationally.

Another intriguing aspect of new information technologies for students of nondemocratic politics concerns how cell phones, e-mail, and Internet websites may empower antidemocratic opposition groups. For example, online "virtual mobilization," as utilized by some Islamic fundamentalist organizations, may serve as a partial surrogate for the marches and rallies of the mass-based, antidemocratic movements of the twentieth century.[25] The use of websites to broadcast decapitations of hostages has proven a potent way for small groups of Islamic insurgents to get their "message" out to a worldwide audience. Students of democratic politics have fruitfully explored how modern communication technologies, especially television, transformed mass-based political parties; students of nondemocratic politics could also gain insight by considering how new technologies affect the strategies and fortunes of nondemocratic opposition groups.

A focus on pluralism, mobilization, and ideology, combined with a focus on the territorially uneven nature of state power and the implications of new information technologies for authoritarian rulers and oppositions, will provide a stronger understanding of the spectrum of modern nondemocratic regimes.

Notes

I thank Gerardo Munck for extensive comments on this chapter. I also appreciate helpful suggestions from Jason Brownlee and Ellen Lust-Okar.

1. On the persistent nondemocratic regimes of the Middle East, see Bellin (2004), Lust-Okar (2005), and Posusney and Angrist (2005).

2. For a related challenge to the "transition paradigm," see the symposium on "Elections Without Democracy" in the *Journal of Democracy* 13/2 (April 2002).

3. On "democracy with adjectives," see Collier and Levitsky (1997).

4. Elections are also a means that nondemocratic regimes have used to maintain control (Hermet 1982; Schedler 2002b). Yet even when they serve this purpose, elections occur infrequently and, hence, are not "everyday forms" of nondemocratic rule.

5. See Brooker (2000: especially Chap. 2), for a good overview and synthesis of earlier efforts to classify nondemocratic systems. The dimension of stateness (how much rulers rule) has been less central to prior work on regimes. See Linz and Stepan (1996) for an important exception.

6. Although military regimes are not extinct, the number of such regimes has clearly decreased since the end of the Cold War. This demilitarization of contemporary nondemocratic regimes, which has not received much attention in the literature, likely results from (1) the increasing illegitimacy of military rule in an international context that favors the appearance of democratic rule: military regimes are among the most patently nondemocratic forms of rule; and (2) the exhaustion in the 1980s and 1990s of the "statist-developmental ideology" that legitimated many military regimes as "developmentalist" during the 1950s, 1960s, and 1970s. One wonders whether the increasing evidence of a return of statist economic interventions, for example, across Latin America, might eventually serve to re-legitimate a role for the armed forces in politics.

7. Still, it should not be taken for granted that military regimes enjoy a total monopoly over the means of coercion: even the high-capacity, bureaucratic-authoritarian regimes of the Southern Cone of Latin America in the 1960s and 1970s faced armed guerrilla insurgencies.

8. Technically, Algeria's regime was a single-party regime led by the National Liberation Front. Yet the military's role became so central by 1992 that it is best characterized as a military–single party hybrid. In Algeria, the military stepped in to put an end to the country's first experiment with competitive elections in 1992, after the Islamic Salvation Front won the first round of two-round legislative elections.

9. The concept of regime reequilibration is from Linz (1978).

10. The best analysis of the transition to democracy in the Philippines is Thompson (1995). See Brownlee (2004) for a fine comparative study of the contrasting effects of elections on the fortunes of nondemocratic rulers in the Philippines, Iran, Malaysia, and Egypt.

11. See also Thompson and Kuntz, Chapter 7 in this book.

12. See also Hermet (1982) on how elections may be an important instrument that helps incumbent nondemocratic elites keep power.

13. See Linz and Stepan (1996) on the interaction of elections, regime institutions, and stateness in Russia, Yugoslavia, and Spain.

14. On the Liberian elections, see Carter Center (n.d.). On usable state apparatuses as a key dimension of democratic and nondemocratic regimes, see Linz and Stepan (1996).

15. The Freedom House political rights and civil liberties indexes are both on a seven-point scale, with a score of 1 indicating a very high degree of political rights and civil liberties. The "average Freedom House score" is the average of a country's scores on the Freedom House political rights index and civil liberties index.

16. According to Schedler (2002b: 48), "closed authoritarian regimes" represent just 16.5 percent of a sample of 192 countries, whereas electoral authoritarian regimes represent 38.4 percent. Still, the category of regimes that are conventionally classified as "closed authoritarianism" includes the world's most populous country, China, as well as other countries with large populations (e.g., Vietnam, Democratic Republic of Congo). Hence, whether or not the number of countries with closed regimes is, in fact, relatively small, a very large share of the world's people still lives under such political forms.

17. The *locus classicus* of the distinction between authoritarian and totalitarian regimes is the work of Juan Linz (1964, 1975).

18. Indeed, even death was more or less orderly and predictable for many victims of totalitarian regimes.

19. For an important analysis of how the distinction between "access to power" and "exercise of power" serves to clarify the conceptualization of political regimes, see Mazzuca (forthcoming).

20. On how state capacity shapes the ability of nondemocratic regimes to govern, see Lucan Way's contribution to this book in Chapter 10.

21. Linz's rich and complex analysis contained numerous other dimensions, for example, which groups were excluded from or, alternatively, allowed to participate in the regime, but these three dimensions were the main ones. See Linz and Stepan (1996) for a revised version of the typology that treats sultanistic and post-totalitarian regimes as distinct categories, rather than as subtypes of authoritarianism.

22. Analytic strategies for studying subnational authoritarian regimes are discussed in Snyder (2001).

23. On e-democracy, see, for example, West (2005).

24. Intensified state surveillance of citizens can also be seen in democratic regimes. For example, to counter crime, downtown Wilmington, Delaware, is blanketed by video cameras connected to the authorities.

25. Any member of a contentious social science department understands well how e-mail can serve as an effective tool for mobilizing support and building coalitions. The observation that advances in information technology may place new tools in the hands of antidemocratic opposition groups raises a number of interesting counterfactual historical questions. For example, what might the Nazi or Bolshevik movements have looked like if they had had access to e-mail, cellular telephones, and websites?

Bibliography

Ai Camp, Roderic. 1985. "The Political Technocrat in Mexico and the Survival of the Political System," *Latin American Research Review* 20/1: 97–118.

Ajulu, Rok. 1995. "A Historical Background to Lesotho's Election of 1993," in *Democratisation and Demilitarisation in Lesotho: The General Election of 1993 and Its Aftermath,* ed. Roger Southall and Tsoeu Petlane. Pretoria: Africa Institute of South Africa, pp. 3–17.

Akindès, Francis. 2004. *The Roots of the Military-Political Crises in Côte d'Ivoire.* Research Report no. 128. Uppsala, Sweden: Nordic Africa Institute, www.nai.uu.se/publ/publeng.html.

Allina-Pisano, Jessica. 2004. "Sub Rosa Resistance and the Politics of Economic Reform: Land Redistribution in Post-Soviet Ukraine," *World Politics* 56 (July): 554–581.

———. 2005. "Informal Institutional Challenges to Democracy: Administrative Resource in Kuchma's Ukraine," Danyliw Research Seminar in Contemporary Ukrainian Studies, Chair of Ukrainian Studies, University of Ottawa, 29 September–1 October.

Anderson, David. 2003. "Le Déclin et la chute de la Kanu," *Politique Africaine* 90 (June): 37–55.

Antonić, Slobodan. 2002. *Zarobljena zemlja: Srbija za vlade Slobodana Miloševića.* Belgrade: Oktrovenje.

Anusorn, Limmanee. 1998. "Thailand," in *Political Party Systems and Democratic Development in East and Southeast Asia,* Vol. 1: *Southeast Asia,* ed. Wolfgang Sachsenroder and Ulrike E. Frings. Aldershot: Ashgate, pp. 403–448.

Aquino, Belinda A. 1987. *The Politics of Plunder: The Philippines Under Marcos.* Manila: Great Books Trading.

Aslund, Anders. 2002. "Is the Belarusian Economic Model Viable?" in *The EU and Belarus: Between Moscow and Brussels,* ed. Ann Lewis. London: Federal Trust, pp. 170–192.

Baker, Bruce. 1998. "The Class of 1990: How Have the Autocratic Leaders of Sub-Saharan Africa Fared Under Democratisation?" *Third World Quarterly* 19/1: 115–127.

———. 2000. "Can Democracy in Africa Be Sustained?" *Commonwealth and Comparative Politics* 38/3 (November): 9–34.

Banégas, Richard. 1997. "Retour sur une Démocratisation Modèle," in *Transitions Démocratiques Africaines,* ed. Jean Pascal Daloz and Patrick Quantin. Paris: Karthala, pp. 23–94.

Barkan, Joel D. 2000. "Protracted Transitions Among Africa's New Democracies," *Democratization* 7/3: 227–243.

Barros, Robert. 2005. "Secrecy and Dictatorship: Some Problems in the Study of Authoritarian Regimes," Political Methods No. 2, Working Paper Series of the IPSA Committee on Concepts and Methods, www.concepts-methods.org.

Bellin, Eva. 2004. "The Robustness of Authoritarianism in the Middle East: Exceptionalism in Comparative Perspective," *Comparative Politics* 36/2 (January): 139–157.

Bernbaum, Marcia, Rafael López Pintor, and Cynthia Sanborn. 2001. "Transparencia: Civil Society Observes Peru's Controversial 2000 Elections, Vigilance Case Study," www.transparencia.org.pe.

Bienen, Henry, and Nicolas van de Walle. 1991. *Of Time and Power: Leadership Duration in the Modern World.* Stanford, CA: Stanford University Press.

Blair, David. 2002. *Degrees in Violence: Robert Mugabe and the Struggle for Power in Zimbabwe.* London: Continuum.

Blume, M. E. 1974. "Unbiased Estimators of Long Run Expected Rates of Return," *Journal of the American Statistical Association* 69/347: 634–638.

Bogdanor, Vernon, and David Butler, ed. 1983. *Democracy and Elections.* Cambridge: Cambridge University Press.

Boix, Carles. 2003. *Democracy and Redistribution.* New York: Cambridge University Press.

Bollen, Kenneth, and R. W. Jackman. 1989. "Democracy, Stability, and Dichotomies," *American Sociological Review* 54: 612–621.

Bollen, Kenneth, and Richard Lennox. 1991. "Conventional Wisdom on Measurement: A Structural Equation Perspective," *Psychological Bulletin* 110/2: 305–314.

Bonner, Raymond. 1988. *Waltzing with a Dictator: The Marcoses and the Making of American Policy.* New York: Vintage.

Booth, John A. 1985. *The End and the Beginning: The Nicaraguan Revolution,* 2nd ed. Boulder, CO: Westview.

———. 1998. "Electoral Observation and Democratic Transition in Nicaragua," in *Electoral Observation and Democratic Transitions in Latin America,* ed. Kevin Middlebrook. La Jolla: Center for US-Mexican Studies, University of California, San Diego, pp. 187–209.

Borneo, Horacio, and Edelberto Torres Rivas. 2001. *¿Por qué no votan los guatemaltecos? Estudio de participación y abstención electoral.* Guatemala: IDEA International, IFE, and UNPD.

Bosco, Joseph. 1992. "Taiwan Factions: Gaunxi Patronage and the State in Local Politics," *Ethnology* 31/2 (April): 157–183.

Boudon, Laura. 1997. "Burkina Faso: The 'Rectification' of the Revolution," in *Political Reform in Francophone Africa,* ed. John F. Clark and David E. Gardinier. Boulder, CO: Westview, pp. 127–143.

Bratton, Michael, and Nicolas van de Walle. 1997. *Democratic Experiments in Africa: Regime Transitions in Comparative Perspective.* Cambridge: Cambridge University Press.

Brett, E. A. 1995. "Neutralizing the Use of Force in Uganda: The Role of the Military in Politics," *Journal of Modern African Studies* 33/1 (March): 139–152.

Brooker, Paul. 2000. *Non-Democratic Regimes: Theory, Government, and Politics.* New York: St. Martin's.

Brownlee, Jason. 2004. "Durable Authoritarianism in an Age of Democracy." PhD diss. Princeton, NJ: Princeton University.

Bruhn, Kathleen. 1997. *Taking on Goliath.* University Park: Pennsylvania State University Press.

Buijtenhuijs, Robert. 1994. "Les Partis Politiques Africains ont-ils des Projets de Société? L'Exemple du Tchad," *Politique Africaine* 56 (December): 119–136.

————. 1998. *Transition et Elections au Tchad, 1993–1997.* Paris: Karthala.

Bujosevic, Dragan, and Ivan Radovanovic. 2003. *The Fall of Milosevic: The October 5 Revolution.* London: Palgrave.

Bunce, Valerie. 2003. "Rethinking Recent Democratization: Lessons from the Postcommunist Experience," *World Politics* 55 (January): 167–192.

Burnell, Peter. 2001. "The Party System and Party Politics in Zambia: Continuities Past, Present, and Future," *African Affairs* 100: 239–263.

————. 2002. "Zambia's 2001 Elections: The Tyranny of Small Decisions, 'Nondecisions' and 'Not-decisions,'" *Third World Quarterly* 23/6: 1103–1120.

Buss, Claude A. 1987. *Cory Aquino and the People of the Philippines.* Palo Alto, CA: Stanford Alumni Association.

Camara, Mohamed Saliou. 2000. "From Military Politization to Militarization of Power in Guinea-Conackry," *Journal of Political and Military Sociology* 28/2 (Winter): 311–326.

Campbell, Ian. 1994. "Nigeria's Failed Transition: The 1993 Presidential Election," *Journal of Contemporary African Studies* 12/2: 179–199.

Canton, Santiago A., and Neil Nevitte. 1998. "Domestic Electoral Observation: The Practical Lessons," in *Electoral Observation and Democratic Transitions in Latin America,* ed. Kevin Middlebrook. La Jolla: Center for US-Mexican Studies, University of California, San Diego, pp. 33–52.

Carey, Henry F. 1998. "Electoral Observation and Democratization in Haiti," in *Electoral Observation and Democratic Transitions in Latin America,* ed. Kevin Middlebrook. La Jolla: Center for US-Mexican Studies, University of California, San Diego, pp. 141–166.

Carey, Sabine C. 2002. "A Comparative Analysis of Political Parties in Kenya, Zambia, and the Democratic Republic of Congo," *Democratization* 9/3 (Autumn): 53–71.

Carothers, Thomas. 1997. "The Observers Observed," *Journal of Democracy* 8/3 (July): 17–31.

————. 2001. "Ousting Foreign Strongmen: Lessons from Serbia," *Carnegie Endowment Policy Brief* 1/5.

————. 2002. "The End of the Transition Paradigm," *Journal of Democracy* 13/1 (January): 5–21.

Carter Center. n.d. "Observing the 1997 Elections Process in Liberia." Atlanta: Carter Center.

————. 1997. *The Observation of the 1996 Nicaraguan Elections,* Special Report. Atlanta: Carter Center.

Carter Center and Council of Freely-Elected Heads of Government. 1990. *Observing Nicaragua's Elections, 1989–1990,* Special Report 1. Atlanta: Carter Center, www.cartercenter.org/documents/1153.pdf.

Carter Center, Council of Freely-Elected Heads of Government, and NDI. 1991. *The 1990 Elections in the Dominican Republic: Report of an Observer Delegation,* Special Report 2. Atlanta: Carter Center.

Case, William. 1993. "Semi-Democracy in Malaysia: Withstanding the Pressures for Regime Change," *Pacific Affairs* 66/1 (Summer): 183–205.

————. 1996. "Can the 'Halfway House' Stand? Semidemocracy and Elite Theory in Three Southeast Asian Countries," *Comparative Politics* 28/4 (July): 437–464.

————. 2004. "Singapore in 2004: Another Tough Year," *Asian Survey* 44/2 (January–February): 115–120.

Centeno, Miguel. 1994. *Democracy Within Reason: Technocratic Revolution in Mexico.* University Park: Pennsylvania State University Press.

Chabal, Patrick, and Jean Pierre Daloz. 1999. *Africa Works.* London: James Currey.

Chao, Linda, and Ramon H. Myers. 1994. "The First Chinese Democracy: Political Development of the Republic of China on Taiwan, 1986–1994," *Asian Survey* 34/3 (March): 213–230.

Chege, Michael. 1996. "Between Africa's Extremes," in *The Global Resurgence of Democracy,* 2nd ed., ed. Larry Diamond and Marc F. Plattner. Baltimore: Johns Hopkins University Press, pp. 350–357.

Chehabi, Houchang, and Juan J. Linz. ed. 1998a. *Sultanistic Regimes.* Baltimore: Johns Hopkins University Press.

———. 1998b. "A Theory of Sultanism 1: A Type of Nondemocratic Rule," in *Sultanistic Regimes,* ed. Houchang Chehabi and Juan J. Linz. Baltimore: Johns Hopkins University Press, pp. 3–25.

———. 1998c. "A Theory of Sultanism 2: Genesis and Demise of Sultanistic Regimes," in *Sultanistic Regimes,* ed. Houchang Chehabi and Juan J. Linz. Baltimore: Johns Hopkins University Press, pp. 26–48.

Cheng, Tun-Jen. 1989. "Democratizing the Quasi-Leninist Regime in Taiwan," *World Politics* 41/4 (July): 471–499.

Christian, Shirley. 1986. *Nicaragua: Revolution in the Family.* New York: Vintage.

Chu, Yun-han. 2001. "The Legacy of One-Party Hegemony in Taiwan," in *Political Parties and Democracy,* ed. Larry Diamond and Richard Gunther. Baltimore: Johns Hopkins University Press, pp. 266–298.

Churchill, Thomas. 1995. *Triumph over Marcos: A Story Based on the Lives of Gene Viernes and Silme Domino, Filipino American Cannery Union Organizers, Their Assassination, and the Trial That Followed.* Seattle: Open Hand.

Clark, John F. 1997. "Congo: Transition and the Struggle to Consolidate," in *Political Reform in Francophone Africa,* ed. John F. Clark and David E. Gardinier. Boulder, CO: Westview, pp. 62–85.

———. 1998. "Foreign Intervention in the Civil War of the Congo Republic," *Issue* 26/1: 31–36.

———. 2002. "The Neo-Colonial Context of the Democratic Experiment of Congo-Brazzaville," *African Affairs* 101/403 (April): 171–192.

———. 2005. "The Collapse of the Democratic Experiment in the Republic of Congo: A Thick Description," in *The Fate of Africa's Democratic Experiments,* ed. Leonardo A. Villalón and Peter VonDoepp. Bloomington: Indiana University Press, pp. 96–125.

Clark, John F., and David E. Gardinier, ed. 1997. *Political Reform in Francophone Africa.* Boulder, CO: Westview.

Cohen, Morris R., and Ernest Nagel. 1934. *An Introduction to Logic and Scientific Method.* New York: Harcourt, Brace.

Collier, David, and Robert N. Adcock. 1999. "Democracy and Dichotomies: A Pragmatic Approach to Choices About Concepts," *Annual Review of Political Science* 2: 537–565.

Collier, David, and Steven Levitsky. 1997. "Democracy with Adjectives: Conceptual Innovation in Comparative Research," *World Politics* 49/3 (April): 430–451.

Collier, Ruth Berins. 1999. *Paths Toward Democracy: Working Class and Elites in Western Europe and South America.* New York: Cambridge University Press.

Compagnon, Daniel. 2000. "Carton Jaune pour Mugabe," *Politique Africaine* 77 (March): 107–116.

Contamin, Bernard, and Bruno Losch. 2000. "Côte d'Ivoire: La Voie Etroite," *Politique Africaine* 77 (March): 117–128.

Cooper, Andrew F., and Thomas Legler. 2001. "The OAS in Peru: A Model for the Future?" *Journal of Democracy* 12/4 (October): 123–136.

Coppedge, Michael, and Wolfgang H. Reinicke. 1990. "Measuring Polyarchy,"

Studies in Comparative International Development 25/1: 51–73.

Cornelius, Wayne, Todd A. Eisenstadt, and Jane Hindley, ed. 1999. *Subnational Politics and Democratization.* La Jolla: Center for US-Mexican Studies, University of California, San Diego.

Crawford, Gordon. 2001. *Foreign Aid and Political Reform: A Comparative Analysis of Democracy Assistance and Political Conditionality.* New York: Palgrave.

Crook, Richard. 1997. "Winning Coalitions and Ethno-Regional Politics: The Failure of the 1990 and 1995 Elections in Côte d'Ivoire," *African Affairs* 96: 215–242.

Dahl, Robert A. 1966. "Preface," in *Political Oppositions in Western Democracies,* ed. Robert A. Dahl. New Haven, CT: Yale University Press, pp. xiii–xxi.

———. 1971. *Polyarchy: Participation and Opposition.* New Haven, CT: Yale University Press.

———. 1989. *Democracy and Its Critics.* New Haven, CT: Yale University Press.

———. 1998. *On Democracy.* New Haven, CT: Yale University Press.

Darden, Keith. 2001. "Blackmail as a Tool of State Domination: Ukraine Under Kuchma," *East European Constitutional Review* 10/2–3 (Spring–Summer): 67–71.

———. Forthcoming. "The Integrity of Corrupt States: Graft as an Informal State Institution," *Politics and Society.*

Datton, Kenneth, John S. Greenies, and Kenneth J. Stewart. 1998. "Incorporating a Geometric Mean Formula into the CPI," *Monthly Labor Review* (October): 3–7.

Decalo, Samuel. 1997. "Benin: First of the New Democracies," in *Political Reform in Francophone Africa,* ed. John Clark and David Gardinier. Boulder, CO: Westview, pp. 43–61.

———. 1998. *The Stable Minority: Civilian Rule in Africa.* Gainesville: Florida Academic Press.

Deegan-Krause, Kevin. 2004. "The Ambivalent Influence of the European Union on Democratization in Slovakia," in *The European Union and Democratization,* ed. Paul Kubicek. London: Routledge, pp. 56–86.

Democratic Elections in Ukraine. 1994. *Report on the 1994 Presidential Elections.* Kiev, Ukraine.

Diamond, Larry. 1989. "Introduction: Persistence, Erosion, Breakdown, and Renewal," in *Democracy in Developing Countries: Asia,* ed. Larry Diamond, Juan J. Linz, and Seymour Martin Lipset. Boulder, CO: Lynne Rienner, pp. 1–52.

———. 1997. "Prospects for Democratic Development in Africa," Essays in Public Policy 74. Stanford, CA: Stanford University, Hoover Institution on War, Revolution, and Peace.

———. 1999. *Developing Democracy: Toward Consolidation.* Baltimore: Johns Hopkins University Press.

———. 2000. "Is Pakistan the (Reverse) Wave of the Future?" *Journal of Democracy* 11/3 (July): 91–106.

———. 2002. "Elections Without Democracy: Thinking About Hybrid Regimes," *Journal of Democracy* 13/2 (April): 21–35.

Diamond, Larry, Juan J. Linz, and Seymour Martin Lipset. 1995. "Introduction: What Makes for Democracy?" in *Politics in Developing Countries: Comparing Experiences with Democracy,* ed. Larry Diamond, Juan J. Linz, and Seymour Martin Lipset. Boulder, CO: Lynne Rienner, pp. 1–66.

Diamond, Larry, and Leonardo Morlino. 2004. "The Quality of Democracy: An Overview," *Journal of Democracy* 15/4 (October): 20–31.

Díaz-Cayeros, Alberto, and Joy Langston. 2003. "The Consequences of Competition: Gubernatorial Nominations and Candidate Quality in Mexico, 1994–2000," Working Paper 160. Mexico City: CIDE.

Dickson, Bruce J. 1998. "China's Democratization and the Taiwan Experience," *Asian Survey* 38/4 (April): 349–364.

Di Palma, Giuseppe. 1993. *To Craft Democracies: An Essay on Democratic Transitions.* Berkeley: University of California Press.

Dix, Robert H. 1994. "History and Democracy Revisited," *Comparative Politics* 27/1: 91–105.

Djukić, Slavoljub. 2001. *Milošević and Marković: A Lust for Power.* Montreal: McGill-Queen's University Press.

Dogan, Mattei, and John Higley, ed. 1998. *Elites, Crises, and the Origins of Regimes.* Lanham, MD: Rowman and Littlefield.

Domes, Jurgen. 1989. "The 13th Party Congress of the Kuomintang: Towards Political Competition?" *China Quarterly* 118 (June): 345–359.

———. 1999. "Electoral and Party Politics in Democratization," in *Democratization in Taiwan: Implications for China,* ed. Steve Tsang and Hung-mao Tien. London: Macmillan, pp. 49–66.

Doorenspleet, Renske. 2005. *Democratic Transitions, 1989–2001: Exploring the Structural Sources.* Boulder, CO: Lynne Rienner.

Downs, Anthony. 1957. *An Economic Theory of Democracy.* New York: Harper-Collins.

Dresser, Denise. 1996. "Treading Lightly and Without a Stick: International Actors and the Promotion of Democracy in Mexico," in *Beyond Sovereignty: Collectively Defending Democracy in the Americas,* ed. Tom Farer. Baltimore: Johns Hopkins University Press, pp. 316–341.

Dunleavy, Patrick, and Helen Margetts. 1995. "Understanding the Dynamics of Electoral Reform," *International Political Science Review* 16/1 (January): 9–29.

Duverger, Maurice. 1954. *Les Partis Politiques.* Paris: Colin.

———. 1980. "A New Political System Model: Semi-Presidential Government," *European Journal of Political Research* 8/1 (June): 165–187.

Eboko, Fred. 1999. "Les Elites Politiques au Cameroun: Le Renouvellement sans Renouveau?" in *Le (Non)Renouvellement Des Elites en Afrique Subsaharienne,* ed. Jean-Pascal Daloz. Bordeaux: Centre D'Etude d'Afrique Noire, pp. 99–133.

Eckstein, Harry. 1992. *Regarding Politics: Essays on Political Theory, Stability, and Change.* Berkeley: University of California Press.

Eisenstadt, Todd A. 2004. *Courting Democracy in Mexico: Party Strategies and Electoral Institutions.* Cambridge: Cambridge University Press.

Eklof, Stephan. 1999. *Indonesian Politics in Crisis: The Long Fall of Suharto, 1996–98.* Copenhagen: Nordic Institute of Asian Studies.

Elklit, Jørgen, and Andrew Reynolds. 2002. "The Impact of Election Administration on the Legitimacy of Emerging Democracies: A New Comparative Politics Research Agenda," *Commonwealth and Comparative Politics* 42/2: 86–119.

Elklit, Jørgen, and Palle Svensson. 1997. "What Makes Elections Free and Fair?" *Journal of Democracy* 8/3 (July): 32–46.

Elster, Jon, Claus Offe, and Ulrich K. Preuss, with Frank Boenker, Ulrike Goetting, and Friedbert W. Rueb. 1998. *Institutional Design in Post-Communist Societies: Rebuilding the Ship at Sea.* Cambridge: Cambridge University Press.

Fairbanks, Charles H. 2004. "Georgia's Rose Revolution," *Journal of Democracy* 15/2 (April): 110–124.

Fish, M. Steven. 1995. *Democracy from Scratch: Opposition and Regime in the New Russian Revolution.* Princeton: Princeton University Press.

———. 1998. "Mongolia: Democracy Without Prerequisites," *Journal of Democracy* 9/3 (July): 127–141.

———. 2003. "The Impact of the 1999–2000 Parliamentary and Presidential Elections on Political Party Development," in *The 1999–2000 Elections in Russia: Their Impact and Legacy,* ed. Vicki L. Hesli and William M. Reisinger. Cambridge: Cambridge University Press, pp. 186–212.

———. 2005. *Democracy Derailed in Russia: The Failure of Open Politics.* New York: Cambridge University Press.

Fish, M. Steven, and Robin S. Brooks. 2000. "Bulgarian Democracy's Organizational Weapon," *East European Constitutional Review* 9/3 (Summer): 69–77.

Fish, M. Steven, and Matthew Kroenig. 2006. "The Legislative Powers Survey and the Parliamentary Powers Index: A Global Study of the Powers of National Legislatures." Unpublished typescript. University of California, Berkeley.

Fishman, Robert M. 1990. "Rethinking State and Regime: Southern Europe's Transition to Democracy," *World Politics* 42/3 (April): 422–440.

Forrest, Joshua B. 2005. "Guinea-Bissau: Democratization in a Divided Political Culture," in *The Fate of Africa's Democratic Experiments,* ed. Leonardo Villalón and Peter VonDoepp. Bloomington: Indiana University Press, pp. 246–266.

Foye, Stephen. 1993. "Civilian-Military Tension in Ukraine," *RFE/RL Research Report.* 18 June.

Franco, Jennifer C. 2001. *Elections and Democratization in the Philippines.* New York: Routledge.

Freedom House. 1989. "Mission to Paraguay." New York: Freedom House.

———. 2005. "Annual Survey of Freedom, Country Ratings, 2005." New York: Freedom House, freedomhouse.org.

Fuh-sheng Hsieh, John. 1999. "Manipulating the Electoral System Under the SNTV: The Case of the Republic of China on Taiwan," in *Elections in Japan, Korea, and Taiwan Under the Single Non-Transferable Vote: The Comparative Study of an Embedded Institution,* ed. Bernard Grofman, Sung-Chull Lee, Edwin Winckler, and Brian Woodall. Ann Arbor: University of Michigan Press, pp. 65–84.

Furley, Oliver. 2000. "Democratisation in Uganda," *Commonwealth and Comparative Politics* 38/3 (November): 79–102.

Gallie, W. B. 1956. "Essentially Contested Concepts," in *Proceedings of the Aristotelian Society* 56. London: Harrison and Sons, pp. 167–198.

Ganev, Venelin I. 2004. "History, Politics, and the Constitution: Ethnic Conflict and Constitutional Adjudication in Postcommunist Bulgaria," *Slavic Review* 63/1 (Spring): 66–89.

Gardinier, David E. 1997. "Gabon: Limited Reform and Regime Survival," in *Political Reform in Francophone Africa,* ed. John Clark and David Gardinier. Boulder, CO: Westview, pp. 145–161.

Garrido, Luis Javier. 1982. *El partido de la revolución institucionalizada: La formación del nuevo estado en México, 1928–1945.* Mexico City: Siglo Veintiuno.

———. 1993. *La ruptura: La Corriente Democrática del PRI.* Mexico City: Grijalbo.

Geddes, Barbara. 1999. "What Do We Know About Democratization After Twenty Years?" *Annual Review of Political Science* 2: 115–144.

———. 2003. *Paradigms and Sand Castles: Theory Building and Research Design in Comparative Politics.* Ann Arbor: University of Michigan Press.

———. 2004. "Authoritarian Breakdown." Unpublished typescript. Los Angeles: UCLA.

Geertz, Clifford. 1983. *Local Knowledge.* New York: Basic.

Gibson, Clark C. 2002. "Of Waves and Ripples: Democracy and Political Change in Africa in the 1990s," *Annual Review of Political Science* 5: 201–221.

Gomez, Terence. 1998. "Malaysia," in *Political Party Systems and Democratic Development in East and Southeast Asia,* Vol. 1: *Southeast Asia,* ed. Wolfgang Sachsenroder and Ulrike E. Frings. Aldershot: Ashgate, pp. 226–228.

Haggard, Stephan. 2003. *The Political Economy of the Asian Financial Crisis.* Washington, DC: Institute for International Economics.

Hartlyn, Jonathan. 1998. *The Struggle for Democratic Politics in the Dominican Republic.* Chapel Hill: University of North Carolina Press.

Hartlyn, Jonathan, Jennifer McCoy, and Thomas Mustillo. 2003. "The 'Quality of Elections' in Contemporary Latin America: Issues in Measurement and Explanation." Twenty-Fourth International Congress of the Latin American Studies Association, 27–29 March, Dallas, Texas.

Hedman, Eva-Lotta. 1998. *In the Name of Civil Society: Contesting Free Elections in the Postcolonial Philippines.* PhD diss. Ithaca, NY: Cornell University.

Heilbrunn, John. 1993. "Social Origins of National Conferences in Benin and Togo," *Journal of Modern African Studies* 31/2: 277–299.

Hempel, Carl Gustav. 1952. *Fundamentals of Concept Formation in Empirical Science.* Chicago: University of Chicago Press.

Herbst, Jeffrey. 2001. *States and Power in Africa.* Princeton, NJ: Princeton University Press.

Hermet, Guy. 1982. "Las elecciones en los regímenes autoritarios: Bosquejo de un marco de análisis," in *¿Para qué sirven las elecciones?* ed. Guy Hermet, Alain Rouquié, and Juan Linz. Mexico City: Fondo de Cultura Económica, pp. 18–53.

Hermet, Guy, Richard Rose, and Alain Rouquié. 1978. "Preface," in *Elections Without Choice,* ed. Guy Hermet, Richard Rose, and Alain Rouquié. New York: Halsted, pp. vii–xi.

Herndández-Rodríguez, Rogelio. 1992. "La división de la elite política mexicana," in *México: Auge, crisis, y ajuste,* ed. Carlos Bazdresh, Nora Bucal, Soledad Loaeza, and Nora Lustig. Mexico City: Fondo de Cultura Económica, pp. 239–265.

Higley, John, and Richard Gunther, ed. 1992. *Elites and Democratic Consolidation in Latin America and Southern Europe.* Cambridge: Cambridge University Press.

Hill, Ronald J. 1991. "The CPSU: From Monolith to Pluralist?" *Soviet Studies* 43/2: 217–235.

Holmes, Stephen. 1997. "What Russia Teaches Us Now: How Weak States Threaten Freedom," *American Prospect* 8/33 (July): 30–39.

———. 2002. "Simulations of Power in Putin's Russia," in *Russia After the Fall,* ed. Andrew Kuchins. Washington, DC: Carnegie Endowment Series, pp. 79–89.

Holmquist, Frank. 2003. "Kenya's Postelection Euphoria—and Reality," *Current History* 102/664 (May): 200–205.

Holston, James, and Teresa P. R. Caldeira. 1998. "Democracy, Law, and Violence: Disjunctions of Brazilian Citizenship," in *Fault Lines of Democracy in Post-Transition Latin America,* ed. Felipe Agüero and Jeffrey Stark. Miami: North-South Center Press of the University of Miami, pp. 363–396.

Horowitz, Donald L. 1996. "Comparing Democratic Systems," in *The Global Resurgence of Democracy,* 2nd ed., ed. Larry Diamond and Marc F. Plattner. Baltimore: Johns Hopkins University Press, pp. 143–149.

Howard, Marc Morjé. 2003. *The Weakness of Civil Society in Post-Communist Europe.* Cambridge: Cambridge University Press.

Howard, Marc Morjé, and Philip G. Roessler. 2006. "Liberalizing Electoral Outcomes in Competitive Authoritarian Regimes," *American Journal of Political Science* 50/2 (April): 362–378.

Howe, Herbert. 2001. *Ambiguous Order: Military Forces in African States.* Boulder, CO: Lynne Rienner.

Huang, Teh-fu. 1996. "Elections and the Evolution of the Kuomintang," in *Taiwan's Electoral Politics and Democratic Transition: Riding the Third Wave,* ed. Hung-Mao Tien. Armonk, NY: M. E. Sharp, pp. 105–136.

Huntington, Samuel P. 1968. *Political Order in Changing Societies.* New Haven, CT: Yale University Press.

―――. 1991. *The Third Wave: Democratization in the Late Twentieth Century.* Norman: University of Oklahoma Press.

Inglehart, Ronald. 2002. *World Values Surveys, 2002,* worldvaluessurvey.org.

Inglehart, Ronald, Miguel Basañez, Jaime Díez-Medrano, Loek Halman, and Ruud Luijkx. 2004. *Human Beliefs and Values: A Cross-Cultural Sourcebook Based on the 1999–2002 Values Surveys.* Mexico City: Siglo Veintiuno.

International IDEA (International Institute for Democracy and Electoral Assistance). 1997. "Code of Conduct: Ethical and Professional Observation of Elections." Stockholm: International IDEA, www.idea.int/publications.

―――. 1999. "The Future of International Electoral Observation: Lessons Learned and Recommendations: Conference Report." Stockholm: IDEA International, www.idea.int/publications.

―――. 2002. "International Electoral Standards: Guidelines for Reviewing the Legal Framework of Elections." Stockholm: International IDEA, www.idea.int/ publications.

Jesudason, James V. 1996. "The Syncretic State and the Structuring of Opposition Politics in Malaysia," in *Political Oppositions in Industrialising Asia,* ed. Garry Rodan. London: Routledge, pp. 128–160.

Joseph, Richard. 1992. "Zambia: A Model for Democratic Change," *Current History* 91/565 (May): 191–201.

―――. 1998a. "Africa, 1990–1997: From Abertura to Closure," *Journal of Democracy* 9/2 (April): 3–17.

―――. 1998b. "Is Ethiopia Democratic? Oldspeak vs. Newspeak," *Journal of Democracy* 9/4 (October): 55–61.

―――. 1999. "The Reconfiguration of Power in Late Twentieth-Century Africa," in *State, Conflict, and Democracy in Africa,* ed. Richard Joseph. Boulder, CO: Lynne Rienner, pp. 57–80.

Kaplan, Abraham. 1964. *The Conduct of Inquiry: Methodology for Behavioral Science.* Scranton, PA: Chandler.

Karatnycky, Adrian, Aili Piano, and Arch Puddington, ed. 2003. *Freedom in the World: The Annual Survey of Political Rights and Civil Liberties 2003.* Lanham, MD: Rowman and Littlefield.

Karl, Terry Lynn. 1995. "The Hybrid Regimes of Central America," *Journal of Democracy* 6/3 (July): 72–87.

Katz, Richard S. 1980. *A Theory of Parties and Electoral Systems.* Baltimore: Johns Hopkins University Press.

Keck, Margaret E., and Kathryn Sikkink. 1998. *Activists Beyond Borders: Advocacy Networks in International Politics.* Ithaca, NY: Cornell University Press.

Kelley, Judith. 2004. "International Actors on the Domestic Scene: Membership Conditionality and Socialization by International Institutions," *International Organization* 58/3: 425–458.

Kerkvliet, Benedict J. Tria. 1996. "Contested Meanings of Elections in the Philippines," in *The Politics of Elections in Southeast Asia,* ed. Robert H. Taylor. Cambridge: Woodrow Wilson Centre Press, Cambridge University Press, pp. 164–183.

Kharitonov, M. A. 2003. *Zvezdy I terny Vladimira Egrova.* Minsk, Belarus: Bonem. www.fsd.uta.fi/aineistot/Introduction_Tampere.pdf.

Khin, Maung Win, and Alan Smith. 1998. "Burma," in *Political Party Systems and Democratic Development in East and Southeast Asia,* Vol. 1: *Southeast Asia,* ed. Wolfgang Sachsenroder and Ulrike E. Frings. Aldershot: Ashgate, pp. 98–156.

Kitschelt, Herbert. 2000. "Linkages Between Citizens and Politicians in Democratic Polities," *Comparative Political Studies* 33/6 (August): 845–879.

Kopstein, Jeffrey S., and David A. Reilly. 2000. "Geographic Diffusion and the Transformation of the Postcommunist World," *World Politics* 53/1 (October): 1–37.

Kravchuk, Leonid. 2002. *Maemo te, shcho maemo.* Kiev, Ukraine: Stolittia.

Krennerich, Michael. 1996. *Wahlen und Antiregimekriege in Zentralamerika.* Opladen: Leske und Budrich.

Krouwel, André. 2000. "The Presidentialisation of East-Central European Countries," European Consortium of Political Research, Joint Sessions of Workshops, Copenhagen, April.

Kubicek, Paul. 2000. *Unbroken Ties.* Ann Arbor: University of Michigan Press.

Kumar, Chetan. 2000. "Transnational Networks and Campaigns for Democracy," in *The Third Force: The Rise of Transnational Civil Society,* ed. Ann M. Florini. Washington, DC: Carnegie Endowment for International Peace, pp. 115–142.

Kuran, Timur. 1995. *Private Truths, Public Lies: The Social Consequences of Preference Falsification.* Cambridge, MA: Harvard University Press.

Kuzio, Taras. 1993. "Coup Talk in Ukraine," *Foreign Report: Economist,* 9 December.

———. 1996. "Kravchuk to Kuchma: The Ukrainian Presidential Elections of 1994," *Journal of Communist Studies and Transition Politics* 12 (June): 117–144.

———. 1997. *Ukraine Under Kuchma.* Birmingham: Centre for Russian and East European Studies, University of Birmingham.

———. 2000. *Ukraine: Perestroika to Independence.* New York: St. Martin's.

Laitin, David. 1998. *Identity in Formation: The Russian Speaking Populations in the Near Abroad.* Ithaca, NY: Cornell University Press.

Langston, Joy. 2002. "Breaking Out Is Hard to Do: Exit, Voice, and Loyalty in Mexico's One-Party Hegemonic Regime," *Latin American Politics and Society* 44/3 (Fall): 61–88.

Ledeneva, Alena. 2001. *Unwritten Rules: How Russia Really Works.* London: Center for European Reform.

Lehoucq, Fabrice. 2003. "Electoral Fraud: Causes, Types, and Consequences," *Annual Review of Political Science* 6: 233–256.

Leones, Errol B., and Meil Moraleda. 1998. "Philippines," in *Political Party Systems and Democratic Development in East and Southeast Asia,* Vol. 1: *Southeast Asia,* ed. Wolfgang Sachsenroder and Ulrike E. Frings. Aldershot: Ashgate, pp. 289–342.

Levitsky, Steven, and Maxwell A. Cameron. 2003. "Democracy Without Parties? Political Parties and Regime Change in Fujimori's Peru," *Latin American Politics and Society* 45/3: 1–33.

Levitsky, Steven, and Lucan A. Way. 2002. "Elections Without Democracy: The Rise of Competitive Authoritarianism," *Journal of Democracy* 13/2 (April): 51–65.

Lewis, Peter M. 1994. "Endgame in Nigeria? The Politics of a Failed Democratic Transition," *African Affairs* 93 (July): 323–340.

Lijphart, Arend. 1984. *Democracies: Patterns of Majoritarian and Consensus Government in Twenty-One Countries.* New Haven, CT: Yale University Press.

Lijphart, Arend, and Carlos H. Waisman. 1996. "Institutional Design and Democratization," in *Institutional Design in New Democracies: Eastern Europe and Latin America,* ed. Arend Lijphart and Carlos H. Waisman. Boulder, CO: Westview, pp. 1–11.

Lindberg, Staffan I. 2002. "Problems of Measuring Democracy: Illustrations from Africa," in *Development and Democracy: What Have We Learned and How?* ed. Goran Hyden and Ole Elgström. London: Routledge, pp. 122–138.

———. 2003. "It's Our Time to 'Chop': Do Elections in Africa Feed Neopatrimonialism Rather Than Counteract It?" *Democratization* 10/2: 121–140.

———. 2004a. "The Democratic Qualities of Multiparty Elections: Participation, Competition, and Legitimacy in Africa," *Journal of Commonwealth and Comparative Studies* 42/1: 61–105.

———. 2004b. "Democratization and Women's Empowerment: The Effects of Electoral Systems, Participation, and Repetition in Africa," *Studies in Comparative International Development* 39/1: 38–53.

———. 2005. "Consequences of Electoral Systems in Africa: A Preliminary Inquiry," *Electoral Studies* 24/1: 41–64.

———. 2006. *Democracy and Elections in Africa.* Baltimore: Johns Hopkins University Press.

Linz, Juan J. 1964. "An Authoritarian Regime: Spain," in *Cleavages, Ideologies, and Party Systems: Contributions to Comparative Political Sociology,* ed. Erik Allardt and Yrjö Littunen. Helsinki: Westermarck Society, pp. 291–341.

———. 1975. "Totalitarianism and Authoritarian Regimes," in *Handbook of Political Science,* Vol. 3: *Macropolitical Theory,* ed. Fred Greenstein and Nelson Polsby. Reading, MA: Addison-Wesley, pp. 175–411.

———. 1978. *The Breakdown of Democratic Regimes: Crisis, Breakdown, and Reequilibriation.* Baltimore: Johns Hopkins University Press.

———. 2000. *Totalitarian and Authoritarian Regimes.* Boulder, CO: Lynne Rienner.

Linz, Juan J., and Alfred Stepan. 1996. *Problems of Democratic Transition and Consolidation: Southern Europe, South America and Post-Communist Europe.* Baltimore: Johns Hopkins University Press.

Linz, Juan J., and Arturo Valenzuela, ed. 1994. *The Failure of Presidential Democracy.* Baltimore: Johns Hopkins University Press.

Liu, I-Chou. 1999. "Campaigning in an SNTV System: The Case of the Kuomintang in Taiwan," in *Elections in Japan, Korea, and Taiwan Under the Single Non-Transferable Vote: The Comparative Study of an Embedded Institution,* ed. Bernard Grofman, Sung-Chull Lee, Edwin Winckler, and Brian Woodall. Ann Arbor: University of Michigan Press, pp. 181–208.

Lohmann, Susanne. 1994. "The Dynamics of Informational Cascades: The Monday Demonstrations in Leipzig, East Germany, 1989–91," *World Politics* 47/1: 42–101.

Lukashuk, Alexander. 1992. "Belarus's KGB: In Search of an Identity," *RFE/RL Research Report* (27 November): 17–21.

Lustig, Nora. 1998. *Mexico: The Remaking of an Economy,* 2nd ed. Washington, DC: Brookings Institution.

Lust-Okar, Ellen. 2005. *Structuring Conflict in the Arab World: Incumbents, Opponents, and Institutions.* Cambridge: Cambridge University Press.

Magaloni, Beatriz. 1999. "Is the PRI Fading? Economic Performance, Electoral Accountability, and Voting Behavior in the 1994 and 1997 Elections," in *Toward Mexico's Democratization: Parties, Campaigns, Elections, and Public Opinion,* ed. Jorge I. Dominguez and Alejandro Poiré. New York: Routledge, pp. 203–236.

Mahoney, James. 2001. *The Legacies of Liberalism: Path Dependence and Political Regimes in Central America.* Baltimore: Johns Hopkins University Press.

Mainwaring, Scott, Daniel Brinks, and Aníbal Pérez-Liñán. 2001. "Classifying Political Regimes in Latin America, 1945–1999," *Studies in Comparative International Development* 36/1: 37–65.

Mainwaring, Scott, and Timothy R. Scully, ed. 1995. *Building Democratic Institutions: Party Systems in Latin America.* Stanford, CA: Stanford University Press.

Mainwaring, Scott, and Matthew Soberg Shugart, ed. 1997. *Presidential Democracy in Latin America.* New York: Cambridge University Press.

Mair, Peter, ed. 1990. *The West European Party System.* Oxford: Oxford University Press.

Maisrikrod, Surin. 1992. *Thailand's Two General Elections in 1992.* Singapore: Institute of Southeast Asian Studies.

Manning, Carrie. 2005. "Conflict Management and Elite Habituation in Post-War Democracy: The Case of Mozambique," in *The Fate of Africa's Democratic Experiments,* ed. Leonardo Villalón and Peter VonDoepp. Bloomington: Indiana University Press, pp. 221–245.

Marcus, Richard R. 2001. "Madagascar: Legitimizing Autocracy?" *Current History* 100/646 (May): 226–231.

Marcus, Richard R., and Paul Razafindrakoto. 2003. "Madagascar: A New Democracy?" *Current History* 102/664 (May): 215–221.

Marshall, Monty G., and Keith Jaggers. 2002. "Polity IV Project: Political Regime Characteristics and Transitions, 1800–2002: Dataset Users' Manual." College Park, MD: Integrated Network for Societal Conflict Research, Center for International Development and Conflict Management, University of Maryland, www.cidcm.umd.edu.

Martin, Denis. 1978. "The 1975 Tanzanian Elections: The Disturbing Six Per Cent," in *Elections Without Choice,* ed. Guy Hermet, Richard Rose, and Alain Rouquié. New York: Halsted, pp. 108–128.

Mauzy, Diane K., and R. S. Milne. 2002. *Singapore Politics Under the People's Action Party.* London: Routledge.

Mayhew, David R. 2004. "Events as Causes: The Case of American Politics," Contingency in the Study of Politics: A Conference in Honor of Robert Dahl, New Haven, CT, Yale University, Department of Political Science, 3–5 December.

Mazzuca, Sebastián. Forthcoming. "Access to Power Versus Exercise of Power: Reconceptualizing Democracy in Latin America," *Studies in Comparative International Development.*

McClintock, Cynthia. 2001. "The OAS in Peru: Room for Improvement," *Journal of Democracy* 12/4 (October): 137–140.

McCoy, Jennifer. 1998. "Monitoring and Mediating Elections During Latin American Democratization," in *Electoral Observation and Democratic Transitions in Latin America,* ed. Kevin Middlebrook. La Jolla: Center for US-Mexican Studies, University of California, San Diego, pp. 53–90.

McFaul, Michael. 2001. *Russia's Unfinished Revolution.* Ithaca, NY: Cornell University Press.

———. 2002. "The Fourth Wave of Democracy and Dictatorship: Noncooperative Transitions in the Postcommunist World," *World Politics* 54 (January): 212–244.

McGowan, Patrick J. 2003. "African Military Coups d'État, 1956–2001: Frequency, Trends and Distribution," *Journal of Modern African Studies* 41/3: 339–370.

Mehler, Andreas. 2005. "The Shaky Foundations, Adverse Circumstances, and Limited Achievements of a Democratic Transition in the Central African Republic," in *The Fate of Africa's Democratic Experiments,* ed. Leonardo Villalón and Peter VonDoepp. Bloomington: Indiana University Press, pp. 126–152.

Middlebrook, Kevin, ed. 1998. *Electoral Observation and Democratic Transitions in Latin America.* La Jolla: Center for US-Mexican Studies, University of California, San Diego.

Mihalisko, Kathleen J. 1997. "Belarus: Retreat to Authoritarianism," in *Democratic Changes and Authoritarian Reactions in Russia, Ukraine, Belarus, and Moldova,* ed. Karen Dawisha and Bruce Parrot. Cambridge: Cambridge University Press, pp. 223–281.

Mill, John Stuart. 1991. *Considerations on Representative Government.* Amherst, NY: Prometheus.

Moestrup, Sophia. 1999. "The Role of Actors and Institutions: The Difficulties of Democratic Survival in Mali and Niger," *Democratization* 6/2 (Summer): 171–186.

Molinar, Juan. 1991. *El tiempo de la legitimidad.* Mexico City: Cal y Arena.

Molomo, Mpho G. 2000. "Understanding Government and Opposition Parties in Botswana," *Commonwealth and Comparative Politics* 38/1 (March): 65–92.

Morlino, Leonardo. 2005. *Democracias y Democratizaciones.* Mexico City: Centro de Estudios de Política Comparada.

Moss, Todd J. 1995. "US Policy and Democratization in Africa: The Limits of Liberal Universalism," *Journal of Modern African Studies* 33/2: 189–209.

Mozaffar, Shaheen, and Andreas Schedler. 2002. "The Comparative Study of Electoral Governance—Introduction," *International Political Science Review* 23/1 (January): 5–27.

Munck, Gerardo L. 2004. "Democratic Politics in Latin America: New Debates and Research Frontiers," *Annual Review of Political Science* 7: 437–462.

Munck, Gerardo L., and Jay Verkuilen. 2002. "Conceptualizing and Measuring Democracy: Evaluating Alternative Indices," *Comparative Political Studies* 35/1 (February): 5–34.

Mundt, Robert. 1997. "Côte d'Ivoire: Continuity and Change in a Semi-Democracy," in *Political Reform in Francophone Africa,* ed. John F. Clark and David E. Gardinier. Boulder, CO: Westview, pp. 182–203.

Nathan, Andrew, and Kelle Tsai. 1995. "Factionalism: A New Institutionalist Restatement," *The China Journal* 34 (July): 157–192.

NDI (National Democratic Institute for International Affairs). 1989. *The 1989 Paraguayan Elections: A Foundation for Democratic Change.* Washington, DC: NDI.

NDI and Carter Center. 2000a. "Statement of the National Democratic Institute for International Affairs/Carter Center March 2000 Pre-Election Delegation to Peru," Lima, March 24, www.ndi.org.

———. 2000b. "Peru Elections 2000: Final Report of the National Democratic Institute/Carter Center Joint Election Monitoring Project," www.ndi.org.

NDI, Carter Center, and Council of Freely-Elected Heads of Government. 1990. *The 1990 General Elections in Haiti.* Washington, DC: NDI.

Nelson, Joan M., and Stephanie J. Eglinton. 1992. *Encouraging Democracy: What Role for Conditioned Aid?* Washington, DC: Overseas Development Council.

Nwokedi, Emeka. 1994. "Nigeria's Democratic Transition: Explaining the Annulled 1993 Presidential Election," *The Round Table* 330 (April): 189–204.

O'Donnell, Guillermo. 1994. "Delegative Democracy," *Journal of Democracy* 5/1 (January): 55–69.

———. 1996. "Illusions About Consolidation," *Journal of Democracy* 7/2 (April): 34–51.

———. 1999. *Counterpoints: Selected Essays on Authoritarianism and Democratization.* Notre Dame, IN: University of Notre Dame Press.

———. 2001. "Democracy, Law, and Comparative Politics," *Studies in Comparative International Development* 36/1 (Spring): 7–36.

———. 2004. "On the Quality of Democracy and Its Links with Human Development and Human Rights," in *The Quality of Democracy: Theory and Practice,* ed. Guillermo O'Donnell, Osvaldo Iazzetta, and Jorge Vargas Cullell. Notre Dame, IN: University of Notre Dame Press, pp. 9–92.

O'Donnell, Guillermo, and Philippe Schmitter. 1986. *Transitions from Authoritarian Rule: Tentative Conclusions About Uncertain Democracies.* Baltimore: Johns Hopkins University Press.

Okoye, Chudi. 1999. "Blocked Transition in Nigeria: Democracy and the Power of Oligarchy," in *Voting for Democracy: Watershed Elections in Contemporary*

Anglophone Africa, ed. John Daniel, Roger Southall, and Morris Szeftel. Aldershot: Ashgate, pp. 158–182.

Ooi, Can Seng. 1998. "Singapore," in *Political Party Systems and Democratic Development in East and Southeast Asia,* Vol. 1: *Southeast Asia,* ed. Wolfgang Sachsenroder and Ulrike E. Frings. Aldershot: Ashgate, pp. 343–402.

Oquaye, Mike. 2000. "The Process of Democratisation in Contemporary Ghana," *Commonwealth and Comparative Politics* 38/3 (November): 53–78.

Organization for Security and Cooperation in Europe/Office for Democratic Institutions and Human Rights. 2003. "Existing Commitments for Democratic Elections in OSCE Participating States." Warsaw: OSCE/ODIHR.

———. 2004. *Report on Partial Repeat Parliamentary Elections in Georgia, 28 March 2004,* Part 2, 23 June.

Ott, Dana, and Melissa Rosser. 2000. "The Electronic Republic? The Role of the Internet in Promoting Democracy in Africa," in *The Internet, Democracy, and Democratization,* ed. Peter Ferdinand. London: Frank Cass, pp. 137–155.

Ottaway, Marina. 2003. *Democracy Challenged: The Rise of Semi-Authoritarianism.* Washington, DC: Carnegie Endowment for International Peace.

Pastor, Robert A. 1995. "Mission to Haiti #3: Elections for Parliament and Municipalities, June 23–26, 1995," Working Paper. Atlanta: Carter Center.

———. 1998. "Mediating Elections," *Journal of Democracy* 9/1 (January): 154–163.

Pavlović, Dušan. 2001. *Akteri i modeli: Ogledi o politici u Srbiji pod Miloševićem.* Belgrade: Samizdat B92.

Peuch, Jean-Christophe. 2004. "Georgia: Critics Say Police Media Intimidation on the Rise," *Eurasianet,* 20 February, www.eurasianet.org/departments/rights/eav022004.shtml.

Posner, Daniel. 2004. *Institutions and Ethnic Politics in Africa.* New York: Cambridge University Press.

Posusney, Marsha Pripsten, and Michele Penner Angrist, ed. 2005. *Authoritarianism in the Middle East: Regimes and Resistance.* Boulder, CO: Lynne Rienner.

Powell, Bingham G. 2000. *Elections as Instruments of Democracy: Majoritarian and Proportional Visions.* New Haven, CT: Yale University Press.

Pridham, Geoffrey C. 1991. "The Politics of the European Community, Transnational Networks and Democratic Transition in Southern Europe," in *Encouraging Democracy: The International Context of Regime Transition in Southern Europe,* ed. Geoffrey Pridham. Leicester: Leicester University Press, pp. 212–245.

———. 1999. "Complying with the European Union's Democratic Conditionality: Transnational Party Linkages and Regime Change in Slovakia, 1993–1998," *Europe-Asia Studies* 51/7: 1221–1244.

Przeworski, Adam. 1991. *Democracy and the Market: Political and Economic Reforms in Eastern Europe and Latin America.* New York: Cambridge University Press.

Przeworski, Adam, Michael E. Alvarez, Joseph A. Cheibub, and Fernando Limongi. 1996. "What Makes Democracies Endure?" *Journal of Democracy* 7/2 (April): 39–55.

———. 2000. *Democracy and Development: Political Institutions and Well-Being in the World, 1950–1990.* New York: Cambridge University Press.

Quandt, William B. 1998. *Between Ballots and Bullets: Algeria's Transition from Authoritarianism.* Washington, DC: Brookings Institution.

Quantin, Patrick. 1997. "Congo: Transition Democratique et Conjoncture Critique," in *Transitions Démocratiques Africaines,* ed. Jean Pascal Daloz and Patrick Quantin. Paris: Karthala, pp. 139–192.

Rae, Douglas. 1971. *The Political Consequences of Electoral Laws.* New Haven, CT: Yale University Press.

Rakner, Lise. 2004. *Economic and Political Liberalization in Zambia, 1991–2001.* Uppsala, Sweden: Nordic Africa Institute.

Rakner, Lise, and Lars Svåsand. 2004. "From Dominant to Competitive Party System: The Zambian Experience, 1991–2001," *Party Politics* 10/1: 49–68.

Razumkov Center. 2004. "The System of Democratic Civilian Control over Law-Enforcement Bodies: Its Effectiveness and Shortcomings," *National Security and Defense* (Kiev, Ukraine) 4: 12–21.

Remington, Thomas. 2001. *Russian Parliament: Institutional Evolution in a Transitional Regime, 1989–1999.* New Haven, CT: Yale University Press.

Rigger, Shelley. 1999. "Grassroots Electoral Organization and Political Reform in the ROC on Taiwan and Mexico," in *The Awkward Embrace: One-Party Domination and Democracy,* ed. Hermann Giliomee and Charles Simkins. Amsterdam: Harwood Academic Publishers, pp. 301–317.

Riggs, Fred. 1966. *Thailand: The Modernization of a Bureaucratic Polity.* Honolulu: East-West Center Press.

Roeder, Philip. 1994. "Varieties of Post-Soviet Authoritarian Regimes," *Post-Soviet Affairs* 10/1 (January–March): 61–101.

Rouquié, Alain. 1982a. "El análisis de las elecciones no competitivas: Control clientelista y situaciones autoritarias," in *¿Para qué sirven las elecciones?* ed. Guy Hermet, Alain Rouquié, and Juan Linz. Mexico City: Fondo de Cultura Económica, pp. 54–89.

———. 1982b. "Conclusión," in *¿Para qué sirven las elecciones?* ed. Guy Hermet, Alain Rouquié, and Juan Linz. Mexico City: Fondo de Cultura Económica, pp. 147–157.

Rueschemeyer, Dietrich, Evelyne Huber Stephens, and John D. Stephens. 1992. *Capitalist Development and Democracy.* Chicago: University of Chicago Press.

Sakwa, Richard. 1998. "Russian Political Evolution: A Structural Approach," in *Rethinking the Soviet Collapse: Sovietology, the Death of Communism, and the New Russia,* ed. Michael Cox. New York: Pinter, pp. 181–201.

Sartori, Giovanni. 1976. *Parties and Party Systems: A Framework for Analysis.* Cambridge: Cambridge University Press.

———. 1984. "Guidelines for Concept Analysis," in *Social Science Concepts: A Systematic Analysis,* ed. Giovanni Sartori. Beverly Hills: Sage, pp. 15–85.

———. 1986. "The Influence of Electoral Systems: Faulty Laws or Faulty Method?" in *Electoral Laws and Their Political Consequences,* ed. Bernard Grofman and Arend Lijphart. New York: Agathon, pp. 43–68.

———. 2001. "The Party Effects of Electoral Systems," in *Political Parties and Democracy,* ed. Larry Diamond and Richard Gunther. Baltimore: Johns Hopkins University Press, pp. 91–106.

Schatzberg, Michael. 2001. *Political Legitimacy in Middle Africa: Father, Family, Food.* Bloomington: Indiana University Press.

Schedler, Andreas. 2001. "Measuring Democratic Consolidation," *Studies in Comparative International Development* 36/2 (Spring): 66–92.

———. 2002a. "The Nested Game of Democratization by Elections," *International Political Science Review* 23/1 (January): 103–122.

———. 2002b. "Elections Without Democracy: The Menu of Manipulation," *Journal of Democracy* 13/2 (April): 36–50.

———. 2004. "Degrees and Patterns of Party Competition in Electoral Autocracies," 100th Annual Meeting of the American Political Science Association, Chicago, 2–5 September.

Schraeder, Peter J. 1994. *United States Foreign Policy Toward Africa: Incrementalism, Crisis and Change.* Cambridge: Cambridge University Press.

Seagrave, Sterling. 1988. *The Marcos Dynasty.* New York: Harper and Row.

Shevtsova, Lilia. 2000. "Can Electoral Autocracy Survive?" *Journal of Democracy* 11/3 (July): 36–38.

Shugart, Matthew Soberg, and John M. Carey. 1992. *Presidents and Assemblies.* Cambridge: Cambridge University Press.

Simon, David J. 2005. "Democracy Unrealized: Zambia's Third Republic Under Frederick Chiluba," in *The Fate of Africa's Democratic Experiments,* ed. Leonardo A. Villalón and Peter VonDoepp. Bloomington: Indiana University Press, pp. 199–220.

Singh, Hari. 2000. "Democratization or Oligarchic Restructuring? The Politics of Reform in Malaysia," *Government and Opposition* 35/4: 520–546.

Sklar, Richard L. 1987. "Developmental Democracy," *Comparative Studies in Society and History* 29/4: 686–714.

Smith, Peter. 2005. *Democracy in Latin America: Political Change in Comparative Perspective.* Oxford: Oxford University Press.

Snyder, Richard. 1992. "Explaining Transitions from Neopatrimonial Dictatorships," *Comparative Politics* 24/4: 379–399.

———. 1998. "Paths Out of Sultanistic Regimes: Combining Structural and Voluntarist Perspectives," in *Sultanistic Regimes,* ed. Houchang E. Chehabi and Juan J. Linz. Baltimore: Johns Hopkins University Press, pp. 49–81.

———. 2001. "Scaling Down: The Subnational Comparative Method," *Studies in Comparative International Development* 36/1 (Spring): 93–110.

Solchanyk, Roman. 1994. "The Politics of State Building: Centre-Periphery Relations in Post-Soviet Ukraine," *Europe-Asia Studies* 46/1: 47–68.

Steinberg, David I. 2001. *Burma: The State of Myanmar.* Washington, DC: Georgetown University Press.

Stepan, Alfred, and Cindy Skach. 1993. "Constitutional Frameworks and Democratic Consolidation," *World Politics* 46/1 (October): 1–22.

Stokke, Olav. 1995. "Aid and Political Conditionality: Core Issues and the State of the Art," in *Aid and Political Conditionality,* ed. Olav Stokke. London: Frank Cass and EADI, pp. 1–87.

Tahi, Mohand Salah. 1995. "Algeria's Democratisation Process: A Frustrated Hope," *Third World Quarterly* 16/2: 197–220.

Takougang, Joseph. 1997. "Cameroon: Biya and Incremental Reform," in *Political Reform in Francophone Africa,* ed. John F. Clark and David E. Gardinier. Boulder, CO: Westview, pp. 162–181.

———. 2003. "The 2002 Legislative Election in Cameroon: A Retrospective on Cameroon's Stalled Democracy Movement," *Journal of Modern African Studies* 41/3: 421–435.

Talbi, Mohamed. 2000. "Arabs and Democracy: A Record of Failure," *Journal of Democracy* 11/3 (July): 58–68.

Tan, Qingshan, Peter Kien-hong Yu, and Wen-chun Chen. 1996. "Local Politics in Taiwan: Democratic Consolidation," *Asian Survey* 36/5 (May): 483–494.

Tate, C. Neal. 1999. "Judicial Defense of Human Rights During the Marcos Dictatorship in the Philippines: The Careers of Claudio Teehankee and Cecilia Munoz Palma," in *Judicial Protection of Human Rights: Myth or Reality?* ed. Mark Gibney and Stanislaw Frankowski. Westport, CT: Greenwood, pp. 123–135.

Taylor, Robert H. 1996. "Elections in Burma/Myanmar: For Whom and Why?" in *The Politics of Elections in Southeast Asia,* ed. Robert H. Taylor. Cambridge: Woodrow Wilson Center and Cambridge University Press.

Thiriot, Céline. 1999. "Sur un Renouvellement Relatif des Elites au Mali," in *Le (Non)Renouvellement Des Elites en Afrique Subsaharienne,* ed. Jean-Pascal Daloz. Bordeaux: Centre D'Etude d'Afrique Noire, pp. 135–154.

Thomas, Robert. 1999. *The Politics of Serbia in the 1990s.* New York: Columbia University Press.

Thompson, Dennis F. 2002. *Just Elections: Creating a Fair Electoral Process in the United States.* Chicago: University of Chicago Press.

Thompson, Mark R. 1995. *The Anti-Marcos Struggle: Personalistic Rule and Democratic Transition in the Philippines.* New Haven, CT: Yale University Press.

———. 1998. "The Marcos Regime in the Philippines," in *Sultanistic Regimes,* ed. Houchang E. Chehabi and Juan J. Linz. Baltimore: Johns Hopkins University Press, pp. 206–229.

Thompson, Mark R., and Philip Kuntz. 2004. "Stolen Elections: The Case of the Serbian October," *Journal of Democracy* 15/4 (October): 159–172.

Throup, David W., and Charles Hornsby. 1998. *Multi-Party Politics in Kenya: The Kenyatta and Moi States and the Triumph of the System in the 1992 Election.* Oxford: J. Currey.

Tien, Hung-mao, and Tun-jen Cheng. 1997. "Crafting Democratic Institutions in Taiwan," *China Journal* 37 (January): 1–27.

Tien, Hung-mao, and Yun-han Chu. 1996. "Building Democracy in Taiwan," *China Quarterly* 148 (December): 1141–1170.

Tsebelis, George. 1990. *Nested Games: Rational Choice in Comparative Politics.* Berkeley: University of California Press.

UNDP (United Nations Development Programme). 2000. *Human Development Report 2000.* New York: Oxford University Press.

United Nations. 2005. "Declaration of Principles for International Election Observation and Code of Conduct for International Election Observers." Commemorated 27 October at the United Nations, New York, www.cartercenter.org/documents/2231.pdf.

Vachudova, Milada. 2004. *Europe Undivided: Democracy, Leverage, and Integration After Communism.* London: Oxford University Press.

Valenzuela, J. Samuel. 1985. *Democratización vía Reforma: La expansión del sufragio en Chile.* Buenos Aires: Ediciones del IDES.

———. 2001. "Class Relations and Democratization: A Reassessment of Barrington Moore's Model," in *The Other Mirror: Grand Theory Through the Lens of Latin America,* ed. Miguel Angel Centeno and Fernando López-Alves. Princeton, NJ: Princeton University Press, pp. 240–286.

van de Walle, Nicolas. 2002. "Elections Without Democracy: Africa's Range of Regimes," *Journal of Democracy* 13/2 (April): 66–80.

———. 2003. "Presidentialism and Clientelism in Africa's Emerging Party Systems," *Journal of Modern African Studies* 41/2 (June): 297–321.

Vanhanen, Tatu. 2000. "A New Dataset for Measuring Democracy, 1810–1998," *Journal of Peace Research* 37: 251–265.

———. 2004. "Polyarchy Dataset: Measures of Democracy, 1810–2002." Unpublished typescript, www.fsd.uta.fi/aineistot/Introduction_Tampere.pdf.

Vengroff, Richard. 1993. "Governance and the Transition to Democracy: Political Parties and the Party System in Mali," *Journal of Modern African Studies* 31/4: 541–562.

Villalón, Leonardo. 1994. "Democratizing a (Quasi)Democracy: The Senegalese Elections of 1993," *African Affairs* 93: 163–193.

Villalón, Leonardo, and Abdourahamane Idrissa. 2005. "A Decade of Transition:

Institutional Experimentation and Inter-Elite Competition in Niger," in *The Fate of Africa's Democratic Experiments,* ed. Leonardo Villalón and Peter Von-Doepp. Bloomington: Indiana University Press, pp. 27–48.

Villalón, Leonardo, and Peter VonDoepp, ed. 2005. *The Fate of Africa's Democratic Experiments: Elites and Institutions.* Bloomington: Indiana University Press.

Way, Lucan A. 2003. "Weak States and Pluralism: The Case of Moldova," *East European Politics and Societies* 17/3 (August): 454–482.

———. 2004. "The Sources and Dynamics of Competitive Authoritarianism in Ukraine," *Journal of Communist Studies and Transition Politics* 20/1 (March): 143–161.

———. 2005a. "Authoritarian State Building and the Sources of Political Competition in the Fourth Wave: The Cases of Belarus, Moldova, Russia, and Ukraine," *World Politics* 57 (January): 231–261.

———. 2005b. "Kuchma's Failed Authoritarianism," *Journal of Democracy* 16/2 (April): 131–145.

Weiner, Myron. 1987. "Empirical Democratic Theory," in *Competitive Elections in Developing Countries,* ed. Myron Weiner and Ergun Ozbudun. Durham, NC: Duke University Press, pp. 3–34.

West, Darrell M. 2005. *Digital Government: Technology and Public Sector Performance.* Princeton, NJ: Princeton University Press.

Whitehead, Laurence, ed. 1996. *The International Dimensions of Democratization: Europe and the Americas.* Oxford: Oxford University Press.

Wilson, Andrew. 1993. "The Growing Challenge to Kiev from the Donbas," *RFE/RL Research Report,* 20 August.

———. 2005. *Virtual Politics: Faking Democracy in the Post-Soviet World.* New Haven, CT: Yale University Press.

Winckler, Edwin A. 1984. "Institutionalization and Participation on Taiwan: From Hard to Soft Authoritarianism," *China Quarterly* 99 (September): 481–499.

Wolf, Thomas P. 2003. "Kula Kwa Kanu, Kura Kwa NARC (Take/Eat from Kanu, Vote for NARC): Money in the Mombasa 2002 General Election," Research Report. Nairobi: Transparency International.

World Bank. 1997. *World Development Report 1997.* New York: Oxford University Press.

Wu, Chung-li. 2001. "The Transformation of the Kuomintang's Candidate Selection System," *Party Politics* 7/1: 103–118.

Wurfel, David. 1988. *Filipino Politics: Development and Decay.* Ithaca, NY: Cornell University Press.

Ying-Mao Kua, Michael. 1996. "The Power Structure in Taiwan's Political Economy," *Asian Survey* 36/3 (March): 287–305.

Zakaria, Fareed. 1997. "The Rise of Illiberal Democracy," *Foreign Affairs* 76/6 (November–December): 22–43.

———. 2003. *The Future of Freedom: Illiberal Democracy at Home and Abroad.* New York: W. W. Norton.

Zubek, Voytek. 1995. "The Phoenix Out of the Ashes: The Rise to Power of Poland's Post-Communist SdRP," *Communist and Post-Communist Studies* 28/3: 275–306.

Zudin, Aleksei. 1999. "Oligarkhiia kak politicheskaia problema rossiiskogo post-kommunizma," *Obshchestvennie nauki i sovremennost'* 1: 45–65.

The Contributors

William Case is associate professor of international business and Asian studies at Griffith University, Brisbane, Australia.

John F. Clark is associate professor of international relations and chair of the Department of International Relations at Florida International University.

M. Steven Fish is associate professor of political science at the University of California, Berkeley.

Jonathan Hartlyn is professor of political science at the University of North Carolina, Chapel Hill.

Philipp Kuntz is lecturer in politics at Dalarna University College, Falun, Sweden.

Joy Langston is professor of political science at CIDE, Mexico City.

Steven Levitsky is associate professor of government and social studies at Harvard University.

Staffan I. Lindberg is assistant professor of political science at the University of Florida.

Jennifer McCoy is professor of political science at Georgia State University and director of the Americas Program at the Carter Center in Atlanta.

Gerardo L. Munck is associate professor at the School of International Relations at the University of Southern California.

Andreas Schedler is professor of political science and chair of the Department of Political Studies at CIDE, Mexico City.

Richard Snyder is associate professor of political science at Brown University.

Mark R. Thompson is professor of political science at the University of Erlangen, Nuremberg.

Nicolas van de Walle is the John S. Knight Professor of International Studies, Associate Dean for International Studies in the College of Arts and Sciences, and director of the Mario Einaudi Center for International Studies at Cornell University.

Lucan A. Way is assistant professor of political science at Temple University.

Index

253

About the Book

Today, electoral authoritarianism represents the most common form of political regime in the developing world—and the one we know least about. Filling in the lacuna, this new book presents cutting-edge research on the internal dynamics of electoral authoritarian regimes.

Each concise, jargon-free chapter addresses a specific empirical puzzle on the basis of careful cross-national comparison. The result is a systematic, clearly structured study of the interaction between rulers and opposition parties in the central arena of struggle under electoral authoritarianism, the electoral battlefield.

Andreas Schedler is professor of political science and chair of the Department of Political Studies at CIDE, Mexico City. Among his publications is *The Self-Restraining State: Power and Accountability in New Democracies.*